Jewish Choices

SUNY Series in American Jewish Society in the 1990s
Barry A. Kosmin and Sidney Goldstein, editors

Jewish Choices

American Jewish Denominationalism

BERNARD LAZERWITZ
J. ALAN WINTER
ARNOLD DASHEFSKY
EPHRAIM TABORY

STATE UNIVERSITY OF NEW YORK PRESS

Published by
State University of New York Press, Albany

© 1998 State University of New York

For information, address State University of New York Press,
State University Plaza, Albany, NY 12246

Production by David Ford
Marketing by Nancy Farrell

Library of Congress Cataloging-in-Publication Data

Jewish choices : American Jewish denominationalism / Bernard Lazerwitz
    . . . [et al.].
        p.   cm. — (SUNY series in American Jewish society in the
    1990s)
    Includes bibliographical references and index.
    ISBN 0-7914-3581-4 (hardcover : alk. paper). — ISBN 0-7914-3582-2
(pbk. : alk. paper)
    1. Judaism—United States. 2. Reform Judaism—United States.
3. Conservative Judaism—United States. 4. Orthodox Judaism—United
States. 5. Jews—United States—Social conditions. I. Lazerwitz,
Bernard Melvin, 1926–   . II. Series.
BM205.J48 1997
296.8′3′0973—dc21   97-3079
                                                                CIP
                                                                r97

10   9   8   7   6   5   4   3   2   1

To our grandparents, parents, and teachers from whom we derived our Jewish choices; to our wives with whom we have shared them; and to our children and their spouses and to our grandchildren, for whom we strive to illuminate a path to similar choices.

Contents

PART I

PART II

List of Tables and Figures

Tables

Figures

American Jewish Society in the 1990s

An Introduction

Jewish Choices: American Jewish Denominationalism is the third monograph to be published in the SUNY series American Jewish Society in the 1990s, based on the Council of Jewish Federation's (CJF) landmark 1990 National Jewish Population Survey. The survey yielded a vast array of statistical data on the demographic, social, and religious characteristics of the Jewish American population. It is being used to provide, in a number of monographs, an in-depth assessment of the major changes and trends in Jewish American life as it approaches the end of the century. To a degree, this monograph series parallels past undertakings by teams of social scientists who analyzed the demographic and social data emanating from United States decennial censuses. A monograph series focusing on the Jewish population is, however, unique. Although a national survey similar in nature had been conducted in 1970, that project yielded comparatively few reports and those were in limited areas of concern.

Recognizing the importance of a comprehensive assessment of the total Jewish American population as the basis for an effective planning agenda, the concept of a national Jewish population survey in 1990 was first considered in 1986 by CJF's National Technical Advisory Committee on Jewish Population Studies (NTAC). The idea was further promoted the following year at the World Conference on Jewish Demography held in Jerusalem, at which plans were developed for a worldwide series of national Jewish population studies undertaken in or around the decennial year. An American survey was seen as a key component of this series. In 1988, CJF officially agreed to conduct a national Jewish population survey in 1990, parallel to the federal decennial census. ICR Survey Research Group of Media, Pennsylvania, was commissioned to conduct the three-stage survey.

In contrast to the 1970 national study, NTAC decided to ensure public access to the 1990 National Jewish Population Survey (NJPS) data as early as possible and to actively encourage wide use and analysis. The success of that effort is evident in the large number of analyses that have been completed or are in process. To date, more than 150 items extensively based on NJPS, such as journal and magazine articles, dissertations, and papers for professional meetings, have been written. These encompass such varied topics as aging, apostasy, the baby boom generation, children, comparisons with international Jewry, comparisons with the larger American population, denominations, fertility, gender equality, geography, intermarriage, Israel connections, Jewish education, Jewish identity, life cycle, mobility, occupation, philanthropy, Sephardim, social stratification, and women's roles. A number of these topics are expected to appear as monographs in the series.

From the outset, NTAC envisioned that a number of scholars would independently produce monographs utilizing NJPS data for in-depth assessment of topics having special relevance for the understanding of Jewish life in America. While planning for the various stages of NJPS, NTAC therefore concurrently acted to identify potential monograph writers. Public notices were placed in a variety of academic journals and invitations were conveyed through a network of professionals, both within and outside of Judaic disciplines. Although funds were raised for the data collection, survey execution, and data processing, no financial support was available for subsidizing data analyses, except for a summary report, *Highlights of the CJF 1990 National Jewish Population Survey*. Thus, potential monograph writers knew from the beginning that they would be participating on a voluntary basis, dependent on whatever resources they could themselves muster. The dedication of the authors to the completion of their respective monographs is gratefully acknowledged. While drawing on basically the same set of data, authors were free to establish their own analytic categories and to apply their own perspectives in interpreting the data. They were also encouraged to draw not only on NJPS, but also on comparative data from other sources, such as local community surveys.

In selecting authors, efforts were made to ensure coverage of key issues and a diversity of topics and to avoid serious overlap in coverage of the same topic. A screening and approval process, in collaboration with the editors at the State University of New York Press, was administered by the series editors, Dr. Barry A. Kosmin, director of research at the Council of Jewish Federations and director of the Mandell L. Berman Institute—North American Jewish Data Bank (NAJDB) at City University of New York Graduate Center; and Dr. Sidney Goldstein, chair of NTAC and G. H. Crooker University Professor emeritus and professor emeritus of sociology at Brown University.

Jeff Scheckner, administrator of NAJDB and research consultant at CJF, with the help of the series editors, coordinated the activities of the monograph writers by arranging meetings at which authors discussed technical aspects of the data and their preliminary findings, fielding daily inquiries about the data set, and circulating periodic informational updates. Much of this activity was necessitated by the fact that NJPS is both a large data set with a complex weighting system (see Appendix A) and that definitional issues complicate any analysis of contemporary Jewish populations. The work of the monograph authors was further enhanced through the coordination of a "buddy" system by which other scholars associated with NJPS provided academic peer review to authors at various stages of manuscript preparation.

The intense interest generated by the initial release of NJPS findings has already significantly affected deliberations within the Jewish American community among communal service workers, religious and educational professionals, and lay leaders. At the same time, the results of early reports have elicited considerable attention among those in the larger American community whose interests focus on the changing religio-ethnic composition of the population and the role of religion in America. This series is intended to provide a comprehensive, in-depth evaluation of American Jewry today, some one hundred years since the massive waves of Jewish immigrants from Eastern Europe began to change the size and character of Jewry in the United States. During the intervening decades, continual change has been the hallmark of the community. The profile of the Jewish population in the 1990s that NJPS delineates both provides a historical perspective and points to the challenges of the future.

Barry A. Kosmin
Graduate Center
City University of New York and
   Council of Jewish Federations
New York, New York

Sidney Goldstein
Population Studies and
   Training Center
Brown University
Providence, Rhode Island

March 1997

Foreword

Andrew Greeley

When I was a very young priest—long before I became a sociologist—the only work my pastor would let me do was teenage work. I didn't mind that because I liked teens—still do as a matter of fact. I did, however, marvel on occasion how little my role was like that of the Old Country clergy. They used to wander around at night breaking up the crossroad dances with their black thorn sticks, while I promoted teenage dances. They tried to keep the gossoons and the colleens separate. I rode on buses with them to picnics. In some respects I had been Americanized. Like many of my Protestant separated brothers, I was now a social service director for teens.

Then, one day, in *Time* magazine, I saw a picture of a Buddhist monk in a sweater on a bus with teens going to a picnic. I understood, finally, the enormous impact American culture and social structure had on religion, on any religion, and on all religions. The monk was a man who should be praying, the rabbi, a man who should be interpreting the law, the priest, a man who ruled the roost from his parish house. We all, however, had become teenage clergy.

Hence, I am not surprised that denominationalism shapes all American religions, including Judaism. But I am fascinated by this study, which documents how the various Jewish denominations have emerged and how they have shaped themselves and been shaped by their members. It is axiomatic in this country, where religious pluralism and voluntarism flourish, that religions organize themselves into denominational structures.

I could not help but reflect as I read this careful and intelligent study that most Jews in other parts of the world would be astonished by the emergence of denominational structures like the ones the authors describe and document. Perhaps they would even be offended. Yet they must be persuaded that this is the way religion works in our country and, if one may say so, it works very well indeed.

I was also intrigued by the way American Jews sort themselves into denominational categories. Orthodoxy declines, Reform increases, but at the same time ceremonial activities increase and so too does synagogue participation, however moderately. One expects such developments in a denominational society in which various groups, on the one hand, tend to pull farther apart and, on the other hand, at the same time coming closer together, at least on the level of symbol, ritual, and story.

This volume, updating an earlier study of American Jews, fills an important gap in our understanding of American Judaism and, I would presume, in the self-understanding of American Jews.

This outsider has always been more optimistic that Judaism would survive in this country than many rabbis have been. *Jewish Choices* confirms that expectation. Judaism does survive and will survive as a denominational religion, both in its external relations and in its internal structure.

I must leave it to others to judge whether such denominationalism is good or bad. It seems to me, however, that it is inevitable.

Preface

[handwritten: BIG QUESTIONS]

In the United States, perhaps more so than in any other society, religious preference is an individual, voluntary choice. Nobody is formally required to affiliate with a religious organization or even to identify with one of its many religious denominations. However, if one does either, we believe that doing so expresses that person's stance on important existential questions. For Jews, the choices concerning denominational preference and synagogue membership express what it means to be a Jew in the United States. In particular, within the context of the voluntarism and individualism of the American way of life, the individual American Jew defines his or her religious preference in response to two related questions:

[handwritten: Confrontation w/ modernity]

1. Should one's Jewish identity be based on modern, Western models of acceptable identities, or should it be based on traditional Judaic models, such as those embodied in Jewish law (*halakha*), as set forth in traditional Jewish texts?

[handwritten: Ethnic vs. religious]

2. Should Jewish identity be essentially religious, that is, based in the synagogue or temple, or should it be essentially ethnic—based in the history and traditions of the more or less autonomous, self-governing Jewish people such as found in the shtetls of Eastern Europe or in the modern state of Israel?

The findings of this study support the contention that the decision to affirm a denominational preference or to join a synagogue is associated with important aspects of one's Jewish life. Moreover, this association is above and beyond the influence of socioeconomic and demographic factors. Of course, in an open society, such as the United States, in which individuals freely choose their religious affiliations, boundaries within and between major faith groups are fluid and permeable. Thus, it is not uncommon for individual Jews raised in one denomination to choose another as an adult or even to marry somebody who is not Jewish, as this study shows.

The study of American Jews poses a very difficult task for survey researchers. American Jews comprise less than three percent of the entire

American population and much of this population is scattered among other American residential households. Thus, the usual techniques of survey research often turn up too few Jewish respondents for careful and sophisticated statistical analysis such as we employ in this book. Fortunately, the two surveys analyzed here were each devoted specifically to finding and interviewing Jewish respondents and took special care and effort to locate them. Overall, the two surveys, the 1971 and 1990 National Jewish Population Surveys (NJPS), have provided an excellent opportunity for scholars, such as ourselves, to study the components and consequences of a Jewish identity. Of course, these surveys, like all surveys, have their limits when compared with other, more qualitative and personal forms of analysis. Still, there is much to be learned even from surveys and the statistics they yield. Moreover, we found the opportunity to study and contrast two surveys conducted just about twenty years apart to be an interesting and challenging task. We hope the academic style and concerns that guided the writing of this book do not obscure the satisfaction we felt in contrasting the two surveys. We hope, too, that what follows is indeed informative and accessible to the nonacademic, nonstatistically inclined reader. Moreover, we trust that our discussion of Jewish choices within the context of the denominationally oriented society, which is the United States, will throw light not only on those Jewish choices, but on the choices of those of other religious persuasions as well.

What follows is a collaborative endeavor. Together, we represent and have faced many of the significant choices that face American Jews. One or the other of us has an affiliation with each of the major branches or denominations of Judaism—Orthodox, Conservative, and Reform. All of us are American-born, but only two of us still reside in the United States. The other two are *olim,* immigrants to Israel from America. We trust that our mutual collaboration and intellectual stimulation has added to the quality of what has been done in this book.

The statistical analyses reported here, especially in chapters 3–7, was primarily the responsibility of the senior author, Bernard Lazerwitz; the conceptual framework used throughout the book, but especially as presented in chapters 1 and 8, was primarily the responsibility of J. Alan Winter, who along with Ephraim Tabory, sought to provide continuity from chapter to chapter and section to section. Arnold Dashefsky was primarily responsible for the sociohistory presented in chapter 2. Each of us, of course, checked and rechecked the entire book to ensure its internal consistency.

As is the case with all human endeavors, ours has its limits. For example, we have sometimes limited the depth of our analysis of a given topic, for instance, intermarriage. We do so because ours is but one book in a series and we often left more detailed analysis of a given topic to others working on other monographs in this series. We have also, with the exception of chapter 2 and some closing remarks in chapter 8, focused our efforts upon the analysis of the responses to the two surveys, 1971 and 1990, and resisted the temptation to go beyond the survey data to more qualitative or historical analysis. We invite others to go beyond the limits of our study and fill in the gaps we have left. In particular, we would hope that others use our analysis of Jews in the United States in comparative studies of the other major concentration of Jews in the world, namely, Israel.

There were, of course, many who helped us with this study or who otherwise made it possible. Among the latter, we wish especially to acknowledge the assistance of the Council of Jewish Federations (CJF) and the Mandell Berman Institute of the North American Jewish Data Bank (NAJDB) at the Graduate School and University Center of the City University of New York, who made the data of the 1990 NJPS available to us. We wish also to thank Sidney Goldstein, chair of CJF's National Technical Advisory Committee, Barry A. Kosmin, CJF's research director and director of NAJDB, and Jeffrey Scheckner, of CJF's research department, without whose cooperation, our work would not have been possible. Additional thanks are also due the Research Foundation of the University of Connecticut. We wish also to thank Zina Lawrence, Jennifer Doling, and David Ford of the State University of New York Press for their efforts in shepherding our work through the various steps from manuscript to book.

In closing, we wish to acknowledge the substantial contribution made to the statistical ideas of this book by the teaching and writing of that outstanding survey statistician Professor Leslie Kish. The data analysis procedures employed here also owe a good deal to the work of Professor Hubert Blalock. They are to be thanked for the best aspects of the methodology employed here, while we accept any blame for its limitations. And finally, we wish to thank Menucha Kanter of Bar Ilan University, Anita Allen and Gina Foster of Connecticut College, and Alyson Bacon of the Center for Judaic Studies and Contemporary Jewish Life of the University of Connecticut for their efforts in various stages of the physical production of our manuscript, and the staffs of the computer centers at Connecticut College and Bar Ilan University for their assistance in dealing with the vagaries of computerized statistical analysis. And, of course, we wish to thank our respective families for their support and forbearance through the long days and nights we devoted to creating this manuscript.

PART I

1

Denominations in American Religious Life

The Jewish community in America can trace its beginnings back nearly three and a half centuries to colonial America. However, its contemporary character has been shaped largely by the massive influx of Jewish immigrants to America from Germany, Russia, Poland, and elsewhere in Eastern Europe in the past 120 or so years, and by their descendants. Jewish immigration to the United States involved more than a mere change of geographic location. It entailed an exposure to the transforming forces of industrialization, urbanization, modernization, and secularization (Goldscheider 1986: 4). Since these forces "logically compelled Emancipation, the end to Jewish exclusion from the polity, economy and society" (Cohen 1983: 18), they helped bring about a fundamental restructuring of the life and institutions of American Jewry. Emancipation, however, was offered conditionally. It required Jews to adjust their communal structures, alter their self-images, change occupations and adapt their cultural orientations and religious practices (Cohen 1983: 18). Those Jews who desired to enter into the mainstream of American society, with all the rewards that might bring, were welcomed. Such welcome was

> contingent upon their either completely abandoning group distinctiveness (i.e., assimilating) or, minimally, reconstructing their group definition so as to comport with the modern . . . social constructs of the voluntary religious group. (Cohen, 1983: 23)

In short, the entry of America's Jews into the mainstream entailed altering what it meant to be a Jew. As Charles S. Liebman notes (1973: 43), the new meaning is largely a creation of Eastern European Jewish immigrants and their descendants. Eastern European Jews understood that to be a Jew meant to be a member of an ethnic community, a more or less autonomous body governed by Jewish law and traditions that functioned within the larger society. In America such a communal identity lacked legitimacy (C. S. Liebman 1973:

3

43). However, the norms of religious tolerance rendered the maintenance of a particular and distinct religious identity acceptable. Such a religious identity could provide a basis for the distinctiveness of being Jewish that immigrants and their descendants sought to preserve. Thus, as Herberg (1960: 187) has noted, among immigrant groups in the United States, "the dissolution of the old ethnic group entailed renewed identification with a religious community." In particular,

> The young Jew for whom the Jewish immigrant-ethnic group had lost all meaning, because he was an American and not a foreigner, could think of himself as a Jew, because to him being a Jew now meant identification with the Jewish religious community. (Herberg 1960: 187)

For Jews alone, unlike other immigrant groups, the "religious community bore the same name as the old ethnic group and was virtually coterminous with it" (Herberg 1960: 187). Thus, while many Italian Catholics, Irish Catholics, and Polish Catholics have become simply "Catholics" as their *ethnic* identity now makes "little difference in Catholic religious beliefs or behavior" (Hammond 1992: 204), Jews remained "Jews," even as the meaning of the term shifted emphasis from peoplehood or ethnicity to religiosity (see Levine 1986; Winter 1991b, 1992). In sum, while America's Jews found it difficult to legitimize distinctive Jewish institutions defined primarily in communal-ethnic-cultural-national terms" (C. S. Liebman 1973: 44), they could more easily legitimize distinctive Jewish *religious* institutions.

It is now possible, therefore, for an American Jew to "establish his Jewishness not apart from, nor in spite of, his Americanness, but precisely through and by virtue of it" (Herberg 1960: 198). Specifically, when it comes to religion, as Kosmin and Lachman (1993: 14) recognize and as did de Tocqueville before them, two crucial and interrelated aspects of Americanness, the American way of life, are voluntarism and individualism. The longstanding heritage of voluntarism in America fosters a spirit of religious individualism that encourages each person to make a personal decision about his/her religious involvement (Wertheimer 1993: 191).

Bellah et al. (Bellah, Madsen, Sullivan, Swidler, and Tipton 1985: 226) recognize that individualism in the United States leads Americans to regard religion as an entirely individual or personal matter that need not entail a commitment to any organized religious group. There is, of course, no established church in the United States. Involvement with organized religion is entirely voluntary. One may be so involved, but one need not be.

Interestingly, the other side of the coin of voluntary religious involvement and the absence of an established church may be a degree of "religious vitality that is absent in other industrial Western societies" (Tiryakian 1993: 45).

I'm a Conservative Jew but no observance of ～ 113N (like Ortho-doxy 25 years ago !)

The magnitude of the American exception to the general pattern of religious involvement in other Western societies can best be seen by comparing the proportion, 51 percent, of Americans who actually assigned great importance to religious belief with the mere five percent that would have done so on the basis of the patterns of involvement in other countries (Wald 1987: 7). "By all normal indicators of religious commitment—the strength of religious institutions, practices and beliefs"—the United States is an exception (Wald 1987: 7). At least insofar as survey data can indicate, there has been little change in the relatively high levels of church attendance, prayer, organizational affiliation, and organizational activity in the past quarter century or more (Greeley 1991: 104).

American individualism, on the other hand, may encourage some, such as Sheila Larson, a nurse interviewed by Bellah et al. (1985: 220–21), to feel perfectly free to name "her religion . . . after herself . . . as 'Sheilaism.'" Indeed, individualism suggests the possibility of over 220 million religions, one for each American (Bellah et al. 1985: 221). Such a possibility is, of course, far from materializing. What is found, under the conditions of voluntarism and individualism, "is the peculiarly American practice of claiming a 'religious preference'" that is voluntary and independent of ascriptive loyalty or other social or group pressures (Roof and McKinney 1987: 67). While religion is privatized and relatively unfettered by custom or social bonds, it is still "a prime idiom by which Americans identify themselves" (Warner 1993: 1077). One's private, optional, religious preference is an important and significant decision, symbolic of how one chooses to live in the world and of how one responds to questions of existential import. For Jews, as we shall see, one key question is: What does it mean to be a Jew in an emancipated society such as America in which there is relatively free access to the political, economic, and social structures?

No matter how private, individualized, and voluntary one's religious preference is, for most Americans, it is a choice made not in a vacuum but rather in an open market of religious alternatives (Roof and McKinney 1987: 67). For most, deciding on a religious preference does not entail, as it did for Sheila Larson, devising a unique or idiosyncratic faith, but rather choosing from among the various denominations present in the American religious marketplace.

> Denominationalism involves being a particular kind of American . . . as much as it does being a particular kind of Christian or Jew. . . . By the same token, full participation in civil society anticipates membership in some denomination. . . . Denomination membership symbolizes commitment to society's highest values, one of which—by the very nature of the historical antecedents of the Enlightenment—is doctrinal pluralism. (Swatos 1981: 221)

Indeed, as Greeley (1972: 231) noted,

> denominations are . . . groups providing means of identification and location within the American social structure. Loyalty to the . . . denomination . . . involves loyalty to the denomination's tradition, and particularly to those elements of the tradition which for reasons of history, geography, culture, or social structure, most sharply differentiate this tradition in the American experience from other traditions. But at the same time the traditions are all perceived, to a greater or lesser extent, as valid patterns of being American, and each in its own way is conceded to be reinforcement for the more general commitments that most if not all Americans accept.

When Greeley and Swatos refer to denominations, they are speaking of the three major religious traditions in the United States: Protestantism, Catholicism, and Judaism. However, what Greeley (1972: 232–33) says about them can be applied to the various denominations within Judaism. Loyalty to a religious tradition is important to defining oneself both as an individual and as an American. In Greeley's view (1972: 233), America is "a denominational society—that is to say, a society in which denominational loyalty . . . will be extremely important to the . . . American for his becoming himself and being an American." As Lazerwitz and Harrison claim in their study of America's Jews (1979: 665; Harrison and Lazerwitz 1982), "a denominationalism based more on variations of belief and religious style than on social or economic division" will be found, a denominationalism reflecting the voluntary choice of an individual pondering on what is meaningful to him or her as an individual and not solely an expression of social or economic status, whether ascribed or achieved. Similar results were found in Roof and McKinney's national survey of English-speaking persons in the continental United States. They find that while the social sources of denominationalism, identified in Niebuhr's (1929) study, namely, class, race, national origin, and region are still relevant, they are no longer as important for individual religious styles as they were in the past (Roof and McKinney 1987: 144–47).

In sum, given the importance of voluntarism and individualism within the American way of life, denominationalism has become a chief means of expressing one's religion in America.

> Insofar as denominations do not absolutize their traditions and practices, they provide alternative places and occasions in which individuals experience belonging and meaning in a multicultural and diverse society. . . . [T]hey preserve and transmit particular, if partial, understandings of God's dealings with humankind and particular, if partial, traditions of piety and moral perspective as guides for practice. (Carroll and Roof 1993b: 349)

Given the voluntarism and individualism of American religious life and the concomitant absence of an established church or religion (see Hammond 1992: 1–18; Swatos 1981), for religion to play such crucial roles organizing social authority or providing a sense of community and group solidarity, organizational identification and affiliation are most important (Kosmin and Lachman 1993: 14). Even for otherwise disaffected baby-boomers, for example, the sense of community provided by affiliation with a church or synagogue is very appealing (Roof 1993: 160). "Denominational loyalties persist, in large part, because "religion provides for Americans not merely 'meaning' but also a sense of 'belonging'" (Carroll and Roof 1993a: 15). The significance of denominationalism is that it provides a structure for the organization of communal relationships relating to the transcendent realm in a pluralistic socio-cultural system (Swatos 1981: 222).

Within the United States, then, with a plethora of denominations, but no established church, communal identification is, generally, by and through one's choice of denominational affiliation. This is not to claim that the long-standing denominational boundaries will remain sharp and unchanged. *B H* Indeed, as Wuthnow (1988: 91) contends, such boundaries are no longer seen as immutable or "even in many cases especially important." Moreover, the boundaries are permeable both within the major faith groups and between them as evidenced by the common occurrence of switching from one denomination to another and by interfaith marriages, respectively. Nevertheless, "it clearly would be overstating the case to suggest that denominationalism no longer carries any weight" (Wuthnow 1988: 97). In fact, the division between religious liberals and religious conservatives is, if anything, deepening (Wuthnow 1988: 164). In short, while differences within the broad groupings of lib- *Similar* eral and conservative denominations, as say, between religiously liberal *to* Episcopalians and Congregationalists may not seem crucial in the choice of *Liberal* denominational affiliation, the difference between them and a religious con- *Jews* servative denomination, such as the Southern Baptists, is still regarded as *+* important.[1] Thus, as Roof's study of baby-boomers concludes (1993: 249), *Cons.* while denominational boundaries may be eroding as Americans grow up *@ the* — knowing very little about their specific denominational religious heritages, *dox* there is still knowledge of what Roof (1993: 249) calls the "general faith traditions—Roman Catholicism, Judaism, Islam, and Protestantism—clustered into its liberal and conservative camps." Consequently, even when not particularly well informed, the expression of denominational preference is not frivolous. It represents an attempt to give voice to one's basic religious faith and beliefs. At their best, denominational preferences have provided a

> *place* in the socio-cultural milieu in such a way that the transient and the
> eternal are harmonized into a meaningful whole in the consciousness of the

participant. Thus, denominations have served to mediate *both God and Country* . . . and so structure within its limits the lives of people whose rootlessness was often painfully obvious. To align with one denomination or another in a community gave one heritage—practically a family—whose boundaries transcended time and place. (Swatos 1981: 223; emphasis in original)

Like Americans in general, Jews in the United States also express their religious preference, voluntarily and individually, by choosing from among the available denominations. For American Jews, the choice of denominations largely entails deciding whether to be an Orthodox, Conservative, or Reform Jew.

Within the context of the voluntarism and individualism of the American way of life, the individual American Jew defines his or her religious preference in response to two related (existential) questions posed by the opening of opportunities in the non-Jewish world to those who want to retain a Jewish identity: *religious/ethnic*

1. Should Jewish identity be essentially a religious identity and thus based in the synagogue, as Emancipation would have it, or is one's Jewishness essentially an ethnic matter, based in the history and traditions of the more or less autonomous Jewish people?

2. Should one's Jewish identity be based on modern, Western models of acceptable identities, as, again, Emancipation suggests, or should it be based on traditional Judaic models, such as those embodied in Jewish law (*halakha*), as set forth in traditional Jewish texts? *tradition/modernity*

Responses to these questions have varied greatly among America's Jews. With respect to the first question, for example, about two-thirds of America's Jews are or have been members of a synagogue. With respect to the question of the use of Western or Jewish models, America's Jews have nurtured three broad variants or branches of Judaism for most of the twentieth century: Orthodoxy (including ultra-Orthodox and modern variants), Conservative denominations (including the Union for Traditional Judaism and the Reconstructionists), and the Reform movement. The basic differences among these variations (to be discussed in the following chapter) is their stance vis-à-vis the competing claims of *halakha* and traditional Jewish texts (see Harris 1994), on the one hand, and the norms of Western, liberal society on the other. The Orthodox tend to resolve such disputes in favor of *halakha* and tradition. The Conservative movement tends to adopt a position that generally follows the practices and norms of American society only when doing so can be justified by *halakha* and tradition, or at least be seen as consistent with them. The

Reform movement gives precedence to the norms of liberal society and does not regard *halakha* as necessarily binding, although they do maintain allegiance to specifically Jewish theology and ethics.

These denominational differences are evident in their respective responses to the question of whether to ordain women as rabbis. The Orthodox movement maintains ancient tradition and does not ordain women as rabbis; the Conservatives have done so recently after long debates as to whether the ordination of women can be justified in light of Jewish law; while the Reform movement has ordained women as rabbis for over two decades, justifying the practice in light of egalitarian, liberal norms. Similarly, while the Orthodox and Conservative movements celebrate two days of Rosh HaShanah, the Jewish New Year, as required by Jewish tradition, the Reform movement celebrates one day, as is consistent with American norms for holiday celebrations. In short, the more traditional the denomination, the more it conforms to the traditional standards of Jewish law and the less it accepts the norms of the larger society.

In any case, while most American Jews affiliate with one of the major denominations, not all do so. There are those who are essentially secular humanists or religious liberals of one stripe or another who regard Jewish ritual, liturgy, and theology as outdated vestigial trappings. They include those who prefer to focus on the great moral and ethical lessons of Judaism, especially as these are consistent with the basic values of American society such as democracy and the belief in the dignity and equality of all humankind. Similarly, American Jewish history has been enriched by debates between secular Zionists and Yiddishists, who agreed that traditional Jewish ritual, liturgy, and theology were not relevant to modern life, yet could still argue as to whether to live that life in a Jewish state, Israel, or in the United States.

In sum, the encounter with Emancipation, the end of the exclusion from the polity, economy, and society, shattered the relative unanimity on the meaning of Jewishness that prevailed in the premodern Jewish communities of the more or less segregated enclaves of the shtetls of Eastern Europe and the ghettoes of medieval Western Europe. In place of widespread agreement on what it meant to be a Jew, there have been multicornered disputes between, and among, adherents of Orthodox, Conservative, and Reform forms of Judaism, secular humanists and political liberals of all persuasions, and those who see synagogue membership as a crucial, basic commitment and those who do not.

Clearly, the more extreme among the organized responses to Emancipation among American Jewry have largely been abandoned. The classical Reform movement, which eschewed any notion that Jews were a people entitled to their own homeland, has largely given way to a Reform movement proud of the role of the Association of Reform Zionists in America (ARZA) and in the world Zionist movement. Even the leadership of Zionist, secular, organizations recognize the centrality of religion in modern American Jewish life (Woocher 1986). Further, while most Jews remain politically liberal, the institutional structures (see A. Liebman 1978) that sustained a secular, liberal Jewish subcommunity have atrophied. Finally, even Orthodox Jewry has made accommodations to new conditions (see C. S. Liebman 1975; Bulka 1983).

Despite the muting of extreme responses, the current responses to the two basic questions that Emancipation posed enable us to group American Jewry into basic categories that represent the combinations of two dimensions. The first entails the simple distinction between those who join a synagogue and those who do not, that is, the response to the first question as to whether or not to base one's identity in religion and, thus, the synagogue. The second dimension entails a fourfold distinction among denominational orientations: one category for each of the three major denominational preferences (Orthodox, Conservative, Reform) and a fourth for those with no denominational preference. This latter dimension entails the response to the second question of whether to use Jewish and/or Western models in shaping one's identity. The eight resulting groupings (and their percentages in the Jewish population in the United States) are:

1. Those who express a preference for Orthodox Judaism and are synagogue members (5%).

2. Those who express a preference for Orthodox Judaism, but who are not synagogue members (2%).

3. Those who express a preference for Conservative Judaism and who are synagogue members (23%).

4. Those who express a preference for Conservative Judaism, but who are not synagogue members (17%).

5. Those who express a preference for Reform Judaism, and are members of synagogues (16%).

6. Those who express a preference for Reform Judaism, but who are not synagogue members (22%).

7. Those who, while they express no denominational preference, are, nevertheless, synagogue members (2%). Some of the members of this grouping may regard themselves as "just Jews," people who wish to affiliate with other Jews and join a synagogue because there is no other Jewish organization with which to affiliate in their Jewish community.

8. Those who express no denominational preference and who are not synagogue members (13%). This grouping may include those who regard themselves as "just Jews." They may be carry-overs of the various secu-

larist Jewish movements: Jews who are indifferent to religion, but who remain active in any of the wide variety of secular Jewish voluntary associations such as the Federation movement or B'nai B'rith. The grouping may also include those who wish to have no Jewish religious or ethnic involvement.

Throughout this book, we shall attempt to identify the important differences among these groupings.

Chapter Preview

After a brief introduction to the social and historical backgrounds of the American Jewish denominations, our primary focus will be on identifying and analyzing the characteristics of individuals in the groupings named above, that is, those American Jews, whether or not members of synagogues, who regard themselves as adherents of one of the three major denominations, Orthodox, Conservative, and Reform, or as Jews without any denominational preferences. Our analysis throughout focuses on the individual. We do not examine organizational structure, either at the local level or at the national; nor do we analyze the rabbinate of the various denominations. We do, however, study how individual American Jews relate, or fail to relate, to the three major Jewish denominations; how individual American Jews express themselves religiously within a denominational framework; and how they combine their denominational orientations with their involvements both in their local Jewish communities and with the community-at-large. We also seek to compare our findings with those about other religious groupings in the United States. In this regard, focusing on one family of religious groups, our work is like that of Roof on localism theory, which is based on studies of Southern Baptists (Roof 1972) and Episcopalians in North Carolina (Roof 1976, 1978), and like that of Roof and Hoge (1980) and Cornwall (1989), who generalize from studies of Catholics and Mormons, respectively.

In sum, as Harrison and Lazerwitz (1982: 369–70) call for, this book analyzes Jewish lifestyles as expressed by and through the various Jewish denominational preferences and through synagogue membership or the lack of one. Denominational preference and synagogue membership are, we contend, excellent indicators, above and beyond the social sources of denominationalism, of the sort of Jewish life one chooses to live in the open, voluntaristic, individualistic, and pluralistic society that is the United States of America.

In the next chapter, we review the history and ideology of the three major Jewish denominations, Orthodox, Conservative, and Reform to provide insight into the meaning of choosing to affiliate with one or another of them. Thus, part I of the book, which consists of the first two chapters, provides a background against which to understand what follows. The first chapter has presented our sociological perspective. The second chapter reviews the social and historical background of the denominations we study.

Part II, which consists of chapters 3 through 6, presents a review of our survey findings based on various statistical analyses of the responses to the 1990 National Jewish Population Survey and, where applicable, that of 1971 as well. The first of these chapters, chapter 3, provides information on the percentage distributions of the adherents of the three major American Jewish denominations and of those with no denominational preference for both the 1971 and 1990 National Jewish Population Surveys (NJPS) and of their general social, economic, and demographic characteristics. Where possible, the characteristics of adherents of Jewish denominations are compared with those of Christians of various persuasions.

In chapter 4 we use a more complex statistical technique, multiple regression analysis, to obtain a more detailed picture of the concomitants of denominational preference and of changes over time between the 1971 and 1990 NJPS. The appendix to chapter 4 (appendix C) describes how the various scales and indices used in this study were constructed.

Chapters 3 and 4 provide a basis for testing our claim that since religious affiliation is now more a matter of personal choice than of social inheritance—more an achieved status based on what one has done or chosen such as one's occupation, than an ascribed status based on what one is or is born into such as one's gender—denominational preferences and synagogue membership are important variables, above and beyond demographic and socioeconomic factors, for understanding how Jews live in the United States.

As noted above, however, we recognize that while denominational preference is an important indicator of how one chooses to be Jewish in the United States, the boundaries within and between the major faith groups have become increasingly permeable. In short, one consequence of religious affiliation having become a matter of choice is that the choice is important to the individual; another consequence, however, is that the boundaries defining various groups become increasingly flexible and permeable as individuals move freely among and between them.

Chapter 5 analyzes changes in denominational adherence from childhood to adulthood as an example of the permeability among Jewish groupings. Chapter 6 discusses the permeability between Jewish and non-Jewish groups by examining how the rate of marriages between Jews and non-Jews varies among adherents of the three major Jewish denominations and those with no denominational preference.

In part III, we first attempt to project some features of the future of American Jewish denominations and then consider policy questions raised by our analyses. Specifically, we begin, in chapter 7, with a projection of what the distribution among the adult Jewish population of the various denominational orientations might look like in 2010. The final chapter, chapter 8, summarizes our findings and offers recommendations for those who wish to bolster Jewish identity and promote Jewish continuity. We offer our recommendations as a focus for discussions of how American Jewry may both survive and thrive in the United States. The book concludes with a set of four methodological appendices. The first discusses the methodology of the 1990 National Jewish Population Survey; the second provides some information on our use of it; the third describes how the various scales and indices used in this study were constructed; and the fourth provides some additional information on the projections we make in chapter 7.

2

A Sociohistorical Overview of
American Jewish Denominations

Happening today w/ California UJ Semenary + NY JTS?

Denominational differences among Jews did not exist during the colonial era in America. The first Jews arrived in the port of New Amsterdam (New York) in 1654 as refugees from Brazil after the latter changed from Dutch to Portuguese control (Sarna 1986). Virtually all were traditional Jews, whom we would today call Orthodox Jews. In the seventeenth century, the divisions among Jews were based on geographic and associated cultural, rather than religious, differences. At this time, Jews were generally viewed as a distinct community both by themselves and by their neighbors. Jewish life had a medieval quality in that what rights Jews had were granted to the community as a whole and not to its individual members. Indeed, until the beginning of the modern era in the late eighteenth century, Jews, as individuals, had no rights and could not function well, if at all, apart from their community (Abrahams 1969).

Matters were quite different in the new United States. From its very creation, the United States granted full citizenship to Jews within its borders as it did to others who chose to immigrate. America, after all, was the first modern, open, and emancipated nation founded on the principles of the Enlightenment. Assimilation into such a nation was greatly facilitated by what Gordon (1964) has called Anglo-conformity, conformity to the norms of the largely white Anglo-Saxon Protestant society of the "Founding Fathers." Most Jews chose such conformity, at least to some extent, but at the same time they did not wish to abandon Judaism.

The First Jewish Denomination: Reform Judaism

One result of the desire both to conform and to remain Jewish is the emergence of the Reform movement in the United States. While the movement originated in Germany, it was developed further by Jews of German ancestry in the nineteenth century in the United States. As such, it represents the first modern Jewish denomination in the United States, where it has flourished in recent years. Reform Judaism has its roots in the struggle after the Napoleonic wars of German Jews for civil rights and citizenship in the various states that later formed Germany. Under the leadership of those Jews who had acquired some measure of wealth and European education, some Jews in Germany revolted against traditional Judaism. They gradually established their own synagogues in which they introduced nontraditional practices, such as using the language of their country for a number of prayers in place of the traditional Hebrew (*Encyclopedia Judaica* 1971: 23–27).

The first Reform temple was formed in 1818, in Hamburg. Its new practices included use of an organ, and de-emphasis on prayers dealing with the hoped for arrival of the Messiah and the restoration of Jews to the land of Israel, then a Turkish province. The Reform movement, encompassing an ever-growing body of religious changes, spread rapidly among wealthier Jews in Germany, England, and France.

The growth of Reform Judaism in the United States was based on the immigration of a sizeable number of German Jews during the 1840s and 1850s, especially after the failure of the Europe-wide revolutions of 1848, and in later years. Congregation Emanu-El of New York City was started in 1845 and became a stronghold of American Reform Judaism. The American rabbinate of the pre–Civil War era was a product of German Jewry. A major force behind the growth of American Reform Judaism was the German-born Rabbi Isaac Mayer Wise.

Rabbi Wise spent his most active years in Cincinnati, Ohio. From there, he aided in the formation of numerous Reform temples (a term preferred to "synagogue" to emphasize the abandoning of the traditional hope for the rebuilding of a Temple in Jerusalem). In 1873, he formed the Union of American Hebrew Congregations, the umbrella organization for Reform temples and the oldest Jewish denominational organization in the United States. He next established Hebrew Union College in 1875 as the American institution for the training of Reform rabbis. Finally, in 1889 he established the Central Conference of American Rabbis for the American Reform movement.

In 1885, the leadership of the Reform movement met in Pittsburgh and adopted a statement of Reform Jewish principles, the Pittsburgh Platform, which marked a radical departure from traditional Judaism. It greatly de-emphasized Talmudic studies; abandoned the Jewish dietary laws; and rejected the religious desire for a Jewish return to the land of Israel, a position that subsequently led the Reform movement to oppose early Zionism. However, it retained and indeed emphasized a commitment to social justice as outlined by the Hebrew prophets.

Post CW?

Early Reform Judaism + its ed. implications

It is not surprising—given the full citizenship Jews enjoyed in the United States, the example of American Protestants developing many different denominations that entailed radical religious shifts from prior European Protestant positions, and the rise to upper- and middle-class status of a growing number of German Jews and their descendants—that American Reform Judaism would produce a format so radically different from traditional Judaism that it constituted a new denomination. The aim of the movement was to enable American Jews to participate fully in the life of the United States. Complete acculturation to the surrounding society was among its major goals. To this end, some Reform congregations shifted their weekly services from Saturday, the traditional Jewish Sabbath, to Sunday, the Christian Sabbath. Reform Jewish education followed the Protestant model in that there was a weekly Sunday school program rather than the traditional daily study. In its earlier years, Reform Judaism became the denomination preferred by many upwardly mobile and upper-class Jews.

For Reform Judaism, the events of the post–Civil War era represented the apogee of denominational divergence from the orbit of traditional Judaism that had dominated American Jewish life for about two centuries. During the twentieth century, the orbit of Reform Judaism, as reflected in the Columbus Platform of 1937, began to move somewhat closer to the more traditional norms. In the decades since the end of World War II, in cognizance of the European Jewish Holocaust and the creation of the State of Israel, many Reform temples have restored a variety of traditional Jewish practices and the movement now strongly supports Israel. It is now more tolerant of traditional Jewish practices that it had previously disdained, such as the dietary laws and wearing *kippot* (yarmulkes or skull caps) at religious services. It has also greatly broadened its membership base to include many Jews of Eastern European descent. In addition, as we shall show in later chapters, many current adherents of Reform Judaism have a background in more traditional movements. These adherents, many of Eastern European rather than German ancestry, are more religiously traditional than those who were reared in the Reform movement itself. The inclusion of these new elements in Reform Judaism is leading the movement in a direction of greater observance of traditional Jewish religious practices. Nevertheless, a degree of fragmentation exists over ideology and personal practices, further amplified by variations in the national ancestry and religious backgrounds of their membership. (For more detailed treatments of Reform Judaism, see Furman 1987; Agus 1975: Fein, Chin, Daucher, Reisman, and Spiro 1972; Blau 1966).

As Wertheimer (1993: 96) noted,

Whereas Reform was formerly a movement that on principle said no to some aspects of Jewish tradition, it is now a movement that is open to all Jewish possibilities, whether traditional or innovative. The guiding principle of Reform today is the autonomy of every individual to choose a Jewish expression that is personally meaningful.

The essential individualism of Reform Judaism resonates well with American culture and its tendency, noted in chapter 1, toward "Sheilaisms," the construction of personally meaningful, even if unique, religious belief systems. Such resonance helps make Reform Judaism a dynamic force in the contemporary United States.

The Counter-Reformation: Orthodox Judaism

The prospect of widespread individualism, for example, of everyone "making *Shabbos*" (observing the Jewish Sabbath), according to one's own lights or not making it at all, led to the emergence of the modern interpretation of traditional Judaism known as Orthodoxy. It sought to reassert the normative religious standards of Judaism embodied in *halakha* (traditional Jewish law) so as to preserve the status quo. Such attempts at reassertion can be dated as far back as 1819, one year after the Hamburg Reform Temple opened in Germany (*Encyclopedia Judaica* 1971: 1486–94).

Thus, from an historical perspective, Orthodoxy is the second movement to be organized as a denomination, first in Germany and later in the United States. It represented an attempt by the traditionalists in the Jewish community to counter the challenge of Reform Judaism.

Today's version of Orthodoxy is an adaptation of the traditional Judaism brought to America by the masses of Eastern European Jewish immigrants in the late nineteenth and early twentieth century. It rapidly replaced the orthodoxy of earlier, largely Sephardic (Spanish and Portuguese), Jewish immigrants. Eastern European Jews had backgrounds that were steeped in traditional Judaism. These persons faced the difficult task of adjusting to life in the United States and the need to earn a living under trying economic circumstances. Children often regarded their immigrant parents as "greenhorns," ignorant of American ways, and they resisted socialization into an Orthodox lifestyle that might inhibit their acceptance of such ways. Formal Jewish education for American-born Orthodox children was not very well conducted. The net result was the rapid abandonment of Orthodoxy by many children of Eastern European Jewish immigrants.

Initially, Orthodox synagogues had little connection with each other. However, American Orthodoxy gradually began to organize itself. The main institution established by those elements interested in perpetuating an Orthodox way of life in the United States was the *yeshiva*, a school for the study of traditional Jewish texts. Many of the *yeshivot* (plural of *yeshiva*) were total, all-

Ed.
- implications

encompassing institutions, insulated, and at times even isolated, from the non-Jewish world, where religious subjects could be the focus of concern and outside influences were shut out. The Etz Chaim Yeshiva was founded in 1886. It served as the basis for the synthesis of religious and secular life through its evolution into Yeshiva College in 1915 and later into Yeshiva University (1945). It represents the largest independent university founded under Jewish auspices. It was followed by theological colleges in Chicago and Baltimore.

National Orthodox organizations were established for Orthodox rabbis, such as the Union of Orthodox Rabbis in the United States and Canada (1902), and the Rabbinical Council of America (1920) founded by more modern English-speaking rabbis than the Union, which included more European, Yiddish-speaking rabbis. Synagogues organized as well and the Union of Orthodox Jewish Congregations of America was founded in 1898.

The contemporary yeshiva day school movement serves as a forum for a synthesis between religious and secular life. After World War II and the Holocaust, Orthodox Jewish survivors made their way to the United States and contributed to the growth of the educational network of Orthodox Jews. Thus, even as many American-born Jews were leaving the Orthodox fold of their childhood for the Conservative and Reform denominations, American Orthodoxy slowly began building a network of full-time Jewish primary grades and high schools that incorporated advanced Jewish education with standard American education.

Orthodox Jewry has made ideological as well as organizational adjustments in America. As Heilman and Cohen (1989: 2) note, Orthodox immigrants from Eastern Europe were essentially inertial in their religious commitments, able to hold on to their Orthodoxy as long as there was no resistance, but without a developed ideology that could facilitate withstanding the challenges of American modernity. However, those Orthodox Jews who migrated just before or after World War II came with a "far more experienced, time-tested, worked-through, volitional Orthodoxy" (1989: 22), with an ideology to support resistance to the corrosive influences of modernity. (For more details on Orthodox Jews, see Heilman 1992; Davidman 1991; Danzger 1989; Bulka 1983; and Helmreich 1982.)

To be sure, while all versions of contemporary Orthodoxy pursue the path of a Judaism based in *halakha*, the traditional Jewish religious code, Orthodox Jewry is not monolithic. There are traditionalists who seek to follow all religious precepts and insulate themselves, their families, and communities from secular influences. However, there is also a "modern Orthodox" movement, the Young Israel movement, that is more accommodating to secular society and seeks to combine tradition with civil society. The first Young Israel synagogue was established in the early years of the twentieth century in New York by Mordecai Kaplan (who later laid the foundation for Reconstructionist

Judaism). The National Council of Young Israel was formed by such modern Orthodox Jews in 1912. It brought rabbis over from Europe and established community-wide organizations to provide better Jewish education and to supervise commerce in kosher products. Nevertheless, of all the Jewish denominations, Orthodoxy remains the most fragmented organizationally, embracing the ultra-Orthodox sects such as the Lubavitcher Hasidim (Habad) as well as the modern Orthodox of the Young Israel movement. For example, Heilman and Cohen point out that some Orthodox rabbinic organizations are contra-acculturative in their orientation and seek

> to promote Orthodox religious Jewish observance above all else, even at the cost of ignoring or spurning contemporary American culture. They eschew dialogue or interaction with those more acculturative rabbis who do not share these commitments. (1989: 27)

In contrast to the Reform and Conservative denominations in the United States, Orthodox synagogues, except those in the Young Israel movement, are by and large separate institutions that have little contact with one another. The Young Israel movement is much more American than the traditional Orthodox synagogue. Young Israel synagogues use a Hebrew prayerbook with English translation. Their rabbis have university degrees and their sermons are in English. Men and women are seated on the same floor, rather than men on the main floor and women, totally apart, in a second-floor balcony. However, in recognition of tradition, there is a wall or barrier (*mehitza*) separating men and women during religious services. There is also a mixed-gender youth movement, a phenomenon that is totally abhorrent to the extreme traditionalists.

The Young Israel synagogues are also part of the Union of Orthodox Jewish Congregations of America. The Union has become one of the leading representatives of modern Orthodoxy. A primary focus of the movement is on ensuring rigid observance of Jewish dietary laws through its *kashrut* division (which grants the OU [Orthodox Union] label certifying that the food bearing it is kosher). It has also established a relatively successful youth movement, the National Council of Synagogue Youth (NCSY), that has mixed-gender activities.

In addition to the development of formal organizations, the development of more informal networks in neighborhoods populated by Orthodox Jews throughout the United States is noteworthy. Another major development in today's Orthodox community is the use of mass media and modern technology, including computer technology, to further religious life. There are Orthodox newspapers and magazines that are quite sophisticated in their layouts and formats. Orthodox radio programs are broadcast in some cities in the United States. "Dial a Daf" (page of the Talmud) phone lines enable subscribers to phone in and listen to a lesson any hour of the day (in a choice of languages). More recently, on-line computer access has made a variety of text-based material available as well. The adjustment of Orthodox life to American culture is also illustrated by the presence of kosher pizza shops and kosher Chinese or Italian restaurants. These are found in more and more Jewish communities throughout the United States. Orthodox leaders often encourage their presence as means of providing Orthodox boys and girls a place to meet.[1] Obviously, secular society does impinge on the lives of American Orthodox Jews. On the other hand, in recent years, there also seems to be greater accommodation to, awareness of, and respect for Orthodox Jews in American society.

As this book shows, the number and proportion of Orthodox Jews in the United States is quite small. However, the denomination may be significant not only for its members, but for the impact it has on the religious patterns and norms of the non-Orthodox community. Nevertheless, competing elements of the Orthodox movement are prone to accuse one another of wavering in their commitment to traditional ways. All are reluctant to be accused of being "reformist" or "too modern." As Waxman (1996, 29) noted,

> Along with modernization, secularization, and the pluralization, denominationally, of Judaism as well as a decline in the authority of the family and community traditions, there has been a marked emphasis on *humra*, greater ritualistic stringency. Despite the often flaunted triumphalism of the Orthodox, the minority status of the Orthodox—who are the overwhelming majority of day school administrators, faculty, and students—has given rise to a siege mentality. Perhaps this should not be too surprising, since triumphalism is almost certainly a defense against the real fear and anxieties.

As Wertheimer concludes,

> Even as Orthodoxy has emerged in the last quarter of the twentieth century as an outspoken and triumphant force, it continues to struggle to cope with modernity and endures an internal *Kulturkampf* between its modern and antimodern wings. (1993: 136)

The Centrist Denomination: Conservative Judaism

Many students of human behavior make use of the concept, introduced by the philosopher Friedrich Hegel, of the dialectic, that is, the notion that every idea or *thesis* calls forth its opposite or *antithesis*, which ultimately results in *synthesis*, or blending of the two. American Jewish denominationalism has experienced something of a dialectic process in the past century and a half or so in

the struggle between the forces of traditional Eastern European Orthodox
Judaism and the modernizers of German Reform Judaism. The conflict has produced the Hegelian outcome of a synthesis in the form of Conservative Judaism,
a denomination, developed in the United States, where the forces of tradition
and modernity met as descendants of Eastern European and German Jewry
struggling to shape a Judaism that would thrive in America. That is, "Conservative Judaism in the United States crystallized its institutions, not in dissent
from Orthodoxy, but in reaction to Reform" (*Encyclopedia Judaica* 1971: 902).

Many tensions were evident in American Judaism at the beginning of the
twentieth century: the radical religious changes brought about by the Reform
denomination versus the organizational response of Orthodoxy to bolster traditional practices; the desire to preserve Jewish ways versus the readiness to
give up whatever Jewish customs were seen as standing in the way of social
and economic advancement in American society. All of these tensions in the
dialectic of denominationalism were bound to create a search for some middle way. Some American Jews surely felt strange amidst the sharply different
customs and higher social status of Reform Judaism, yet could not accept the
rigidity of Orthodoxy. Out of the difficulties felt by both ordinary Jews and
rabbinical leaders emerged a resolution to the dialectic in the form of the Conservative denomination, a home-grown American response to the tensions felt
by Jews in the United States.

This response was furthered by the efforts of Rabbi Sabato Morais in
establishing the Jewish Theological Seminary of America (JTS) in 1886 in
New York City. JTS subsequently became dedicated to seeking out a middle
way between the Reform and Orthodox versions of Judaism. It began a period
of major growth in 1902 with the assumption of its presidency by Rabbi
Solomon Schechter. An alumni association had already begun in 1901. It grew
into the Rabbinical Assembly of America by 1902 and was formally incorporated as such in 1929.

As JTS became known, and as its rabbinical graduates became the heads
of synagogues, knowledge of its orientation spread among American-born
Jews. The number of synagogues with an orientation similar to that of the
Jewish Theological Seminary grew rapidly and they formed the United Synagogue of America in 1913.

Typically, the liturgy of the synagogues of the Conservative movement
contains much more Hebrew than that found in Reform congregations. Many
of the adherents of the Conservative movement observe *kashrut*, the traditional Jewish dietary laws. They were also much more in favor of the early
Zionist movement than were Reform Jews. The joint seating of men and
women is a good indicator of how changes have taken place within the Conservative movement. The more traditional synagogues retained separate seating for men and women for a longer time than did the less traditional

synagogues. In short, Conservative synagogues have sought to retain the flavor of the Jewish traditions of the old country while moving nearer to the surrounding American social environment.

The pull of the forces of tradition and of accommodation are illustrated by two relatively recent changes within Conservative Judaism. On the one hand, there are the accommodations represented by the decision to educate women as rabbis. On the other hand, there is the expansion of Solomon Schechter day schools, which provide both Jewish and general education for Conservative youth in the elementary, and even high school, grades. The denomination also gives considerable emphasis to Jewish summer camp programs. Its Camp Ramah program is widely regarded as an effective instrument of furthering Jewish identity and commitment to the Conservative movement.

In the tradition of denominationalism in the United States, Conservatism has endured the splitting off of two much smaller movements from its more liberal and more traditional wings, respectively (Silverman 1994). The first split, in 1954, was that of the more religiously liberal Reconstructionists. More recently, the Union for Traditional Judaism was formed in reaction against the decision of the Jewish Theological Seminary to accept women into their rabbinical studies program. (Only one percent of our survey respondents declare themselves to be Reconstructionists, even fewer, less than half a percent, declare themselves to be Traditionalists. Despite the substantial interest in these groups and the changes they may portend for American Jewry, their small numbers preclude their being examined separately in the statistical analysis reported in subsequent chapters.)[2]

The most trenchant sociological analysis of Conservative Judaism remains that offered by Marshall Sklare (1972; but see also Rosenblum 1983 and Siegel 1977). Sklare (1972: 246) explained the dramatic rise of Conservative Judaism:

> [C]ertain needs were so accentuated in the Jewish community as to require a greater degree of adjustment on the part of Orthodoxy than it was able to make. Distinguished by a pervasive interest in group survival, individuals who shared a similar class position, degree of acculturation, and a common background in the Judaism of Eastern Europe, established the first "Conservative" synagogue chiefly during the second and third decades of the [twentieth] century.

However, even though Sklare was writing at the time of Conservative Judaism's peak, he (1972: 281) believed it possible to discern its potential decline:

> [T]he immediate reasons for the drop in Conservative morale at the very zenith of Conservative influence include the emergence of Orthodoxy, the problem of Conservative observance, and the widespread alienation among Conservative young people from the American culture.

As noted above, in our discussions of Reform and Orthodox Judaism, inherent tensions exist within each of these movements. No less is true of Conservative Judaism. As the *Encyclopedia Judaica* noted (1971: 906):

> The Conservative movement has always shown great capacity for maintaining institutional unity amidst great conflict. To continue such unity amidst even greater diversity is the problem which it, perhaps more than either Reform or neo-Orthodoxy, will have to face in the next generation.

In the generation since these words were written, the Reconstructionists on the left have developed as an independent denomination and, on the right, the Union for Traditional Judaism has emerged. As noted above, in the contemporary context, the leaders of the Conservative movement have concluded:

> American Judaism has entered a "virulently denominational age" of religious polarization [and] . . . resolved to assert in the public arena the correctness of Conservative Judaism's recently modified, yet still centrist position. (Wertheimer 1993: 159)

Denominational Development in Historical Retrospect

Table 2.1 presents a summary, based primarily on the work of Glazer (1989) and Sklare (1971), of the history of denominational development within Jewry in the United States. It highlights the *historical period* and the predominance of various ethnic and generational groups and associated *population changes*. The remaining columns show the kinds of *adjustment* Jews experienced within each historical period, both *economic* and *political*, and the related *social* and *religious changes* that the former helped to create.

Denominational Differences:
Homosexuality as a Case in Point

There are a variety of social and political issues on which the denominations diverge. Perhaps no other controversy more sharply reveals the essential denominational differences than that in discussions of homosexuality. These differences are revealed in the following responses by Orthodox, Conservative, and Reform spokespersons as to their respective positions on this matter as quoted in the *Hartford Jewish Ledger*, the Hartford Jewish community newspaper (January 20, 1995, p. 20).

TABLE 2.1

Phases in American Jewish History:
Social Characteristics and Adjustments

Time Frame & Dominant Group	Economic Adjustment: Dominant Occupation	Political Adjustment: Level of Anti-Semitism	Social Adjustment: Degree of Assimilation	Religious Adjustment: Denominational Development
1654–1825 Sephardic	Merchant	Barriers exist	Assimilated to Anglo-Saxon culture	"Dignified" traditional Judaism dominant
1825–1880 German	Peddling	Low level	Assimilated, but maintain separate, "ghetto-like" communities	Reform emerges
1880–1920 East European 1st generation	Skilled factory worker	Rising with racism and nativism	Assimilated, but still maintain separate communities	Orthodox and Conservative emerge
1920–1945 East European 2nd generation	White collar; entrepreneurs; professionals	Peaks	Increased, still in separate communities	Rise of Conservative Judaism
1945–1967 East European 3rd generation	Family business; professionals	Declining	Increased move to suburbs; "gilded" ghettoes emerge	Conservatives dominant; reform rises again
1967–present East European 4th generation	Professionals; corporate business	Latent	Polarization with assimilation; metropolitan dispersal	Reform challenges Conservative for dominance

An Orthodox Viewpoint

Rabbi Pinchas Stolpher, executive vice president of the Union of Orthodox Jewish Congregations of America, presents an Orthodox viewpoint:

> A gay Jew is a person suffering from a sickness. We should help him deal with the problem with warmth and sympathy. We certainly should include him in the synagogue. But we believe the standard set by the Torah is an eternal and immutable one. Our definition of homosexuality as an abomination remains intact.
>
> We believe every human being is capable of exercising moral control over his behavior. We reject the notion that this is an alternative and acceptable lifestyle. Through rabbis and educators, I know of many young people who experimented with homosexuality as adolescents. Most give it up as a childish fling. There's a very broad spectrum of homosexuality, and many individuals do not look upon it as something that can't be changed.
>
> There's no question that people rationalize what's in the Torah, especially people who struggle. The Talmud says, "A person who sins twice and then a third time convinces himself his sin is permissible."

A Conservative Viewpoint

A Conservative viewpoint is provided by Shammai Englemayer, director of communications at the Conservative movement's Jewish Theological Seminary:

> We want to make clear to one and all that none of us tries to pass judgment on people. We want to be as open as possible to everyone. We encourage synagogues and institutions not to turn people away because of their lifestyle. Discrimination is anti-religious.
>
> The only thing we can't do is allow gay rabbis. We have an *halakhic* problem with that. We have to interpret the Torah's prohibition of this lifestyle as a prohibition against religious leadership. If a gay or lesbian person agreed to be celibate, it would technically be permissible to ordain him or her. But that's a heavy burden. It's not the fact of being gay or lesbian that's a *halakhic* problem, but the acting on it. Our movement is founded on the basis of *halakha*. That makes it very, very difficult to approve of a gay synagogue. If a group of Jews—and I realize this is a terrible comparison for gays and lesbians—wanted to start a synagogue for people who were non-Shabbat observers or non-kosher, we wouldn't recognize that synagogue.
>
> The issue is causing a lot of grief in the movement on all fronts. We want to think of ourselves as a modern movement that recognizes its members' needs and aspirations. Even those saying "no" for the most part would want to say, "yes." But then we can't call ourselves what we call ourselves a movement based on *halakha*. If we were to give in to the side that wants recognition of gay rabbis, our movement is over. If we stand our ground, a schism develops. It's a no-win situation. No one is taking it lightly.

A Reform Viewpoint

Rabbi Lynne Landsberg, associate director of the Reform movement's Religious Action Center, presents a Reform point of view:

> For us, it's a non-issue. If you're gay and Jewish, the only part that matters is that you're Jewish. This is not to say there aren't issues the Reform movement has to work out. Sacramental issues, for example, haven't yet been formally addressed. But our attitude is that this is not a matter of tolerance; it's a matter of equality.
>
> The Reform movement considers Jewish law to be its guideline. We study and make Torah real for our lives. There are going to be times when biblical dictates and the realities of modern Jewish life don't easily coincide. This is one of them. It's something with which we grapple.

In essence, the Orthodox rabbi rejects homosexuality "as an abomination" based on biblical and rabbinic dicta. The Conservative representative reveals the dilemma of this movement in trying not "to pass judgment on people," but needing to adhere to traditional Jewish law that rejects homosexuality based on biblical references as the Orthodox representative argued. The Reform rabbi explains that Jewish law is only a guideline and not binding on "the realities of modern Jewish life."

While these statements graphically reveal the essential ideological differences among the denominations, most American Jews, even those with a denominational preference, may well be unable to articulate these points with any clarity. Perhaps, those who belong to a temple or synagogue may find it a bit easier to state their denomination's viewpoint. However, we believe that the choice of a particular denomination is based not so much on detailed knowledge of its specific positions as it is on an awareness of where that denomination falls on broad and multifaceted continua from the traditional to the more modern, that is, from strict observance of Jewish law and tradition (as represented in *halakha*) to greater and greater willingness to modify those traditions and laws to meet the demands of accommodating to the modern (non-Jewish) world. On that continuum, the Orthodox, including the various Hasidic sects, are clearly on one side, usually called the "right." The Reform movement, including perhaps the Society for Humanistic Judaism, which accepts Reform liturgy but rejects theism, is on the other side of the continuum, on what is usually called the "left." The Conservative denominations are somewhere in the middle. The new Union for Traditional Judaism, more to the right, is closer to the Orthodox, and the somewhat older Reconstructionist movement, more to the left, is closer to the Reform.

The Social Psychology of
American Jewish Denominationalism

Following the brief introduction to the three major American Jewish denominations—the Reform, Orthodox, and Conservative—with their offshoots, we turn to the focus of this book: a concern with the characteristics of those American Jews who regard themselves as followers of one of these denominations or as being Jews without any denominational preference. We do not examine the practices of the synagogues of these three denominations, their organizational structure at a local or national level, or the rabbinate of these denominations. Rather, we study how American Jews, as individuals, relate to these three denominations, or fail to relate to them, how American Jews express themselves religiously within a denominational framework, and how American Jews combine their denominational orientations with their involvements in their local Jewish communities, their overall localities, and their social relations with America's other citizens.

What we examine, as pointed out by Harrison and Lazerwitz (1982: 369–70), are Jewish lifestyles as expressed by and through a preference for one of the major Jewish denominations or through a nondenominational position. Denominational preference, then, symbolizes how individuals view themselves both as Americans and as Jews. Denominational preference is, we believe, a most useful indicator of a person's Jewish lifestyle, with significance above and beyond socioeconomic status or demographic factors. Denominational preference is associated with a lifestyle reflected in what one eats and the religious rituals performed in one's home, with one's choice of a synagogue, and with one's relation with non-Jews including the choice of friends and even the choice of a spouse.

The importance of denominational preference is understandable from a social psychological perspective that holds that one's identity is based on an internalized orientation that is shaped by individual, group, and social factors. Among the major factors forming an American Jew's identity are those that define how one regards one's Jewish background.

In the past, being Jewish was largely a matter of ascription, a matter of birth rather than choice. More recently, the situation has changed. Being Jewish is now to an important degree a matter of choice and not simply a matter of descent. Moreover, it is increasingly plausible to decide that even if one has Jewish parents, being Jewish need have no significance in one's own adult life. One may decide to have no religious affiliation and one need not be involved with any Jewish community. Even one's spouse or children may not be Jewish. Being Jewish may be a matter of ancestry and not an important aspect of one's adult life. The identities of such individuals may be constructed on the basis of being an American of a certain educational level, occupation, or profession, or with certain political beliefs.

However, for most Jews in America, being born into a Jewish family and being raised as a Jew results in a Jewish identity that one wishes to acknowledge and express. Such expression finds outlets in a preference for an American Jewish denomination and for finding a place within the organized Jewish community. Despite the fact that the amount of ritual observance and the degree of involvement in organized Jewish life varies considerably even among members of a single Jewish congregation, a denominational preference may well reflect an internal feeling of who one is and who one is not. Of course, many factors enter into the choice of a particular synagogue or temple: family ties, location, cost, and reactions to the rabbi and even to the physical facilities. However, we believe such a choice basically reflects one's identity as a Jew and as an American. For example, by choosing to join a Reform congregation, a Jewish adult is saying not only that he/she is an adherent of the Reform movement, but that he/she is not Orthodox or Conservative, that he/she is less, rather than more, traditional. The ensuing chapters will try to quantify the characteristics of adherents of the major Jewish denominations, as well as those with no preference, as revealed by the 1990 National Jewish Population Survey. The findings will also explore to what extent preferences are associated with differing levels of synagogue and communal activities and the degree to which there is continuity or change over the past two decades since the first Jewish population survey in 1971.

Summary

The transformation of Eastern European Jewry from its isolated, even pariah, status in the various Eastern European nations to full participation in American society was accompanied by Jewish efforts to reduce the religious and communal differences that separated them from their fellow citizens. These efforts resulted in the expansion of a Reform denomination, first formed in Germany in the nineteenth century, which eliminated whatever traditional Jewish customs its adherents felt were blocking full integration into their adopted society. There were also those Jews who refused to eliminate traditional Jewish religious and communal practices and who helped to create modern Orthodoxy in the United States. In between these two religious endeavors, the Conservative denomination emerged as a search for what its adherents regard as a middle way between the Orthodox reluctance to change and the Reform willingness to do so.

In the United States, these movements have developed into full-fledged denominations within the context of a denominational American society.

American Reform Judaism initially followed a path of "radical change." However, in the decades since World War II, the Reform denomination has moved in the direction of greater acceptance of traditional ways. Meanwhile, Orthodoxy has modernized itself and created an extensive Jewish school system. The Conservative denomination, in its most developed form, is an American creation. It has endeavored to retain as much of the Jewish tradition as possible while making as few reinterpretations as necessary in the light of conditions in contemporary American society.

In a sense, American Judaism is somewhat like a symphonic orchestra playing variations on common themes, those of traditional Judaism. The Reform are the first to play and then the Orthodox respond. Subsequently, Conservative Judaism joins in (and Reconstructionism responds to them). However, since there is no conductor and each denomination plays according to its own interpretation of the score, the result is not always as harmonious as a symphony.

As with all Americans, Jews have undergone a great deal of change under the impact of industrialization, urbanization, secularization, and modernization. These same forces have, of course, influenced American Protestants, who, as a result, have undergone considerable religious and communal changes. However, while American Protestants have faced such changes aware of their foundational role in the creation of many of the cultural institutions of the United States, American Jewry (like American Catholicism) has had to face these forces initially aware of their status as an immigrant minority in the United States. Hence, many of the changes in American Jewish denominationalism are the result of their struggles to acculturate and assimilate so as to narrow the differences between them and their fellow, predominantly Christian, Americans.

PART II

3

A General Description of the Adherents of American Jewish Denominations

This chapter begins our study of the general characteristics of the adult adherents of American Jewish denominations by presenting an overview of the findings from two surveys of the American Jewish population. The first survey is the 1971 National Jewish Population Survey (1971 NJPS). It pictures the American Jewish community as of 1971; the second, as of 1990 (1990 NJPS). Throughout this book, the emphasis will be upon contrasting the findings of these two surveys.

We begin this chapter with a review of how the two surveys were conducted and of what is required to render them comparable and usable for our purposes. We then describe how our two main variables, denominational preference and synagogue membership, are defined operationally by the questions asked in the two surveys. Then the variables whose relationships to denominational preference and synagogue membership we are interested in are identified and the techniques to make them usable in our statistical analyses are described. The remainder of the chapter is then devoted to a description of the distributions of denominational preferences and synagogue memberships in 1971 and 1990 together with their relationships to important demographic and socioeconomic variables and to various measures of involvement in Jewish life and the life of American society at large.

The Two Surveys

The 1971 NJPS data were obtained from a combination of samples from local Jewish federation lists and a complex, multistage, disproportionately stratified, area cluster sample design for Jewish housing units not on federation lists. The 1971 survey yielded 5,790 interviews at a 79% response rate. (For a detailed explanation of the 1971 NJPS sample design, see Lazerwitz 1974a.)

The 1990 NJPS sample was obtained by selecting residences from among all United States residential telephones by a process known as Random Digit Dialing (RDD). This process obtained a probability sample of households, using a screening interview, in which at least one resident was then Jewish, or had a Jewish parent. Within these households, one sample Jewish respondent was selected by the "next birthday method of respondent selection" (see Salmon and Nichols 1983).

The 1990 survey obtained 2,441 interviews through the use of a two-stage interviewing procedure that first screened all telephone sample respondents for eligibility and, some time later, recontacted them for the actual interview. The response rate for the initial screening interview was 63%; the response rate among those screened and actually interviewed in the second stage was 68%, for a combined (0.63 × 0.68) rate of 43%. (After clarification of final eligibility, the final response rate is nearly 50%.)

In order to compare the two surveys it is necessary to understand how each defines "who is a Jew." The focus on comparing two surveys also requires that we use comparable categories to define denominational preferences and the battery of background or socioeconomic variables that we examine. We will discuss the matter of comparability first and then turn to a description of findings from the two surveys.

The Population of Interest

The goal of probability surveys is to enable one to generalize from sample findings to the population that has been sampled. Our concern is with the adult Jewish population of the United States. To ensure comparability between the two surveys we have adopted the definition of an adult used in the first, 1971, survey: anyone twenty years of age or older.

Within sampled housing units, respondents were selected by a probability process from among all resident Jewish adults. The sampled housing units were obtained by complex sample design methods that were different for each survey.

Since there are varying numbers of Jewish adults in sampled households, it is necessary to adjust or "weight" the statistics derived from respondent answers to survey questions for the number of Jewish adults in a sampled household. The use of such adjustments or "weights" compensates for the fact that some households have more Jews in them than others. That is, since only one adult in a given household has been interviewed, a potential respondent in a household with two Jewish adults is more likely to be interviewed (one chance in two) than, for example, somebody in a household of three adult Jews (one chance in three).

Statistical analysis calls for additional weights or adjustments to ensure equality in the probability of a sample housing unit's being selected for the survey. Since the two surveys (1971 and 1990) used different sample designs, the additional housing unit weight factors are different for each survey. However, the goals of our analysis require comparability between the 1971 and 1990 surveys. Therefore, we do not use the weights or adjustments used by those who work only with the 1990 survey. Rather, as was done in 1971, we use a weighting system for the 1990 survey that is based on the number of Jewish adults in sample housing units.[1]

Our population of interest, the population about which we will present our conclusions or generalizations, then, is the population of Jews, twenty years or age or older, as that population is defined on the basis of a weighted, statistically adjusted sample of individual respondents chosen from within the sampled households. To understand who is in that population, it is necessary to understand who is defined as a Jew and thus eligible for inclusion in the sample.

Who is a Jew?

The first requirement of any Jewish population survey is to decide whom to include as a Jew. The decision is not easily arrived at given the differences among various official and personal definitions of who is a Jew. For example, Orthodox Jews officially define a Jew as anybody born of a Jewish mother, whether or not the father is Jewish, while Reform Jews will accept as a Jew one who is raised as a Jew even if one's father, but not one's mother, is Jewish. In any case, the 1971 survey did not ask directly about religious preference. Rather, it recognized that Jews could regard themselves as Jewish by their religion or as Jewish in an ethnic sense. It asked respondents "Are you Jewish?" This direct question was qualified by responses to subsequent questions about whether a respondent was born Jewish, is Jewish now, or had a father or mother who was born Jewish.

The 1990 survey determined who is a Jew by initially asking about religious preference. If the household respondent said, "Jewish," the screening questions stopped there and the household was deemed eligible for the survey. If the response was "not Jewish," then further questions were asked about whether the person or anybody else in the household considered themselves Jewish, was raised Jewish or had a Jewish parent. The 1990 survey was, then, designed to include respondents who are not currently Jewish, but who have recent Jewish ancestry.

Each approach to the question of who is a Jew rests on a respondent's self-definition. The 1971 survey did not initially seek to differentiate between those who regarded themselves as Jewish by religion from those who regarded themselves as Jewish by some other criterion. Later in the interview, the 1971 survey did seek to determine which of the Jewish respondents had little or no Jewish religious involvement but regarded themselves as Jewish by ethnic or parental background. The 1990 survey, by contrast, sought to distinguish among those who were Jews by religion, those who regarded themselves as without any religion but as Jewish nonetheless, and those who have at least one Jewish parent but who did not regard themselves as Jewish.

To ensure comparability between the two surveys with regard to Jews who have no current religious preference, the approach of the first survey is followed. In the first survey, those respondents who were raised as Jews but said they had no religious preference at present were placed into a category called "no Jewish denominational preference." The same approach has been followed with those eligible for the 1990 survey who claimed no religious preference.

Some difficulties do arise when applying the 1971 approach to the 1990 survey, particularly with regard to those respondents who had either a Jewish father or Jewish mother, but who were born into, raised in, and now profess a non-Jewish religion. In our analysis of Jewish denominational preferences, we have excluded respondents who have converted from Judaism to another religion or who were never Jewish themselves even if they had a Jewish parent. Such respondents were rare in the first survey. Just 10 respondents in 1971 reported converting away from Judaism; and only 48 persons reported themselves as never having been Jewish even though they had a parent who was born Jewish. These 58 cases represent a small proportion (about one percent) of the total 5,790 cases in the 1971 survey.

The situation is much different for the respondents in the 1990 survey which, for its own purposes, sought to include so-called "core" Jews, "both Born Jews and Jews by choice as well as those Born Jews without a current religion" and all the other "non-core" Jews (Kosmin, Goldstein, Waksberg, Lerer, Keysar, and Scheckner 1991: 4). There are 536 respondent households in which all the members consider themselves as Christian and as never having been Jewish even though one of them had a parent who was born Jewish.[2] These respondents constitute a considerable proportion (22%) of the 2,441 respondents in the 1990 survey. Since the individuals concerned are not considered Jewish by our definition, members of these 536 survey households are not included in our analysis. In addition, the 1990 survey included some twenty-five respondents who, while originally Jewish, had converted to another religion. These respondents are similarly excluded from our analysis. Converts to Judaism, on the other hand, are counted as Jews. As a result of the need to establish consistency in the definition of who is a Jew in our analyses of the two surveys, we use only 1,905 of the original 2,441 interviews for 1990.

Denominational Preferences
and Synagogue Membership

In each survey, respondents were asked the following question with regard to their Jewish denominational preferences: "Referring to Jewish religious denominations, do you consider yourself to be Conservative, Orthodox, Reform, Reconstructionist, or something else?" Those who answered, "Orthodox," "Conservative," or "Reform" were coded as such (1 for Orthodox, 2 for Conservative, 3 for Reform). As in 1971 (see Lazerwitz and Harrison 1979), and to ensure comparability between it and the 1990 survey, we recoded the handful of Reconstructionists as Conservative, the denomination in which their movement began. Respondents who said they were "traditional" or "traditionalist," an even smaller group than the Reconstructionists, were recoded as Orthodox. Respondents who indicated they were "just Jewish," "secular Jews," or in any case not Orthodox, Conservative, Reform, Reconstructionist, or traditionalist, were classified into a fourth code category, those with no denominational preference.

Respondents were also asked, "Are you or any member of your household currently a member of a synagogue or temple?" If so, they were then asked if their synagogue or temple was Conservative, Orthodox, Reform, or Reconstructionist. Since synagogue or temple memberships are generally provided as family memberships, it can be assumed that the membership includes our Jewish respondent. Other studies using the 1990 NJPS, which includes some respondents we do not define as Jews, might need to be more careful in distinguishing family and individual members.

Analysis of the 1971 survey (Lazerwitz 1979; Lazerwitz and Harrison 1979) showed that important insights into denominational preferences are gained by dividing those with a given preference into those who are synagogue members and those who are not members. Doing so yields the eight combinations of denominational preferences and membership noted in our introductory chapter. The number of interviews with respondents who consider themselves Orthodox but are not synagogue members, and the number who have no denominational preference but yet are synagogue members, are each too few for statistical analysis. Hence, most of the tables in this book report on only the remaining six combinations of denominational preference and synagogue membership: Orthodox synagogue members, Conservatives members and nonmembers, Reform members and nonmembers, and those with neither a denominational preference nor a synagogue membership.

Background Variables

The initial description of the data of this study will relate denominational preference and synagogue membership to a number of demographic and socioeconomic factors that sociologists of religion since Niebuhr (1929), as reflected in textbooks in the field such as Hargrove (1989) or Johnstone (1988), have long regarded as the social sources of denominational preferences and/or synagogue memberships. The demographic factors we consider are: gender, age, generations in the United States, marital status, and number of minor children in the household. The socioeconomic factors are: education, occupation of family head, and family income. A central purpose of this study is to determine if such demographic and socioeconomic factors are related to our two central variables—denominational preference and synagogue membership—and, more importantly, if they account for any relationship between these two central variables and both the sort of Jewish life respondents choose to live in the open, pluralistic society that is America and the manner in which they relate to certain aspects of American society in general.

Seven variables are used to describe a respondent's past and current Jewish involvements, that is, the sort of Jewish life they have led or are leading. The 1971 and 1990 surveys include two measures of a respondent's Jewish background: the Jewish characteristics of a respondent's childhood home and his/her Jewish education. Current Jewish involvements are reflected in attendance at religious services, home religious practices, involvement in Jewish primary groups, activity in Jewish community voluntary associations, and orientation toward Israel. Finally, we examine the relationship of denominational preference and synagogue membership to such matters as involvement in general community voluntary associations, degree of political liberalness, and religious intermarriage as aspects of respondents' involvements with general, non-Jewish, components of American society.

The questions from the 1990 survey pertaining to each of the variables just noted were formed into scores and indices in a manner as identical as possible to corresponding scores and indices in the 1971 survey. For example, the various questions in the 1990 survey pertaining to Jewish education were scored as similar questions had been in 1971. The scores were then added to form a summary measure or indicator of the amount of one's Jewish education. All the scores on the summary measure of Jewish education were then arrayed from highest to lowest. The highest scoring third on the summary measures were recorded as "high" (1) on Jewish education; the middle third, as "moderate" (2); and the bottom one-third, as "low" (3) on Jewish education. In this manner, the extent of their Jewish education is reflected in two measures for each respondent: the sum of scores on individual questions about Jewish education (the scale form) and their relative ranking as high, moderate, or low (the index form). The use of both scales and indices is dictated by the requirements of our statistical procedures. A similar procedure was employed with each of the variables pertaining to Jewish background and involvement. For the sake of clarity or brevity, the tables presented below often report only the percent of respondents at the highest level on the indicated variable.[3]

Characteristics Associated with
Differing Denominational Preferences

This section presents information on general, sociologically significant, characteristics of adherents of American Jewish denominations and for those without any denominational preference. Such information will typically be given for both 1971 and 1990. The chapter begins with some basic information about the distribution of our two basic variables, denominational preference and synagogue membership, and the relationship between them. It then presents a series of initial, univariate, and bivariate analyses of the relationship of demographic, socioeconomic, and religious variables to denominational preference and synagogue membership, which provide a basis for more sophisticated multivariate analysis in the next chapter. The chapter concludes with a comparison of the characteristics of adult adherents of the major Jewish denominations with similar characteristics for Protestants and Catholics.

Denominational Preference and
Synagogue Membership: 1971 and 1990

The denominational preferences among respondents is reported in table 3.1, first for all respondents and then, respectively, for those who are synagogue members and for those who are not. These distributions differ not only over time, but from one another. That is, the distributions of denominational preferences among those who are and who are not synagogue members are distinctly different.[4]

As shown in section A of table 3.1, the percentages preferring the Conservative denomination and those with no preference remained stable from 1971 to 1990. However, in the nearly twenty years between the two surveys, the percentage of Orthodox has fallen from 11% to 6%, reducing the proportion with that denominational preference to just about half of what it was in 1971. The proportion who prefer the Reform movement has grown some six percentage points, from 33% to 39%. The percentage of adults who are synagogue members, 48% in 1971 and 47% in 1990, has also remained relatively stable.

The denominational preferences for those who are synagogue members and for those who are not, are reported in table 3.1, sections B and C, respectively. Interestingly, the distributions of specific denominational preferences

TABLE 3.1
Jewish Adult Denominational Preference
and Synagogue Membership, 1971 and 1990

A. Denominational Preference of All Respondents	1971	1990
Orthodox	11%	6%
Conservative	42%	40%
Reform	33%	39%
No Preference	14%	15%
Base	100%	100%
n	5,790	1,905
B. Denominational Preference of Synagogue Members	1971	1990
Orthodox	14%	10%
Conservative	49%	51%
Reform	34%	35%
No Preference	3%	4%
Base	100%	100%
C. Denominational Preference among Not Syn. Members	1971	1990
Orthodox	7%	4%
Conservative	35%	31%
Reform	33%	41%
No Preference	25%	24%
Base	100%	100%

among those with and without a synagogue membership differ not only from each other, but also over time. For example, in 1990, while the more traditional denominations, the Orthodox and Conservative, constitute 46% of all adult Jewish preferences, they are 61% of the preferences of synagogue members in that year. For 1990, when those who are not synagogue members (section C, table 3.1) are compared to all Jewish adult respondents (section A), the percentage who are more traditional, Orthodox, or Conservative, changes from 35% to 46%; the percent of those who prefer the Reform denomination

TABLE 3.2
Percentage of Jewish Adult Synagogue Memberships
by Denominational Preference, 1971 and 1990

	Synagogue Membership	
Denomination	1971	1990
Orthodox	66%	72%
Conservative	57%	59%
Reform	51%	43%
No Preference	11%	13%
For All Adults	48%	47%
n	2,429	752

is relatively stable, going only from 41% to 39%; while those without a preference, who are 15% of all respondents, are 24% of those who are not synagogue members.

More importantly, while the percent preferring the Conservative and Reform denominations in 1990 are almost identical in the total adult population (40% and 39%, respectively), Conservative is a more common preference (51%) than Reform (35%) among those who are synagogue members. Those who consider themselves Orthodox are considerably more common (10%) among synagogue members than among nonmembers (4%). Finally, as expected, the percent with no denominational preference is much higher among those who are not synagogue members (24%) than among those with a synagogue membership (4%). Reform, which is the most popular denominational preference (41%) among those who are not synagogue members, is second to Conservative among synagogue members. In other words, as we shall see from table 3.2, denominational preference and synagogue membership are related. A higher percentage of members relative to nonmembers is found among the more traditional, Orthodox and Conservative, denominations.

There is a steady decrease in 1971 and again in 1990, in the percentage of Jewish adults who are synagogue members as we move from the Orthodox to the Conservatives, to the Reform and finally to those with no denominational preference (table 3.2). Thus, while in both 1971 and 1990, at least two-thirds of those who choose the Orthodox denomination and nearly three-fifths of those who prefer Conservatism are synagogue members, only about half in 1971, and even fewer in 1990, of those who say they are Reform Jews are synagogue members. Regardless of the year, only slightly more than a tenth of those with no denominational preference are synagogue members. (Given their small absolute numbers in both 1971 and 1990, further statistical analysis will not be possible of those who prefer the Orthodox denomination but yet are not synagogue members and of those who are synagogue members but yet have no denominational preference.)

The 1990 survey also asked respondents who were not currently synagogue members if they had ever been members. Nineteen percent of those not currently members reported they had been synagogue members in the past. Overall, then, in 1990, 85% of adult respondents report a preference for one Jewish denomination or another, 47% were currently synagogue members, and 19% had been synagogue members. Only 34% of the adults had never been members of a synagogue or temple.

Demographic and Socioeconomic Concomitants of Denominational Preference: 1971 and 1990

As noted above, it has been commonplace, since Niebuhr's (1929) classic study, for sociologists of religion to contend that denominational preference, at least among Protestants in America, may reflect little more than demographic and socioeconomic status differences. Similar claims have been made with respect to church membership. One aim of this study is to determine if such is the case among Jews in the United States, or whether denominational preferences and synagogue membership have an influence on and relationship to religious and nonreligious lifestyles above and beyond the admitted importance of demography and status.

An earlier study of the 1971 survey (Lazerwitz and Harrison 1979), as expected, did find some demographic and socioeconomic status differences among Jews that were related to denominational preference and synagogue membership. For example, Lazerwitz and Harrison (1979) found that members of Reform synagogues were disproportionately women; that those who preferred the Reform denomination, but were not synagogue members, were disproportionately young; and that over half of the Orthodox synagogue members were foreign-born. In 1971 there was a clear socioeconomic status gradient: members of Reform temples were the most educated group, followed by Reform Jews who were not synagogue members and members of Conservative synagogues. Conservative Jews who were not members of synagogues ranked next on education, while Orthodox Jews were least likely to have a considerable amount of secular education.

Table 3.3 provides information on these matters for 1990. The 1971 relationships have virtually disappeared. That is, as we claimed in chapter 1, denominational preferences and synagogue membership are more and more becoming lifestyle choices reflecting religious and identity issues and less and

TABLE 3.3

Demographic Characteristics by Adult Jewish Denominational Preferences and Synagogue Membership, NJPS, 1990

Characteristics	Orthodox Member	Conservative		Reform		No Preference
		Member	Not Member	Member	Not Member	Not Member
A. % women	48%	53%	53%	53%	50%	41%
B. Age of Adults						
20–39 yrs.	46%	32%	37%	42%	48%	44%
60+ yrs.	30%	32%	31%	16%	20%	26%
C. Adult U.S. Generations						
Foreign-born	28%	11%	7%	5%	4%	10%
U.S.-born parents	23%	44%	46%	70%	67%	56%
D. Adult Socioeconomic Status						
Univ. graduate	64%	70%	52%	80%	63%	65%
$80,000 or more family income	7%	26%	11%	35%	20%	17%
E. Home has children						
5 or younger	26%	13%	13%	17%	15%	19%
6–17 yrs.	18%	16%	9%	23%	12%	13%

less matters of demography or status. However, not all demographic and status differences have disappeared. The Orthodox are still more likely than other groupings to be foreign-born and members of Reform synagogues still enjoy the highest socioeconomic status. (Just over half of the members of Reform synagogues and of both groups of Conservative Jews, that is, synagogue members and nonmembers, are women.) Reform Jews who are synagogue members have the lowest percentage of adherents sixty years old or older. Orthodox and Conservative Jews, the latter whether synagogue members or not, are the most likely to be sixty years old or older. Interestingly, the Orthodox group has a large contingent of young adults between the ages of twenty and thirty-nine that is just about as large as that among Reform Jews, whether synagogue members or not, and among those with no preference.

Orthodox Jews remain the group that has the most individuals with foreign-born parents and the fewest individuals with American-born parents. The reverse is true for Reform Jews, whether synagogue members or not: about two-thirds have American-born parents, and only about one in twenty have foreign-born parents. Conservative Jews are in an intermediate position, between the Orthodox and Reform, with respect to whether their parents are foreign-born or American-born. In 1971, Jews with no denominational preference were the most likely of all the groupings to have American-born parents; now they rank behind Reform Jews, whether synagogue members or not.

Moreover, whereas in 1971, under three-quarters of third generation (or more) American Jews had a denominational preference, by 1990 85% do. Denominational preference has grown among Jews whose families have long been in America. Denominationalism, as we have argued, is more likely to be found among "Americanized" Jews.

Those who prefer the Conservative denomination, but who are not synagogue members, are the least likely, about one chance in two, of all Jews to be college graduates both in 1971 and 1990. Members of Reform synagogues are the most likely, four out of five, to be college graduates. Among the other four categories, Orthodox Jews, Jews with no denominational preference, Conservative synagogue members, and Reform Jews who are not synagogue members, about two in three are college graduates.

Not surprisingly, given the data on education and the relationship of education and income, similar patterns are found with respect to family income. As in 1971, in 1990, members of Reform synagogues are most likely, about one chance in three, to be in families earning $80,000 or more. Among both Reform and Conservative Jews, synagogue members are more likely than those who are not members to be in families earning a high income of $80,000 or more. The difference of some fifteen percentage points in both cases may reflect the high cost of synagogue membership. On the other hand, Jews who have no denominational preference (and no synagogue membership) are more likely to be among those with a high income than are Orthodox Jews who are synagogue members. This difference supports Winter's (1985, 1989, 1991a) finding that the value or significance of such membership, as well as its cost, are factors in deciding whether to join a synagogue or temple.

Overall, with regard to education and income, the gradient in socioeconomic status that existed in 1971 from a low among the Orthodox to a high among Reform synagogue members and nonmembers with Conservative synagogue members and nonmembers in between, no longer pertains. Indeed, members of Conservative synagogues now rank just behind members of Reform synagogues, and ahead of Reform Jews who are not members of synagogues, on both education and family income. The groupings of Reform Jews who are not synagogue members and of Jews with no denominational preferences, as in 1971, have quite similar compositions with respect to their education and income. As in 1971, Orthodox Jews and Conservative Jews who are not members of synagogues rank the lowest with respect to secular education and income. However, in 1990, the Orthodox group includes a somewhat higher percentage of college graduates than do Conservative Jews who are not members of synagogues.

As Sklare and Greenblum (1979: 181–98) found to be the case on the suburban frontier and as Cohen (1983: 124–31) found, synagogue membership is related to one's stage in the family life cycle. In particular, those having school-age children in the home are more likely than others to be synagogue members. We also find (section E, table 3.3) that synagogue members are more likely to have children between six and seventeen years of age in their homes than are respondents who are not members of synagogues, whether Conservative or Reform (the only groupings with enough respondents who are both members and nonmembers to enable statistically meaningful comparison). However, the percentage with children under six years of age is alike, or virtually so, among respondents who are synagogue members and nonmembers, again whether they are Conservative or Reform. Synagogue membership, then, is related not just to having young children, but to having children of school age.

The relationship between family life cycle and synagogue membership also emerges clearly when those respondents who have never been synagogue members are compared to those who are or have been members (table 3.4).[5] (Given the small number of Orthodox Jews who are not synagogue members, this analysis is confined to a comparison of Conservative and Reform Jews.) Consistent with what is shown above in table 3.2, proportionally fewer Conservative adherents have never been synagogue members than are found among adherents of Reform Judaism. In both denominations, those who have never been members are considerably younger than those who have been, but are not currently, synagogue members. Moreover, Reform Jews who have never been synagogue members are younger than Conservative Jews who have never been members. In both denominations, those who have young

TABLE 3.4
Contrasting Past Synagogue Members with Never Synagogue Members
for the Conservative and Reform Denominations, 1990

	Conservative	Reform
Membership Distribution		
Now Member	59%	43%
Was Member	19%	22%
Never Member	22%	35%
Age		
Was Member		
Under 40	23%	25%
40–64	47%	49%
65 and more	30%	26%
Never Member		
Under 40	49%	62%
40–64	33%	32%
65 and more	18%	6%
Children in Home		
Was Member		
5 years or less	8%	7%
6–17 years	7%	8%
Never Member		
5 years or less	15%	18%
6–17 years	9%	13%
Marital Status		
Was Member		
Single	11%	14%
Married	68%	70%
Divorced or other	21%	16%
Never Member		
Single	29%	31%
Married	53%	56%
Divorced or other	18%	13%
Now Intermarried		
Was Member	11%	17%
Never Member	23%	41%

children in their homes are somewhat more likely to have never been members than are those who are not now, but used to be, members. Furthermore, the proportion of Reform Jews with children at home who have never been synagogue members is somewhat higher than the proportion of Conservative Jews with children at home who have never been members.

Those who have never been members of synagogues or temples are more likely to be single than those who have past, but not current, memberships. Finally, those who have never been synagogue members are also more likely than past members to be intermarried, a matter we examine more closely in chapter 6. There are proportionally more intermarried couples among Reform Jews then among Conservatives Jews, whether the comparison involves those who have never been members of synagogues or temples or those who have allowed their memberships to lapse.

In sum, those who are not now synagogue or temple members are a heterogeneous group that includes older former synagogue members and young adults who are either single or married with small children. In other words, as Sklare and Greenblum (1979: 181–98) and Cohen (1983: 124–31) found, synagogue membership is related to one's place in the family life cycle, higher among those with small children at home than for those earlier in the cycle, that is, those who are single or young marrieds without small children, and for those later in the cycle, whose children have left home.

Finally, we turn our attention to another variable often thought a source of religiosity, namely, the size of one's local community. Roof (1972, 1976, 1978), for example, has developed *localism* theory, which holds, in part, that the maintenance of a religious commitment in a highly differentiated modern society such as America's is aided by a localistic perspective more common in small rather than large communities. Lazerwitz (1977) has found a relationship between Jewish religious involvement and community size. More recently, Horowitz (1994) has suggested that community size may be a factor in Jewish involvement. However, these studies do not clarify whether sheer numbers of Jews work to increase Jewish involvement by providing the critical mass needed for a large variety of different activities or if small size means one has to, and often does, work harder at being Jewish.

Specifically, we examine the relationship of denominational preference to the size of the Jewish community in which one resides. The distribution of denominational preference in the variously sized communities do not differ significantly when a distinction is made between synagogue members and nonmembers. Consequently, these differences are not reported here.[6]

For our analyses, seven categories of community size are employed:

1. The largest, with over 1,000,000 Jews, which consists of New York City and its metropolitan area

2. The next largest (about 500,000 in each area), which includes the Los Angeles and Miami metropolitan areas

3. Those communities with approximately 200,000 or 300,000 Jews, namely, the metropolitan areas of Chicago, Philadelphia, Boston, and Washington, D.C.

4. The eleven communities estimated to have from 40,000 to 150,000 Jews

5. Some eighteen Jewish communities estimated to have less than 40,000, but more than 15,000 Jews

6. Communities estimated to have less than 15,000, but more than 3,000 Jews

7. Communities estimated to have fewer than 3,000 Jews

Table 3.5 shows the distribution of Jewish denominational preference in the various categories of Jewish community size. Orthodox respondents, clearly, are concentrated in the New York City metropolitan area as, indeed, are all the other groups, although not to the same extent.

In communities of about 500,000 Jews (the Miami and Los Angeles areas) and those of about 200,000 to 300,000 Jews (the Boston, Chicago, Philadelphia, and Washington D.C. areas), the proportion of Orthodox is lower and the proportion of Conservatives is a bit higher than the national Jewish percentage. The proportion with no denominational preference is lower than the national Jewish percentage in communities of 500,000 or more Jews (Los Angeles and Miami).

Among the smaller communities, 150,000 or fewer Jews, the Orthodox exceed the national Jewish percentage only in those communities of between 40,000 and 150,000. Such communities, though relatively small, would still be large enough to support an adequate range of special Orthodox needs such as for kosher butchers. Reform Jews are slightly more common than the national percentage in small communities with 150,000 Jews or less. Overall, 43% of Reform Jews live in these smaller Jewish communities. The proportion with no denominational preference is higher than the national percentage in communities of fewer than 15,000 Jews.

Religious and Jewish Community Involvement:
1971 and 1990

We turn now turn from a concern with the relationship between our two central variables—denominational preference and synagogue membership—and important social structural differences, as reflected in demographic variables

TABLE 3.5
Jewish Denominations by Jewish Community Size, NJPS, 1990

Jewish Community Size	Orthodox	Conservative	Reform	No Pref.	Nationally
1 million plus (NYC metro area)	57%	31%	27%	33%	31%
Around 500,000 (Los Angeles and Miami metro areas)	6%	15%	15%	10%	14%
200,000–300,000 (Chicago, Philadelphia, Boston, Washington, D.C., metro areas)	8%	20%	15%	17%	17%
40,000–150,000 (11 Jewish communities)	15%	10%	14%	9%	12%
15,000–39,999 (18 Jewish communities)	3%	9%	9%	7%	8%
3,000–14,999	7%	6%	9%	9%	8%
Under 3,000	4%	9%	11%	15%	10%
BASE	100%	100%	100%	100%	100%

and socioeconomic status, to a concern with the relationship between the two main variables as indicators of a respondent's Jewish lifestyle. Specifically, we compare the various preference and membership groupings with respect to religious activities such as synagogue attendance and the performance of Jewish religious rituals at home, as well as with respect to other aspects of a Jewish life such as a Jewish educational background, involvement in Jewish primary groups and voluntary organizations, and relationship to Israel.

In 1971, there was a clear rank ordering among the six groupings examined here with respect to both religious practices and other aspects of Jewish life (Lazerwitz and Harrison 1979). The highest ranking were Orthodox Jews (all of whom were synagogue members), followed by Conservative synagogue members and then Conservative Jews who were not synagogue members. Members of Reform temples were ranked next followed by Reform Jews who were not temple members. Jews who had no denominational preference (and also no synagogue membership) ranked the lowest.

As shown in table 3.6, the earlier rank order, with minor exceptions, still holds in 1990. There appears to be four divisions with respect to Jewish involvement in 1990. In rank order they are: (1) Orthodox Jews; (2) members of Conservative synagogues; (3) Conservative Jews who are not synagogue members and Reform Jews who are synagogue members; and, finally, (4) Reform Jews who are not synagogue members and those with no denominational preference. This rank ordering supports our contention that denominational preference is an indicator of our respondents' Jewish lifestyle and that synagogue membership is something of a "multiplier" of the influence of denominational preference. Thus, Jewish involvement decreases as we move from the Orthodox, to the Conservative, to the Reform, to those with no denominational preference, and is higher among synagogue members than among nonmembers.

There is, however, one notable exception to these overall rankings. Reform Jews who are not members of synagogues, who are like Jews with no denominational preferences with regard to most of the indexes considered in table 3.6 are considerably more likely to be involved in Jewish organizations. With respect to this variable, the two groupings of adults with denominational preferences but no synagogue memberships, namely, the Conservative and the Reform, are very similar to one another and somewhat unlike those who have no denominational preference. Overall, those with both a denominational preference and a synagogue membership are about two or three times more likely than those with only a denominational preference to be involved with Jewish organizations other than the synagogue; however, the latter, those with a preference but no membership, are three and a half times more likely to have such involvement than those who are not synagogue members and also have no denominational preference. It would appear, then, that Jewish involvement is a matter of the interaction of denominational preference (the more traditional the choice, the more the involvement) and synagogue membership (members are more involved than nonmembers). *what about black hat orthodox? what Jewish orgs?*

Consequential Dimension of Denominational Preference

We have suggested that the expression of a denominational preference and membership in a religious organization are ways in which Americans locate themselves within the social and political structures of their society. That is, we have suggested there is, to use Glock and Stark's (1965: 21) term, a "consequential dimension" to religiosity, a dimension reflected in "attitudes and behaviors in secular areas of life." Here we examine two quite different

TABLE 3.6

Percentage Having High Levels of Jewish Involvement by Adult Jewish Denominational Preferences, NJPS, 1990

Denominational Groups

Jewish Involvement Indices	Orthodox Members	Conservative		Reform		No Preference
		Member	Not Member	Member	Not Member	Not Member
Jewish educ. (8 yrs. or more)	54%	59%	33%	39%	20%	19%
Syn. attend. is 25 times or more annually	76%	30%	7%	18%	2%	2%
Home relig. practices*	91%	57%	23%	21%	10%	5%
Jewish primary groups**	92%	57%	35%	31%	16%	10%
Jewish organization activity***	74%	64%	26%	52%	21%	6%
Ties to Israel****	75%	51%	30%	28%	20%	19%

* Shabbat candles; Kiddush; Hanukkah candles; kosher home
** Most friends Jewish; neighborhood Jewish; opposes intermarriage
*** Member several Jewish orgs.; works 20+ hrs. per month for Jewish orgs.; gave money to Jewish orgs.
**** Visited Israel and emotionally involved with it

aspects of secular life in America, involvement with voluntary organizations in the general community and political views measured in the 1971 and 1990 surveys that otherwise focused on involvements in Jewish life.

With respect to involvement with general, non-Jewish community organizations, if, as we have argued, having a denominational preference is a way of "fitting into" American society, then those with a denominational preference will be more involved with the general, non-Jewish community than those who have no preference, whom we regard as somewhat peripheral to the society. However, unlike the case with religious involvement, secular involvements need not increase as we move from the Orthodox, to the Conservative, to Reform branches of Judaism. We do expect that those with a preference for Orthodoxy, as noted in chapter 1, will stand somewhat apart from the ways of American society, preferring their own way (halakha) to Western or American ways. Thus, the Orthodox should be somewhat less involved than those who prefer the Conservative or Reform denominations, which are more willing to accommodate to the demands of the larger society. Table 3.7 provides some information to test our predictions.

Consistent with the views just expressed, members of either Conservative or Reform synagogues are indeed more involved with the general community than are members of Orthodox synagogues, who are the least involved. Similarly, among those who prefer the Conservative or Reform denominations, those who are synagogue members are more active in the general community than those who are not members. However, contrary to our prediction, those with no denominational preference, and indeed, with no synagogue membership, are not the least involved. Rather they are about as likely to be involved with general community voluntary associations as are members of either Conservative or Reform synagogues and more so than those with a denominational preference but who are not synagogue members.

Overall, the synagogue members of both the Reform and Conservative denominations are most apt to be active in both Jewish and general community voluntary associations. The Reform and Conservative Jews who are not synagogue members are quite alike in having lower levels of activity.

With respect to political views, as noted in chapter 1, it is a commonplace to note that Jews as a group are considerably more likely to place themselves on the liberal end of the political spectrum than other groups in the United States (see also table 3.11). They are, as Lipset and Raab (1995: 138) observe, "still on the left," and "well within the liberal camp of the Democratic Party" (Feingold 1995: 115). That Jews are consistently on the liberal side of the American political spectrum despite their relatively high socioeconomic status is something of a departure from the usual pattern in the United States in which political allegiance is strongly related to economic status (Glazer 1995: 133). Chief among the explanations that have been offered for this placement

TABLE 3.7
Adults with a High Level of General Community Involvement and
Who Feel Politically Liberal by Denomination and Synagogue Membership, NJPS, 1990

| Indices | Orthodox Member | Conservative | | Reform | | No Preference |
		Member	Not Member	Member	Not Member	Not Member
General community organization activity*	17%	42%	27%	44%	31%	44%
Politically liberal	23%	40%	34%	39%	44%	56%

* Member of several general community organizations and also gave to non-Jewish charities

is that Jews have identified with the liberal values of the Enlightenment, which provided them with an escape from the restrictions of the pre-Enlightenment era (Cohn 1958; Lipset 1960: 243–44). If that is so, then the degree of liberalness among Jews should increase as one moves from adherents of a denomination less willing to accept Enlightenment values, the Orthodox, to the Reform, whose adherents are more willing to embrace these values. Those who prefer the Conservative denomination would presumably take an intermediate position on the political spectrum. The pattern should be even stronger among those with synagogue memberships, more exposed to the teachings of their respective denominations, than among those without. Those without a denominational preference should be more like the general American population than they are like other Jews, that is, somewhat less likely to be politically liberal. They should differ even more from "Jewishly" involved Jews. Table 3.7 provides information to test these predictions.

As predicted, synagogue members, whether in Conservative or the Reform synagogues, are more likely to be politically liberal than those who prefer the Orthodox denomination. In addition, consistent with our predictions, even those Conservative and Reform Jews who are not members of a synagogue are more likely to be politically liberal than are Orthodox Jews. However, those individuals with no denominational preference are something of an anomaly. They are more likely to be liberal than are members of Conservative or Reform synagogues and more likely to be so than Conservative or Reform Jews who are not synagogue members.

In 1971, those without a denominational preference were most likely to be politically liberal. Moreover, in 1971, Reform Jews, whether synagogue members or not, were the next most likely to be liberals, and Conservatives who were not synagogue members, the least likely. Orthodox Jews and members of Conservative synagogues were in the middle of the political spectrum. The 1990 patterns are a bit closer to what we expect, on the basis of our discussion in chapter 1, than they were some twenty years ago. The influence of denominational preference and synagogue membership, as we have said, is stronger now than it was then.

Jewish Denominations within the Context
of America's Denominational Structure

As noted in chapter 1, America is a denominational society. The purpose of this section is to place the various Jewish denominational groupings within the overall context of the American denominational structure by comparing them to their Christian counterparts. Significantly, this is the first time such denominational comparisons can be made in which Jews can be differentiated by their denominational preferences. Given the relatively small proportion of Jews in the population of the United States, national American surveys do not yield a sufficient number of Jewish respondents to meaningfully differentiate one group of Jews from another. Thus, until now, American denominational studies regarded all Jews as just "Jews," in contrast to Christians, among whom various distinctions could be made. Thus, differences between Jews and non-Jews could be studied, but not differences among Jews, between one Jewish denominational grouping and another.

Our data on non-Jews were obtained from the National Opinion Research Center (NORC) of the University of Chicago. NORC conducts an ongoing series called the "General Social Surveys" (GSS). Typically, these surveys ask a number of questions about a respondent's religious, civic, and political involvements. By combining surveys from a number of consecutive years, it is possible to obtain an adequate number of interviews with Protestant respondents, who prefer one of a wide variety of denominations, and with Roman Catholics.

We have chosen the surveys done in the years 1985 through 1989 (the latest years available to us when we were doing our analysis). We categorized respondents who claimed no religious preference in the NORC surveys in much the same way as we did for the 1971 and 1990 National Jewish Population Surveys. Specifically, respondents who claimed no religious preferences were classified as Protestant if their parents were Protestant and as Catholic if their parents were Catholic. Such a classification approach serves to increase the number of Protestants and Catholics who can be considered marginal members of their respective groupings. The NORC GSS studies define an "adult" as anyone eighteen years or older, rather than twenty or older as we do. Fortunately, the number of eighteen- and nineteen-year-olds in the study is very small. In order to avoid a further source of possible uncontrolled variation only white GSS respondents are included.

The GSS surveys classify Protestants into twenty-seven denominational categories. In turn, GSS groups these categories into three denominational families: fundamentalist, moderate, and liberal. These categories are roughly analogous to those of Orthodox, Conservative, and Reform Jews. (The small number of Protestants with no denominational preference were grouped with the liberal denominations.) Given the limited information available, it is not possible to compare the various groupings of Jews and Christians on all the dimensions used in our study of the Jewish population alone. However, we can contrast the groups in terms of their secular education, attendance at religious services and location on a political spectrum from conservative to liberal.

Table 3.8 contrasts the various Protestant and Jewish groupings and the Roman Catholics with respect to their secular education. It is clear from this table that each of the Jewish groupings includes, proportionately, far more

TABLE 3.8
Comparing Protestants, Catholics, and Jews by Education

Religious Group Adults	Highest Degree				
	H.S. or Less	Voc. & Jr. Coll.	B.A.	Grad. Studies	Base
Protestants (GSS)					
Fundamentalist	86%	3%	8%	3%	100%
Moderate	75%	4%	15%	6%	100%
Liberal	71%	5%	16%	8%	100%
Catholics (GSS)	78%	4%	12%	6%	100%
Jews (NJPS '90)					
Orthodox	38%	3%	39%	20%	100%
Conservative	35%	6%	30%	29%	100%
Reform	28%	7%	40%	25%	100%
No Denom. Pref.	32%	6%	32%	30%	100%

TABLE 3.9
Comparing Protestants, Catholics, and Jews by Religious Attendance

Religious Group Adults	Never	1–2 times per year	3–11 times per year	Monthly	13+ times per year	Base
Protestants (GSS)						
Fundamentalist	11%	19%	11%	7%	52%	100%
Moderate	15%	22%	14%	9%	40%	100%
Liberal	22%	27%	14%	8%	29%	100%
Catholics (GSS)	12%	19%	11%	7%	51%	100%
Jews (NJPS '90)						
Orthodox	6%	17%	12%	7%	58%	100%
Conservative	9%	29%	26%	16%	20%	100%
Reform	16%	42%	24%	9%	9%	100%
No Denom. Pref.	43%	44%	6%	3%	4%	100%

individuals with college and graduate educations than any of the Christian groups. Even those who prefer the Orthodox Jewish denomination are more likely to have B.A. degrees or graduate studies than are members of any of the Christian groupings.

Table 3.9 provides information on attendance at religious services for each of the various Christian and Jewish religious denominations. The table reveals that fundamentalist Protestants, Catholics, and Orthodox Jews have the highest rates of attendance at religious services and that these rates are reasonably equivalent to each other. Liberal and moderate Protestants, and Conservative Jews are the next most likely to attend religious services. Reform Jews and Jews with no denominational preference are the least likely to attend.

Table 3.10 provides information on the political positions of members of the various Christian and Jewish groupings by locating them on a scale of political viewpoint from liberal to conservative. The contrast between the various Jewish groupings, on the one hand, and Protestants and Catholics, on the other, is rather sharp. The Christian groups are heavily concentrated in the "middle of the road" category. Some 70% or more of both Protestants with a denominational preference and of Catholics are middle of the road. Among Jewish groupings, with the exception of the Orthodox, liberals outnumber middle-of-the-roaders. Among Protestants, political conservatives outnumber liberals regardless of denominational preference or, indeed, the lack of one. The same is true among Catholics. For Jews, only among the Orthodox do the number of conservatives outnumber the liberals.

In summary, each Jewish grouping is considerably more educated than any of the Christian religious groupings. However, with respect to religious attendance and scores on the politically liberal-conservative scale, Orthodox Jews are rather similar to Christians. Religious attendance among Conservative Jews is much like that among the religiously liberal Protestant denominations.

Reform Jews and Jews with no denominational preference differ a good deal from the other groups, be they Christian or Jewish. Their attendance at religious services is lower and their concentration on the liberal end of the political spectrum is higher. When the very high educational levels of Reform Jews and Jews with no denominational preference are included in the picture, these two groupings differ considerably from the other American religious groups. Moreover, Jews with no denominational preference appear to be marginal both to America's denominational system in general and to the American Jewish community. These extremely well-educated and politically quite liberal Jews, as the data of this chapter have consistently shown, are seldom involved in Jewish religious or Jewish communal institutions.

The marginality of Jews with no denominational preference is again shown in table 3.11, which reports on three indicators of involvement with

TABLE 3.10

Comparing Protestants, Catholics, and Jews
on a Liberal-Conservative Political Scale

	Liberal-Conservative					
	Extremely Liberal	Liberal	Middle of Road	Conservative	Extremely Conservative	Base
Protestants						
Fundamentalist	2%	6%	70%	19%	3%	100%
Moderate	1%	10%	70%	17%	2%	100%
Liberal	2%	12%	71%	13%	2%	100%
Catholics	2%	10%	73%	13%	2%	100%
Jews						
Orthodox	2%	21%	41%	30%	6%	100%
Conservative	5%	36%	37%	21%	1%	100%
Reform	5%	41%	39%	14%	1%	100%
No Denom. Pref.	28%	33%	22%	16%	1%	100%

TABLE 3.11
Christian Involvements of Jewish Adults
by Denominational Grouping, NJPS, 1990

Jewish Denominational Grouping	Usually Has Christmas Tree	Household Has a Church Member	Attends Church 3 Times or More Per Year
Orthodox Member	0%	0%	0%
Conservative			
Member	2%	0%	0%
Not member	20%	2%	4%
Reform			
Member	10%	0%	1%
Not member	26%	5%	2%
No Preference			
Not member	42%	13%	13%
No Pref., Not Member, & in a Jewish-Christian marriage	74%	27%	25%

the Christian community: whether or not the respondent's household usually has a Christmas tree during the holiday season, household membership in a Christian church, and attendance at Christian religious services. Clearly, synagogue members, whatever their denomination, rarely engage in these practices. While a noteworthy minority of Jews who are not synagogue members, but who have a denominational preference, may have Christmas trees in their houses during the holiday season, they rarely are in households in which a member has joined a church and they rarely attend church services. However, as table 3.11 shows, among Jews with no denominational preference, a large percentage (42%) have Christmas trees in their houses. Indeed, among those Jews who have no denominational preference and who are married to a Christian, a large majority (74%) have Christmas trees in their houses. They are also at least twice as likely as any other category of Jews to be in a household which includes a member of a church or to attend church services, although the frequency of their church attendance does not approach that of Protestants, or even that of Protestants with no denominational preference. It would appear that as a group, Jews with no denominational preference are marginal not only to the Jewish community, but to Christian religious institutions as well even if married to a Christian.

Summary and Conclusions

This chapter has sought to do the following: to provide an overview of the distribution of and interrelations among our two main variables, denominational preferences and synagogue memberships among American Jews, both in 1971 and 1990; to examine the relationship of demographic and socioeconomic status and our two central variables and differentials in the Jewish involvements and consequential variables (involvement with general community voluntary associations and political stance) among the various denominational groupings; and, finally, to contrast Protestant, Catholics, and Jews on certain key demographic, socioeconomic status, and religious variables.

The major trend over the years with respect to Jewish denominational preferences has been the continual decline in the proportion of Orthodox among American Jewish adults, from 11% in 1971 to 6% in 1990. During this same time period, those who prefer the Reform denomination grew from 33% to 39%. The Conservative denomination and the proportion of Jews without any denominational preference remained nearly constant during this time span, as has the proportion who are synagogue members. However, there has been an increase in synagogue membership among the Orthodox and a decrease among the Reform.

While the proportions of the American Jewish adult population in 1990 who prefer the Conservative or Reform denomination, respectively, is just about equal, Conservative Jews are more likely to join synagogues. Those who prefer the Conservative denomination constitute 51% of synagogue members, while the Reform, only 35%. A solid majority of Orthodox and Conservative Jewish adults are synagogue members. Only a minority (43%) of Reform adherents are synagogue members. Thus, while Reform may be on its way to being the denomination preferred by a plurality of American Jewish adults, that preference is often not accompanied by actual membership in a synagogue or temple. As one would expect, only a small proportion of Jews without a denominational preference are synagogue members.

The Orthodox and Conservative denominations have more adherents who are sixty years old or older than do the other two categories. Nevertheless, the Orthodox also have a sizeable proportion of its numbers from twenty to thirty-nine years of age as do the Reform and those with no denominational preference. The Conservative groupings appear to be the aging ones.

Furthermore, 44% of Orthodox homes have children seventeen years old or younger, more than any of the other groupings, although, not much more than the 40% among Reform synagogue members. The denominational "extremes," thus, have the greatest growth potential. In any case, households with children six to seventeen years old are clearly most apt to include synagogue members. Having children of Jewish school age promotes joining synagogues.

With regard to socioeconomic status, members of Reform and Conservative synagogues rank highest. Reform Jews who are not synagogue members and those with no denominational preferences are next highest in socioeconomic status. The lowest ranking groups on socioeconomic status are Orthodox and Conservative Jews who are not synagogue members.

It seems that the Orthodox denomination has reached the end of its historic decline. It now includes a sizeable number of well-educated young people just beginning their careers. The level of education among the Orthodox is increasing and, as the young adults of this group advance in their careers, their income levels will likely increase.

On the whole, when the denominational groupings are contrasted with regard to Jewish religious and Jewish community involvement, the Orthodox are the most involved, both in 1971 and in 1990, followed by Conservatives. Reform Jews are the next most involved; those with no denominational preference are the least involved. Ritterband (1993) reports equivalent findings for New York area Jews in 1981.

The pattern with respect to involvement in the general, non-Jewish, community is somewhat different. In 1990, the Jewish adults most active in general community organizations were the synagogue members among the Conservative and Reform denominations. Those with no denominational preference were as likely to be active in the general community as are Conservative and Reform synagogue members. The Orthodox were the least active in general community organizations, while Conservative and Reform Jews who were not synagogue members hold an intermediate position with respect to activity in the general community.

In 1990, by far the most politically liberal were those respondents with no denominational preference. Reform Jews, whether synagogue members or not, and Conservative synagogue members were next most likely to consider themselves liberal politically. Conservatives Jews who were not synagogue members and Orthodox Jews were the least likely to consider themselves political liberals.

A comparison of the Jewish adult denominational groupings with the Christian population reveals several interesting findings. Orthodox and Reform Jews and Jews with no denominational preference are like Catholics in having a sizeable proportion of their numbers in the younger age groups. Each of the Jewish groupings, including those with no denominational preference, have considerably more education than any of the Christian groups. Fundamentalist Protestants, Catholics, and Orthodox Jews are the denominational groupings

High level of ed implies Jewish ed offering had better be sophisticated

with the highest levels of attendance at religious services. Conservative Jews are similar to religiously liberal Protestants with regard to religious attendance. Reform Jews and Jews with no denominational preference are the least likely to attend religious services.

When asked to place themselves on a scale from politically liberal to conservative, members of each of the Christian groupings tend to see themselves as middle-of-the-road, while the Jewish groupings are concentrated on the liberal side. Orthodox Jews are the most politically conservative Jewish grouping. Jews with no denominational preference are, by far, the most politically liberal with the Reform group, second.

Jews with no denominational preference constitute a rather unique group, especially when contrasted with Protestants. They attend religious services less, are more apt to be politically liberal, and are more highly educated. Indeed, while just 1% of Protestants (1) have at least a college degree, (2) claim to be liberal politically, and (3) attend religious services infrequently, some 29% of Jews with no denominational preference have these three characteristics.

Finally, most of the Jews who are marginal to Judaism and to the Jewish community, including even those who have married non-Jews, are not, themselves, entering into American Christian society. Rather, they are entering into a small category of purely secular Americans. Such Jews appear to be marginal to both American Jewish and American Christian societies.

Despite the findings presented in this chapter indicating the importance of denominational preferences and synagogue membership, the absence of statistical controls leaves the claim that demographic and/or socioeconomic factors may account for the results untested. Thus, the next chapter focuses on the use of the statistical techniques and controls that enable us to determine if denominational preference and synagogue membership have an influence above and beyond that of demographic variables and the components of socioeconomic status.

4

The Components and Consequences
of Jewish Involvement

We have argued that religious denominational preference and synagogue affiliation are significant indicators of how individual Jews choose to adjust to an
individualistic, open, religiously pluralistic society such as the United States.
We have already examined the general characteristics of individuals with different denominational preferences and of those with and without synagogue
membership. In this chapter, we shall use multivariate statistical techniques to
investigate the importance of denominational preference and synagogue membership above and beyond that of demographic and socioeconomic factors.

The statistical technique used in this part of our study is path analysis
(Blalock 1969). This technique, like regression analysis, enables us to determine the influence of one variable on another while holding statistically constant the influence of many other variables. Every effort has been made to
render the 1971 and 1990 analyses as similar as possible variable by variable,
index by index. The procedures used in each study are equivalent.

The first step in a path analysis is to specify the order in which the variables are to be entered into the statistical equations. Not all of these variables
are, in fact, prior in time, as called for by the strict logic of the statistical
analysis. However, those that appear early in the equation serve as controls,
that is, their influence is held constant statistically when we look at the influence of the variables of central concern here, namely, denominational preference and synagogue membership. Our use of path analysis is concerned with
its ability to control for the influence of many variables simultaneously.

The resulting analysis provides two statistics of interest: the standardized
coefficient of regression value (beta); and the squared multiple correlation
coefficient (R^2). Beta, the standardized coefficient of regression, indicates
how much a dependent variable changes for each unit of change in one of its
independent variables above and beyond the impact, or influence, of any other

independent variable. The squared multiple correlation coefficient, R^2, indicates how much of the variation (or variance) of a dependent variable is explained by the combined impact or influence of all the independent variables of the regression equation. (For an elaboration of the involved statistics, refer to Sonquist, Baker, and Morgan, 1971; Andrews and Messenger, 1986; Andrews, Morgan, and Sonquist, 1969; and Blalock, 1969 and 1979.)[1]

The variables that we use, in order of their appearance in the relevant equations, are:

1. *Demographic variables*, namely, gender, age, the number of minor children in the household, marital status, and the number of generations one's family has been in the United States

2. *Socioeconomic variables* such as the level of secular education, the occupation of the family head, and family income

3. *Jewish background factors:* Jewish characteristics of the childhood home and years of Jewish education in one's youth

By placing these three sets of variables first in the equation, the influence of demographic and socioeconomic factors as well as of Jewish background factors are statistically controlled in this analysis when we look at the significance of denominational preference and synagogue membership, which come next in the equations. This statistical technique enables us to determine whether or not denominational preference and synagogue membership are related to a number of other aspects of the respondent's Jewish and non-Jewish involvements above and beyond the influence of demographic characteristics, socioeconomic status, and the Jewish background of the respondents.

The particular aspects of our respondents' Jewish involvement in which we are interested are: attendance at religious services, religious practices at home, involvement with Jewish primary groups, activity in Jewish voluntary associations, and orientation toward Israel. We are also interested in the respondents' involvement with community organizations in the non-Jewish community.

The responses to the questions on each survey pertaining to the variables just noted were scored by giving the variable specific code numbers or points for each response. With respect to questions about one form or another of Jewish involvement, more points were given for answers that indicate more Jewish involvement. The scores for questions belonging to a particular dimension, for example, home religious practices, were added to form a simple summary measure. The frequency distribution for people with the various possible scores was then determined. Finally, the frequency distributions were divided into those scoring in the highest third, the middle scoring third, and the lowest scoring third. The result is a set of two measures for each respondent, a *scale score*, the sum of the responses to a series of related items, and an *index score*, the placement into a high, medium, or low category. The scale and the index score are each used at different points in our statistical analysis.[2]

The procedures just outlined were used to analyze the responses in the first national Jewish population survey of 1971. The same procedures have been used to analyze the 1990 survey in order to maintain comparability over time. Thus, there are three sets of model data available to us: (1) 1971 data; (2) the 1990 data; and (3) where questions are sufficiently similar, a data set combining the 1971 and 1990 survey responses.[3] Not all questions are sufficiently similar in the two surveys to justify combining them into one data set.

Time, the years between the two surveys, can be considered a variable by itself. The survey year for a respondent is simply entered along with his/her responses. In this chapter, we will look first at the 1990 survey and then at the combined results in order to detect changes over time.

This presentation will hypothesize that denominational preference and synagogue membership are more important in 1990 than they were in 1971. It does so because it is assumed that in the intervening twenty years the accommodation among Jews in America to living in an individualistic, open, religiously pluralistic society has advanced. Hence, the various 1971 regression models have been built anew in order to compare the patterns found earlier with those found in the 1990 survey.[4]

The Models

The Jewish Community Involvement Model

We hold that denominational preference and synagogue membership are important above and beyond demographic factors, socioeconomic status, and even the specifics of one's Jewish background. In order to test this hypothesis, we use an extensive model composed of ten regression equations in which demographic factors, socioeconomic status, and Jewish background are included. These are presented in table 4.1. Each line of that table represents a separate multiple regression equation. The control variables for the regression equation on a given line, for instance, the demographic and socioeconomic variables, appear first. They are followed, one by one, by the various Jewish variables. For example, the dependent variable of the first regression equation line is childhood Jewish background. The cell values are the beta coefficients of the predictive regression equation formed by the demographic and socioeconomic control variables. The squared multiple correlation coefficient appears in the last table column. It indicates how much of the variance in the dependent variable, childhood Jewish background, is explained by the combined impact or influence of the control variables.

TABLE 4.1
Betas and Squared Multiple Correlations of the Jewish Community Involvement Model, NJPS, 1990

Dependent Variables	Demographic Variables					Socioeconomic Variables			Jewish Variables									R²
	Gender	Age	Life Cycle	Marital Status	U.S. Gener.	Educ.	Head Occ.	Family Income	Childhood Jewish Background	Jewish Educ.	Denom.	Syn. Memb.	Syn. Attend.	Home Relig. Practice	Jewish Primary Groups	Jewish Org. Activity	Israel Orientation	
Childhood Jewish Background	.04	.09	.02	.02	.32	.05'	−.06	.03'										.15
Jewish Education	.10	−.12	.04	.02	.10	.16	.04'	.08	.29									.15
Denomination	−.08	.02'	.03'	.03'	.11	.03	.03'	.04	.45	.16								.27
Synagogue Membership	−.11	.13	.14	.04'	.05'	.11'	.04'	.13	.06	.23	.25							.23
Synagogue Attendance	.01	.02	.04	.03	.04'	.03	.04	−.07	.06''	.12	.22	.43						.37
Home Religious Practices	−.03	−.12	.01'	.05	.11	.05'	.04'	−.01	.06	.03	.36	.14	.30					.49

(continued on next page)

TABLE 4.1 (continued)

Dependent Variables	Demographic Variables					Socioeconomic Variables						Jewish Variables						R²
	Gender	Age	Life Cycle	Marital Status	U.S. Gener.	Educ.	Head Occ.	Family Income	Childhood Jewish Background	Jewish Educ.	Denom.	Syn. Memb.	Syn. Attend.	Home Relig. Practice	Jewish Primary Groups	Jewish Org. Activity	Israel Orientation	
Jewish Primary Groups	-.06	.08	.01	.03	.15	-.03	.03	.05	-.01	.06	.25	.10	.10	.26				.39
Jewish Organization Activity	-.08	.12*	.08	.08*	.05*	.07	.02*	.21	.04	.12	.05	.19	.14	.09	.14			.40
Israel Orientation	-.04	-.07	.02*	.03*	.28	.11	.02*	.04	.03*	.14	.13*	.01	.04*	.10	.11	.12		.30
General Comm. Org. Activity	-.02	.05*	.05*	.07	.11*	.20	.05	.21	.04	-.02	-.12	-.01	.07*	-.05	-.14	.30	.03	.26

Note: An asterisk means beta category values are not monotonic. A minus sign means (a) the smaller the independent values, the larger the dependent value; or, (b) for gender, men have smaller or less traditional values than women.

The model dependent variables appear one after another down the left-hand side of the table. Each Jewish variable is introduced into the model first as a dependent variable and then, in subsequent equations, it becomes an explanatory variable in the regression equation for the next Jewish variable appearing on the line below. Thus, childhood Jewish background changes to an explanatory variable for the second table line with regard to Jewish education.

Normally, regression equations are monotonic, that is, as scores on the independent or control variables move up or down, so, too, do those on the dependent variable. When such a monotonic increase or decrease fails to occur for a pairing of a dependent variable and one of the control or explanatory variables, an asterisk has been placed next to the regression coefficient in table 4.1. When the relationship between two variables is negative, that is, when the value of a dependent variable decreases when a paired control or Jewish variable increases, or increases when the independent or control variable decreases, the regression coefficient value is negative. (When two variables increase or decrease together, the regression coefficient is positive.)

When regression coefficients have an absolute value of 0.20 or greater, the relationship is considered "strong"; when the absolute value is from 0.10 to 0.19, it is regarded as "moderate," and it is considered "weak" when the absolute value is less than 0.10. As before, a cell value or regression (beta) coefficient indicates the strength of the association of an explanatory or control variable upon the given dependent variable above and beyond all the other variables of that equation line.

We look first at the relationship of the various control variables to our central variables, denominational preference and synagogue membership. Then we examine how the two central variables are related to measures of involvement in Jewish life and in the general (non-Jewish) community.

None of the demographic factors and none of the components of socioeconomic status are related to denominational preference at a statistically significant level. However, the number of generations a respondent's family has been in the United States relationship to denominational preference falls just short of statistical significance. First-generation Americans may be more likely to be Orthodox, the second, may be more likely to be Conservative, and the third, Reform.

Childhood Jewish background is, however, strongly related to denominational preference and to Jewish education. Denominational preference is not based on demographic or socioeconomic factors, but is a choice made in relation to what it means to be a Jew in the United States. This choice is, of course, influenced by one's early Jewish education or childhood Jewish background and perhaps to the number of generations one's family has been in the United States.

Synagogue membership is more strongly related to our control variables than is denominational preference. For example, older respondents and those with higher family income are more likely to be synagogue members. The moderate relationship between gender and synagogue membership falls just short of statistical significance. Finally, those with school-aged children are more likely to be synagogue members than those who not do have school age children. Synagogue membership is not related to childhood Jewish background. However, it is related to both Jewish education and denominational preference.

As shown in table 4.1, denominational preference is strongly related to other indicators of one's religiosity, above and beyond the influence of demographic factors, socioeconomic status, and one's Jewish background. In particular, it is strongly related to synagogue membership and attendance, and religious practices in a respondent's home. It is also strongly related to involvement with Jewish primary groups. However, denominational preference is, at most, weakly related to involvement with Jewish community organizations and only moderately related to the respondent's orientation to Israel. The more traditional a denomination is, the less active are its adherents in non-Jewish communal organizations.

Interestingly, the relationship between denominational preference and orientation to Israel is not monotonic. The mean orientation score is highest among the Orthodox, somewhat lower among the Conservatives and among those with no denominational preference, and lowest among the Reform.

Synagogue membership is strongly related to synagogue attendance. Nonmembers, understandably, attend synagogue services much less often than members. Synagogue membership is moderately related to the frequency of home religious practices. Some of these practices, especially those relating to Passover or Hanukkah, are, perhaps, as much a statement of involvement with the Jewish people and its heritage as they are observances of religious ritual. Thus, they may be relatively common among both synagogue members and nonmembers. In any case, synagogue membership is moderately related to involvement with Jewish community organizations, that is, with Jews outside the confines of the synagogue. Finally, synagogue membership is not related to either the respondent's orientation toward Israel, to Jewish primary group involvement or to involvement in organizations in the general, non-Jewish, community.

There are important differences in the model relationships for denominational preference and synagogue membership. Denominational preference is considerably more closely associated with home religious practices and Jewish primary group involvement; synagogue membership is considerably more closely associated with synagogue attendance and somewhat more so with involvement in Jewish organizations. Denominational preference is more closely associated with areas of individual behavior outside the synagogue. Synagogue membership is differentially associated with involvement in voluntary associations. Similar findings were obtained from the 1971 survey (Lazerwitz and Harrison 1980). It showed that denominational preference is indicative of a broader, more communal orientation toward Judaism and the Jewish community. On the other hand, synagogue membership involves people in institutional influences not likely to be encountered outside of the synagogue and heightens participation in the more institutionalized aspects of Jewish life.

Table 4.2 gives the beta values for 1971 for denominational preference and synagogue membership. These values can be compared with the equivalent beta values of 1990 as seen in table 4.1. We have predicted that denominational preference and synagogue membership would be more significant in 1990 than in 1971 as reflected by higher beta values. Contrary to our expectations, the 1971 and 1990 values are similar for the most part. However, the 1990 values for denominational preference are larger for childhood Jewish background, Jewish primary group involvement, and orientation to Israel. For synagogue membership, the 1990 values are larger for home religious practices and Jewish primary group involvement, but smaller in 1990 with respect to orientation to Israel.

As studies of the 1971 NJPS have shown (Harrison and Lazerwitz 1982; Lazerwitz and Harrison 1979, 1980), Jews in the United States had adopted the American denominational structure by 1971. That adaptation has remained stable since then.

A "Combined" Model

In this section, we examine the results of the 1971 and 1991 surveys to determine if the passage of time in the nearly two decades between the two surveys has had an influence. If the passage of time is associated with an

TABLE 4.2
Betas for Impact of Denomination and Synagogue Membership
on Involvement Variables, NJPS, 1971

Variables	Denominations	Synagogue Member
Childhood Jewish Background	.15	−.07
Jewish Education	.20	.28
Synagogue Attendance	.23	.43
Home Religious Practices	.35	.05
Jewish Primary Groups	.19	.00
Jewish Organization Activity	.02	.15
Israel Orientation	.06	.13
Gen. Community Organization Activity	−.11	.01

increase in the scores on variables in the 1990 survey over those in 1971, the beta for time will be positive and the relationship is said to have strengthened. If the relationship has weakened, there will be a negative beta.

We cannot assess the influence of time on our respondents' childhood Jewish backgrounds. The questions in this area on the two surveys are too dissimilar and too few to permit construction of comparable indexes.

In table 4.3, time is strongly and negatively related to involvement in Jewish primary groups and has a strong positive relationship to orientation to Israel. The strong negative relationship indicates that involvement in Jewish primary groups has decreased considerably from 1971 to 1990 and reflects the increased rate of intermarriage. The strong positive relationship involving the index of orientation toward Israel indicates a considerable strengthening of that orientation. The strengthened commitment to Israel may reflect the success of Jews in finding ways to express a commitment to Israel that is compatible with, and even expressive of, their commitments to the United States.

There is a moderate, positive, relationship between time and synagogue attendance and home religious practices. Both synagogue attendance and home religious practices have increased over time. Perhaps, as we have implied, religious modes of being Jewish are increasingly understood as the "proper" mode. In any case, time is also moderately, albeit negatively, related, to activity in general community organizations and weakly, and again negatively, related to involvement with Jewish communal organizations, indicating that both forms of involvement have decreased slightly.

In sum, our analysis reveals that between 1971 and 1990, synagogue attendance and home religious practices have increased and orientation toward Israel has strengthened. On the other hand, the degree of involvement in Jewish primary groups and in both general and Jewish organizational activities has decreased since 1971.

Further light can be shed on changes in American Jewry between 1971 and 1990 by examining average synagogue attendance. Lazerwitz (1964: 430) provides information on synagogue attendance in the United States for 1957 that was derived from survey data gathered by the Survey Research Center of the University of Michigan. Table 4.4 presents the information on average synagogue attendance in 1957 and averages from the 1971 and 1990 National Jewish Population Surveys. For the National Jewish Population Surveys, but not for the University of Michigan survey, information is available on the synagogue attendance of Jews with differing denominational orientations. Average synagogue attendance for American Jewish adults shows no change over the fourteen years from 1957 to 1971 and a small increase from 1971 to 1990. There is an increase in synagogue attendance in each denominational grouping. These specific increases support the result, indicated by the positive beta values in table 4.3, that synagogue attendance increased overall from 1971 to 1990.

TABLE 4.3
Beta and Multiple Correlation Values for the "Common" Jewish Community Involvement Model, NJPS, 1971 and 1990 Combined

Dependent Variables	Gender	Age	Life Cycle	U.S. Gen.	Educ.	Occ.	Inc.	Time	Jewish Education	Denom.	Syn. Memb.	Syn. Att.	Home Rel.	J. Prim.	J. Org.	Israel Orient.	R²
Jewish Education	.24	.05	.05	.07	.08	.03	.03	.02									.08
Denom.	-.06	.03	.05	.20	.12	.06*	.04	.03	.18								.11
Synagogue Members	-.09	.12	.14*	.03	.10	.10	.14	.02	.18	.27							.22
Synagogue Attendance	-.01	.05	.04	.09*	.09	-.02	.02	.13	.09	.24	.47						.40
Home Religion	-.03	-.09	.04*	.15	.04*	.03*	-.04	.12	.09	.31	.13	.30					.41
Jewish Prim.	-.10	.15	.04*	.14	-.04	.01*	.04	-.22	.05*	.16	.01	.04	.15				.26
Jewish Org.	-.11	.23	.07*	.06*	.08*	.06	.12	-.08	.09	.10*	.15	.12	.11	.06*			.30
Israel Orient.	.01	.04*	.11*	.13	.14	.12*	.04*	.23	.07	.02*	.01	.08*	.09*	.13*	.15		.15
Gen. Com.	.04	.08	-.07	-.08	.10	.07	.16	-.11	.03*	-.10	.02	.07	-.04	-.08	.44	-.05	.34

Note: (a) An asterisk indicates mean values are not monotonic; (b) a minus sign by a beta indicates that a male mean value is less than a female mean value; (c) the lower the dependent value, the higher the independent value; or, (c) 1990 "TIME" value is less than the 1971 value.

TABLE 4.4
Average Synagogue Attendance by Year and Denomination

Year	All	Orthodox	Conservative	Reform	No Pref.
1990	12	27	15	10	4
1971	10	20	12	8	3
1957	10	—	—	—	—

TABLE 4.5
Average Synagogue Attendance by Year, Denomination, and Synagogue
Membership after Controls for Demographic and Socioeconomic Variables

Group	1971	1990
Orthodox Synagogue Members	24	32
Conservative Synagogue Members	17	20
Reform Synagogue Members	13	16
Conservative Nonmembers	5	8
Reform Nonmembers	4	5
No Preference Nonmembers	1	3

The changes noted in table 4.4 do not take into consideration any of the seven control variables of the "common" model presented in table 4.3. These controls are, however, used for the information presented in table 4.5. That table reports the regression analysis of synagogue attendance in which statistical controls are applied for gender, age, life cycle, generations in the United States, education, occupation, and income. The equation reported in table 4.5 allows for an examination of the relationships among denominational preference, synagogue membership and synagogue attendance above and beyond the influence of the control variables.

Table 4.5 indicates there has been a clear increase in synagogue attendance, apart from the influence of the control variables, for Orthodox, Conservative and Reform synagogue members and for Conservative Jews who are not synagogue members. The increase is substantial among Orthodox Jews (all of whom are synagogue members), moderate for Conservative Jews, whether synagogue members or not, and moderate for Reform synagogue members. The changes in synagogue attendance among those without a denominational preference and among Reform Jews who are not synagogue members are too small to be considered meaningful.

The increase in synagogue attendance could be an artifact of the change in wording in the question about synagogue attendance from reference to the past twelve months in the first (1971) survey to a reference to "about how often do you personally attend" used in 1990. Yet these findings do have a consistent pattern of relationships with synagogue membership, primarily showing an increase in attendance. Some 61% of respondents fall into categories of denominational preference and synagogue membership associated with likely increases in synagogue attendance. It does seem likely that the patterns seen here are not random events, especially not for those who prefer Orthodox Judaism.[5]

These results are consistent with research by Sklare and Greenblum on changes in the sixties and the seventies in the suburban Jewish community of "Lakeville." Sklare and Greenblum (1979: 83) noted an overall tendency for stabilization in the amount or frequency of religious observances among American-born Jews of American-born parents:

> The more advanced generation, exposed to a less demanding religious regimen, narrows the gap between itself and its parents. . . . Among those with minimal religious training, the higher level of observance achieved by more advanced generations applies to both home practices and synagogue attendance. . . . [T]he more advanced generations maintain a higher observance level, despite the fact that their [secular] educational achievement is considerable. . . . The formal education of the second generation may have provided them with ideological support for their rejection or radical modification of the "foreign" elements in the religious system of their immigrant parents. For the third generation, general learning no longer presents such a stark contrast with the more acculturated religious pattern of their parents. (Sklare and Greenblum 1979: 84–87)

These comments are in general agreement with the conclusions of Schnapper's (1983) study of French Jewry that despite the increasing acculturation that accompanies the succession of the generations and the very high levels of general education achieved by Jews in France, the decline in religious observance has halted and even reversed.

Overall, our comparisons of the 1971 and 1990 surveys indicate that the importance of denominational preference and synagogue membership had been established by 1971 and increased slightly since then. The passage of time has also seen increased synagogue attendance, more Jewish religious practices in respondents' homes and a stronger orientation toward Israel. However, involvement in Jewish primary groups and in Jewish community voluntary organizations has decreased. It would appear that over time the meaning of being Jewish in the United States has come to focus more on religious aspects centered in the synagogue and on home-based religious practices, such as a *seder* or lighting Hanukkah candles, but less on involvement with Jews outside these settings. The increased orientation to Israel, however, appears to be an exception to the general trend toward a Jewishness based more on religious practice and participation and less on ethnic ties or involvements.

Summary and Conclusions

Ascribed demographic status and achieved socioeconomic status have often been thought, following Niebuhr (1929), to so dominate religious choice in the United States as to render those choices insignificant in and of themselves for predictive analytic purposes. The view that the apparent influence of denominational preference and synagogue membership is merely the result of other factors with which they are correlated has not been supported. To the contrary, the findings presented in this monograph indicate that the manner in which our respondents live their lives as Jews in the United States is influenced considerably by decisions concerning their denominational preferences and whether to affiliate with a synagogue. Moreover, a comparative analysis of the 1971 and 1990 surveys indicates that denominational preference and synagogue membership have retained, and even slightly increased, their influence in the nineteen years between these two surveys.

Interestingly, denominational preference and synagogue membership are each associated with different facets of Jewish life. Denominational preference is clearly associated with non-institutionalized expressions of Jewish life in the areas of religious practices in the home and of socializing with other Jews. Synagogue membership, on the other hand, is associated with aspects of institutional involvement such as attendance at synagogue services and activity in Jewish voluntary associations.

Our analyses also indicate that there has been a moderate increase in synagogue attendance and in observance of home religious practices along with a considerable strengthening of the orientation toward Israel. There has been a decline in involvement in Jewish primary groups and a moderate decline in activity in both Jewish and non-Jewish organizations. Overall, it would appear that Jews in the United States are gradually stabilizing their religious practices while reducing their degree of involvement with other, non-synagogue, features of Jewish communal life. In other words, the meaning of being a Jew in the United States has increasingly come to focus on the twin pillars of religious involvement and Israel and not on with whom one socializes or how one is involved in the voluntary association sector of American Jewish life.

5

Jewish Denominational Switching

Permeable Boundaries Among Jews in the United States

Chapters 3 and 4 have demonstrated the importance of denominational preference. However, since this is a society in which one is free to choose one's religious affiliation, it is not surprising that denominational boundaries in the United States are permeable and switching between them occurs frequently. Newport (1979) reports that 25% to 32% of the American population have switched religions or denominations. A later study finds that approximately 35% of all Americans claim to belong to a denomination that is different from the one in which they were raised (Sherkat and Wilson 1992). Sullins (1993) finds somewhat less switching. He reports that the NORC General Social Surveys conducted from 1973 to 1990 show that only 16% of adult Protestants have switched from the denomination in which they were raised to another Protestant denomination (Sullins 1993: table 2). Four percent have become Catholic; an additional 6% now have no denominational preference; and virtually none have become Jewish. He also notes that switching from one Protestant denomination to another did not increase in the 1970s and 1980s, and may, indeed, have decreased slightly (Sullins 1993: 408). Sullins's data (1993: table 2) also indicate that 87% of his admittedly small number of respondents reared as Jews remain so as adults, 9% have no denominational preference as adults, 2% become Catholic, and a bit over 1% become Protestants. Hadaway and Marler (1993), in a further analysis of the 1973–1990 General Social Surveys, finds that the size of liberal Protestant denominations has remained fairly constant, the size of conservative Protestant denominations has increased slightly, while Catholics and moderate Protestant denominations have decreased slightly. Among those with no denominational preference, switching to a denominational preference has increased slightly. However, they find that switching between denominational families has declined slightly (Hadaway and Marler 1993). Overall, Christians in America switch denominations "more today than they did in the early 1970s, but when they switch they are more likely to remain in the same larger denominational family" (Hadaway and Marler 1993: 102).

Greeley and Hout (1988: 79) find the major change is from religious affiliation to no affiliation and that among Protestants the result of switching among the various liberal and conservative denominations is a net loss for the mainline or liberal denominations. Kelley (1977), Babchuk and Whitt (1990), Bromley (1988), and Roof and McKinney (1987) similarly maintain that Protestantism has been undergoing a definite shift toward its conservative denominations. Sullins, on the other hand, like Hadaway and Marler (1993), finds most denominational switching among Protestants is within, rather than across, the broad families of liberal, moderate, and conservative denominations; that is, "switching close to home" characterizes Protestantism as a whole (Sullins 1993: 416).

The reasons for denominational switching are somewhat varied. Some persons do so in order to join the denomination of their spouse. Thomas (1963: 172) estimates this figure at about 30%; Newport (1979), at around 40%. About 20% change as a result of moving to an area without a church of their previous preference; about 14% change because they prefer the religious beliefs of another church. Newport (1979) writes that upward socioeconomic mobility is related to switching to the higher social status Protestant denominations and that marriage to a spouse with a different religion produces a 40% shift in religion. Hadaway and Marler (1993: 110) find that the most important factor determining whether a person will switch from the denomination in which they were reared to another as an adult is "family involvement in a single denominational tradition." They conclude that switching is very unlikely among Americans "socialized in a single denominational tradition by religiously active parents and who marry someone within the same tradition" (Hadaway and Marler 1993: 110).

Denominational Switching Among American Jews

This chapter examines switching, among Jews in the United States, from the denomination in which one was raised to another as an adult. If denominational preference has become a matter of individual choice among American Jews, as we have argued, then the permeability of boundaries between Jewish denominations as reflected in the amount of switching among them should approach that found among Protestants. Since the 1990 survey asked respondents for current denominational preference and for the denomination in which they were raised, it is possible to contrast current denominational preference with the denomination of one's childhood.

Not my experience

Overall, as shown in table 5.1, the pattern among our adult Jewish respondents is clearer than that among Protestants. There has been practically no net switching to the more traditional denominations. On the contrary, the percentage of adults who now prefer the more religiously liberal Reform denomination is some thirteen percentage points higher than it was when these same respondents were children. By way of contrast, the percentage of adults who choose Orthodox Judaism is some sixteen percentage points below what it was among these respondents when they were children. There is, on the other hand, very little difference between the percentage raised in the Conservative denomination or without any preference and the current percentages, respectively.

Table 5.1, however, presents only the overall, aggregate, picture. It does not reveal the dynamics of change among denominations. For example, as we shall see regarding the Conservative movement, what appears as little change overall, masks considerable movement in and out of the denomination. Table 5.2, which shows the current denominational distribution for each of the four

TABLE 5.1
Childhood and Current Denominational Preferences
for All Adult Jewish Respondents, NJPS, 1990

Denomination	Childhood	Current
Orthodox	22%	6%
Conservative	39%	40%
Reform	26%	39%
No Preference	13%	15%
Base	100%	100%

TABLE 5.2
Childhood Denomination by Current Preference
for All Adult Jewish Respondents, NJPS, 1990

	Was Raised			
Is Now	Orthodox	Conservative	Reform	No Pref.
Orthodox	24%	1%	0%	5%
Conservative	52%	62%	9%	20%
Reform	16%	28%	79%	28%
No Preference	8%	9%	12%	47%
Base	100%	100%	100%	100%

possible points of origin, the three major Jewish denominations and no preference, reveals the more detailed picture. It reveals that among those raised
Orthodox, just 24% are still Orthodox, 52% have switched to the Conservative denomination, 16% to the Reform, and 8% now declare that they have no
denominational preference. The decline in the proportion who are Orthodox
is further highlighted by the fact that very few adults raised in any other
denomination switch to Orthodoxy.

The Conservative denomination has also experienced some significant
losses despite increasing slightly to some 40% of the adult Jewish population
from the 39% raised as Conservative Jews. Some 38% of those reared as Conservatives have switched to another denomination as adult: 28% have become
Reform; 9% now have no preference; and a mere 1% have become Orthodox.

The Reform denomination has been the major beneficiary of shifts in
Jewish denominational preferences. Whereas only 26% of American Jews
were raised as Reform Jews, 39% now prefer that denomination. Moreover, it
has retained 79% of those reared as Reform Jews, while losing just about none
to the Orthodox, 9% to the Conservative, and 12% to no preference. Some
28% of those reared as Conservative Jews are now Reform Jews, as are some
16% of those reared within Orthodoxy.

The percentage of Jews with no denominational preference appears to be
basically stable, increasing only slightly from 13% reared without a preference to 15% who now have no preference. However, the overall pattern masks
considerable change. Just 47% of those reared without a denominational preference remained in this category as adults. Among those reared with no preference, 5% have become Orthodox, 20% have become Conservative, and
28% have become Reform. On the other hand, these losses have been more
than overcome by the 8% reared as Orthodox who now have no preference,
the 9% reared as Conservative, and 12% reared as Reform Jews who now
have no denominational preference.

Overall, 56% of survey respondents have remained in the denomination in
which they were raised—a level well below that among Protestants and
Catholics in the United States. The Reform denomination is most likely to retain
those reared in it. The Conservative denomination has been somewhat less successful in this regard, and the Orthodox even less so. Thirty-four percent of the
respondents have switched to a less traditional denomination, and 10% have
switched to a more traditional denomination. The Reform denomination has
gained 41% of the switchers, the Conservative denomination has gained 37% of
them, 19% have changed from having a denominational preference to having
none; and the Orthodox have gained just 3% of the switchers, contrary to the
often heard claim of a widespread return to Orthodoxy (Danzger 1989).

As a result of the differences in the patterns of "switching" and "staying,"
(summarized in table 5.3) each grouping is composed of a different mixture

TABLE 5.3
Denominational Composition by Stayers and Switchers, NJPS, 1990

Present Denom.	Raised in Denom.	Switched from Orth.	From Conserv.	From Reform	From No Pref.	Base
Orth.	82%	—	8%	*	10%	100%
Conserv.	60%	28%	—	6%	6%	100%
Reform	53%	9%	28%	—	10%	100%
No Pref.	43%	12%	24%	21%	—	100%

* = less than 1%

of "switchers" and "stayers." The Orthodox denomination, for example, is dominated by its stayers, who constitute over four-fifths of that denomination. A smaller proportion, but still a majority, of the Conservative and the Reform denominations, is comprised of those who have stayed in the group in which they were reared. However, over a quarter (28%) of those who currently prefer the Conservative denomination were raised as Orthodox; the same proportion (28%) of the Reform group were raised as Conservative Jews. Only a small proportion (9%) of those who now prefer Reform Judaism, were raised as Orthodox Jews.

Only among the category of those who have no current denominational preference do we find a minority (43%) are "stayers"—individuals reared in the grouping they now prefer as adults. The majority of those now without a denominational preference were reared in one of the three denominations: some (12%) were reared as Orthodox Jews, more (21%) as Reform Jews, and still more (24%) as Conservative Jews. The overall trend, then, is to move from a more to a less traditional denominational preference.

The shift among denominations is generally in small steps toward a less traditional denomination, that is, from Orthodox to Conservative, or Conservative to Reform, not Orthodox to Reform. Those who now prefer Conservative Judaism include some who were raised as Orthodox Jews, but proportionately few who were raised as Reform Jews. Among those who now prefer Reform Judaism, there are proportionally more who were raised as Conservative Jews than as Orthodox.

Table 5.4 puts these changes into an historical context by viewing the shifts in terms of the number of generations a respondent's family has been in the United States. If our contention that Americanization brings with it the view that denominational preference is a matter of choice, then switching should increase as the number of generations one's family has been in the United States increases. Since the great majority of Jewish immigrants within

TABLE 5.4
Adult Denominational Shifting by U.S. Generation, NJPS, 1990

Denomination	Preference in 1st U.S. Gen.		Preference in 2nd U.S. Gen.		Preference in 3rd or More U.S. Gen.	
	When Child	Now	When Child	Now	When Child	Now
Orthodox	41%	21%	40%	9%	10%	3%
Conservative	27%	43%	35%	50%	40%	34%
Reform	12%	19%	14%	28%	36%	48%
No Preference	20%	17%	11%	13%	14%	15%
Base	100%	100%	100%	100%	100%	100%

the last 120 years were reared in rather traditional settings that, as noted in chapter 1, are the least supportive of Western ways among the major Jewish denominations, increased Americanization would mean movement away from Orthodoxy.

In their childhood, just about 40% of the first (foreign-born) generation and of the second (native-born Americans of foreign-born parents) were raised as Orthodox Jews. However, as we have just suggested, there are fewer Orthodox among our adult Jewish respondents. Only 21% of the first and 9% of the second generation currently consider themselves to be Orthodox. The predicted shift out of Orthodoxy continues into the third generation (native-born Americans of native-born parents). Among the third generation (and beyond), 10% were raised as Orthodox Jews, but only 3% now prefer Orthodoxy.

The percentage who are reared as Conservative Jews increases in the second generation in the United States. Among those who are second generation Americans, 50% of the respondents consider themselves to be Conservative Jews. Among adults of the third generation (and beyond) only 34% currently prefer the Conservative denomination.

The substantial growth in the Reform denomination is also consistent with our prediction and begins with adults of the second generation and continues into the third generation. In fact, Reform is the leading preference by the third generation (and beyond) for American Jewish adults.

Remarkably, despite all the denominational shifts, the percentage with no denominational preference remains rather stable from generation to generation perhaps reflecting the increasing importance of having a religious preference discussed in chapter 1. Among first-generation American Jews, some 20% report they were reared with no preference; 17% have no preference as adults. In the third generation, the corresponding figures are 14% reared with no preference and 15% currently without a preference.

Overall, it appears that there has been the predicted Americanization as the second generation left Orthodoxy for the Conservative denomination. In the third generation there has been a shift to the Reform from the Conservative denomination as the process of Americanization increases. Of course, acculturation or Americanization among American Jews has not occurred without some countermovements seeking to preserve Jewish ways. Among these movements is the growth of the Jewish day school.

As might be expected, the tendency to switch denominations is slowed among those who have a Jewish day school education. A Jewish day school education is now common among Orthodox young people and increasingly common among Conservative and even Reform Jews. Among those survey respondents who are now between the ages of 20 to 59 and who are graduates of elementary grade Jewish day schools, 66% of those who were Orthodox in childhood have remained Orthodox and 89% of those who were Conservative in childhood have remained Conservative. (The numbers for Reform Jews are too small for analysis.) Thirty percent of the day-school-educated Orthodox respondents have become Conservative; 7% of the day-school-educated Conservative respondents have become Orthodox, with only 4% of them having become Reform. A religious day school education certainly promotes denominational retention. Among those who do switch, such religious education may be instrumental in inducing movement from a traditional denomination to a less traditional one rather than a transfer to the ranks of those with no denominational preference. Hadaway and Marler (1993) similarly find that childhood religious socialization among Christians also reduces the likelihood of denominational switching. *Ed implications of community day schools?*

Concomitants of Denominational Switching

The pattern of denominational switching among Jews in the United States shown above and its association with the number of generations one's family has been in the United States support our views on the relationship of Jewish acculturation to denominational preferences. It does not, however, address the question of the possible differences in the Jewish involvements of stayers and switchers and of the impact of those differences on the major denominational groupings. These latter questions are addressed by the information in table 5.5.

Table 5.5 presents the percentages who score high on the indices of Jewish education, home religious practices, involvement in Jewish primary groups, activity in Jewish voluntary associations, attendance at synagogue services, and synagogue membership introduced in chapter 3. The table shows

TABLE 5.5

Religious and Community Involvement Characteristics for
Denominational Stayers and Switchers, NJPS, 1990

Denominational Changing	8 yrs.+ Jewish Education	Often Attends Synag.	Home Religious Practices (a)	Jewish Primary Groups (b)	Jewish Organiz. Activity (c)	General Organiz. Activity (d)	Is Synag. Member
Remained Orthodox	52%	56%	77%	80%	61%	16%	69%
All Now Orthodox	50%	58%	80%	82%	62%	16%	72%
Orth. to Conserv.	52%	27%	52%	54%	55%	36%	62%
Remained Conserv.	49%	15%	39%	45%	43%	36%	57%
All Now Conserv.	48%	20%	43%	48%	48%	36%	59%
Conserv. to Reform	36%	11%	15%	26%	39%	42%	49%
Remained Reform	34%	6%	10%	19%	27%	31%	36%
All Now Reform	28%	9%	15%	23%	34%	36%	43%

Key: (a) Shabbat candles + Kiddush; Hanukkah candles; kosher homes
(b) Most friends Jewish; neighborhood Jewish; opposes intermarriage
(c) Member several J. orgs.; 20 hrs. mo. + work for J. org.; donates $ to J. organizations
(d) Member several gen. comm. org.; donates $ to non-Jewish organizations

that the percentages scoring high on these indices is lower for those who are denominational switchers than for those who remained in the denomination from which they switched. Only on the index of activity in general community voluntary associations are the switchers more likely to score higher than those who stayed in the denomination they left. These differences are small, but the patterns are too consistent to be mere random happenings. Of course, since the changes reported in the table are from Orthodox to Conservative and from Conservative to Reform Judaism, that is, from more to less traditional, such results are to be expected.

Similarly, when switchers are compared to those who were reared in the denomination to which they switch, they tend to be more active. In fact, there is only one exception to the pattern: those switching from the Conservative denomination to the Reform are more likely to be active in general community voluntary associations than those who have remained Conservative or Reform. Thus, in general, the activity level of switchers, with regard to the indices used here, falls between that of those in the denomination they are leaving and those in the denomination into which they have moved.

The presence of consistent differences between denominational stayers and switchers raises the question of how much influence the new members—who are, as Hadaway and Marler (1993: 111) say of Christian switchers, typically "more fervent than stayers"—have on their new denominations. The answer for the Orthodox denomination is "very little," since it receives few switchers.

The influence of switchers on the other denominations may be more pronounced. Those Jews who switch from a more to a less traditional denomination are often more Jewishly involved than the overall membership of their newly acquired denomination. For the Conservative and Reform denominations, the switchers or "new recruits" bring more traditional patterns and raise the percentage of those who are observant and involved for the denomination as a whole. The actual impact, of course, will vary from congregation to congregation depending on the relative number of stayers and switchers in a particular synagogue or temple and on the original orientation within it.

Whatever the consequences of switching on the various denominational groupings, we may still ask what social factors are associated with the observed shifts. We discuss these factors next. In so doing, we will exclude shifts among Jews now married to a non-Jew. Intermarriage will be treated in the next chapter.

The data in this section are from interviews with the 628 respondents who are now in a marriage in which both spouses were born to Jewish parents or raised Jewish. By studying married couples only we limit the confounding influence of life cycle found to be important in the previous chapters. Among these respondents, some 34% report they were reared as Orthodox, 39% as

Conservative, 20% as Reform, and 7% report they were raised with no denominational preference. The number of interviews from those raised either as Reform Jews or with no preference and now married to another Jew are too few to permit complex statistical analysis. Therefore, they are not considered in the following discussion.

In the analysis which follows, those whose current denominational preference is the same as that of their childhood are called "stayers" and those who have changed denominations, "switchers," regardless of whether they were raised as Orthodox or Conservative Jews. The result is a "staying-switching" binomial (two category) variable formed by coding switchers as "0" and stayers as "1." Two sets of independent or predictor variables will be used in the analyses to help understand who switches and why. The first set consists mainly of demographic and socioeconomic variables. It includes: gender, age, number of generations one's family has been in the United States, childhood Jewish education, family life cycle, respondent's education, the occupation of the family head, family income (in the year prior to the survey), and geographic mobility. The question about geographic mobility asked where a respondent lived before moving into his/her current residence. The responses were: "always lived here," "lived in same city," "lived in a different city in this state," or "lived in another state." Since respondents were not asked to specify when they switched denominations, if they did, it is not possible to determine if switching came before or after moving from one residence to another.

The second set of predictor variables consists of Jewish activities: frequency of synagogue attendance, extent of home religious practices, synagogue membership, degree of involvement in Jewish primary groups, and activity in Jewish voluntary associations.[1]

The analysis of the relationship of these variables to whether one is a "stayer" or a "switcher" entailed the use of the complex multiple regression technique, Multivariate Nominal Scale Analysis (MNA) described in Andrews and Messenger (1986). It enables the researcher to determine the influence or impact (beta values) of each predictor variable upon the decision to stay or switch apart from the impact of any of the other predictor variables. (A negative beta value is associated with switching; a positive, with staying.) In this way it is possible to evaluate the relationship of one variable, for example, gender, independent of the influence of any other variable. Our use of MNA clearly shows that for all respondents gender, Jewish education, family income, activity in Jewish voluntary associations, and synagogue memberships are weakly associated with denominational switching.[2] For purposes of clarity, these variables are not noted in table 5.6, which reports the other results of the use of MNA.

Table 5.6 shows the results of analyses done separately for those reared as Orthodox and Conservative Jews. The pattern of association between stay-

TABLE 5.6
MNA Impact Factors Associated with Denominational Shifts
for Couples Born into Jewish Families and with
Orthodox or Conservative Childhoods, NJPS, 1990

	Impact Factors for Respondents with	
Characteristics	Orthodox Childhoods	Conservative Childhoods
I. Prior to Survey		
Age	−.15	−.17
Children in Home	.34	−.15
U.S. Generation	.14	.18
Education	−.04	.17
Occup. Family Hd.	−.14	−.09
Mobility	−.17	.12
II. At Time of Survey		
Synag. Attend.	.20	.24
Home Relig. Pract.	.14	.28
Jewish Prim. Grps.	.23	.13
n	208	243

ing or switching and the various demographic and socioeconomic status variables is different for those reared as Orthodox or as Conservative Jews. For example, Orthodox respondents with preschool children are the least likely to change denomination, as indicated by the association between staying and children in the home, while among those raised Conservative respondents in households with preschool children are more likely to have switched denominations.[3]

The number of generations one's family has been in the United States has just about the same influence on the denominational switching of Conservative and Orthodox Jews. In both case, there is more denominational shifting among the more Americanized third-generation Americans than among those of an earlier generation.

The negative association between age and switching indicates there has been more switching among older than among younger respondents. Such a result is understandable if, as we have contended, the notion that one chooses rather than "inherits" a religious preference has been growing among Jews over time.

The degree of secular education is not associated with denominational switching among those reared as Orthodox Jews to a statistically meaningful degree. For those reared as Conservative Jews, there is more switching among those with a low education level. Among both Orthodox and Conservative Jews, as occupational status declines, so too does the amount of switching. Finally, our multivariate analysis, which controls for the influence of other variables, is consistent with the bivariate analysis, which did not use such controls, in Goldstein and Goldstein (1996: 180–84) in showing that geographic mobility is not consistently related to switching among those reared as Conservatives, but is among those reared Orthodox. Respondents reared as Orthodox who have done any kind of moving, whether between cities or between states, are considerably more likely to switch out of Orthodoxy than are those respondents, reared as Orthodox, who report no moving.

Among the measures of current Jewish activities and practices, greater synagogue attendance, more home religious practices, and greater involvement in Jewish primary groups are clearly associated with less switching, regardless of whether one was reared as an Orthodox or a Conservative Jew.

In sum, among both Orthodox and Conservative respondents married to Jews, denominational switching is lower among those who attend synagogue more frequently. Whether the increased attendance is the cause or effect, we cannot be sure. In any case, denominational switching among the married Orthodox respondents is less common among those with young children at home and among those involved with Jewish primary groups. Among the Orthodox, then, family and friends seem to play a role in switching. Among married Conservative respondents, family and friends are less important and engaging in home religious practices, more so.

Summary and Conclusions

The information presented in this chapter reveals the permeability of denominational boundaries among Jews in the United States.[4] More specifically, it highlights the historic decrease in the proportion of Orthodox Jews in the United States. This decrease appears whether one compares the denomination in which a survey respondent was raised with his/her present denominational preference or whether one looks at changes over the number of generations a respondent's family has been in the United States.

In the years represented by the lives of respondents to the 1990 survey, the proportion who are Orthodox Jews has declined considerably. The proportion who prefer Conservative Judaism appears relatively stable, but the stability is more apparent than real. The Conservative denomination has gained enough adherents from among those reared as Orthodox to offset its sizeable losses to the Reform denomination.[5]

Those with no denominational preference also constitute an unstable category. Almost as many adults adopt a denominational preference, even though not raised with one, as decide against having a denominational preference despite having been reared with one.

The major beneficiary of Jewish interdenominational movement has been the Reform denomination. While just 26% of survey respondents report being raised Reform, 39% claimed this denomination preference as adults in 1990.

The major trend in the denominational switching among Jews in America has been from Orthodox to Conservative and from Conservative to Reform. Thirty-four percent of the switches have been from a more to a less traditional denomination. Only 10% have been from a less to a more traditional denomination. There may be a debate among religious researchers about whether or not the more conservative Protestant denominations are growing (Kelley 1977; Hadaway 1978; Roof and McKinney 1987). However, there can be no debate over the considerable decline in the Jewish Orthodox denomination and the switch to the less traditional Jewish denominations.

The Conservative denomination is most preferred among second generation Jews, native-born Americans of foreign-born parents. Among them, 50% identify themselves as Conservative Jews. Among third-generation (and more) American Jews, native-born Americans of native-born parents, only 34% identify with the Conservative denomination. While only 28% of second-generation American Jews identify with Reform Judaism, 48% of those who are third-generation (or more) Jews do so.

Overall, 44% of American Jewish adults have switched denominations. This frequency of change is somewhat more than the 15% to 35% reported for white Protestants earlier in the introduction to this chapter.

On the whole, denominational switchers tend to be less Jewishly involved than are those who stay in the denomination in which they were reared. However, switchers tend to be more Jewishly involved than the adherents of the denominations into which they move. American Jewish denominations may then be "pulled" in more traditional directions by their "incoming" people.

Those reared as Reform Jews are most likely to remain in the denomination of their childhood; those reared as Conservatives are next most likely to retain their denomination of origin, while the Orthodox are least likely. Those reared without a denominational preference fall between those reared Conservative and those reared Orthodox with respect to remaining in the grouping in which they were reared.

Sources of Denominational Switching

The studies of American Protestants referred to at the beginning of this chapter, identify a variety of factors associated with denominational switching. In particular, the following factors have been named:

Factors in switching

1. Whether a person is raised in a religiously liberal or traditional denomination (there is more switching among those raised in liberal denominations)

2. Geographic mobility (the more mobile, the more switching)

3. Amount of childhood religious education (the more religious education, the less switching)

4. Frequency of religious observances (more observances, less switching)

5. Changes in socioeconomic status (upwardly mobile persons tend to switch more)

6. Gender (women tend to switch less)

7. Intermarriage (intermarried switch more than intramarrieds)

Our analysis of Jewish denominational switching shows some of the same factors at work, although not necessarily in the same manner. The most important point about Jewish denominational switching is the shift away from Orthodoxy. Moreover, this shift appears to be the result of particular generational and historical factors. For example, it is related to the number of generations one's family has lived in the United States, that is, to a process known as Americanization. It also appears to be a result of the historical fact of the Emancipation of Jews as discussed in chapter 1. In any case, the switch from the more traditional Orthodox to the less traditional Conservative and Reform forms of Judaism constitutes a movement opposite that of the switching from the more liberal to more traditional denominations earlier found among Protestants and from the pattern of remaining with broad denominational families found more recently.

Other factors, however, are found to work in similar manners among both Protestants and Jews. Geographic mobility, for example, is associated with an increased likelihood of denominational switching for both Protestants and Jews.

Among Jewish adults 20 to 59 years of age who received a Jewish day school education, the tendency to remain in the denomination in which one was reared is much stronger. Among those with a day school education from Orthodox backgrounds, 66% remain Orthodox. Among those with a day school education from Conservative backgrounds, 89% have remained Conservative.

Among both Protestants and Jews, the more religiously observant one is, the less likely one is to have changed denominations. The regression analysis reported above (table 5.6) indicates that the greater the frequency of synagogue attendance, the more one partakes in home religious observances and the greater one's involvement in Jewish primary groups, the less likely one is to switch denominations. This pattern is similar to that found among Christian Americans by Hadaway and Marler (1993).

American Jews have undergone considerable change in their socioeconomic status. For example, Lazerwitz (1961: 573; 1979: 659) reports that while 16% of Jews had four years or more of college in 1957, by 1971, 35% had reached this level. Moreover, the 1990 NJPS reports that 62% of American Jews had four years or more of college. In a matter of thirty-three years, about a generation, the percentage of Jews who are college graduates increased almost fourfold. However, the regression analysis reported above (table 5.6) indicates that differences in social status, as measured by years of secular education or income, are related to denominational switching only weakly and/or inconsistently.

Contrary to studies among Protestants, which show men are more likely than women to switch denominations, the data reported in this chapter indicate that Jewish men and women are about equally likely to switch denominations. Since we do not have information on the denominational background of a respondent's spouse, we cannot determine the effect of a marriage between Jews reared in different denominations upon denominational switching. However, as will be seen in the next chapter, intermarriage between a Jew and a non-Jew is associated with considerable denominational switching.

Denominational Predictions

Keeping in mind the risks of prediction, it is possible, using the analyses reported in this chapter, to make some informed, albeit tentative, forecasts about denominational growth, decline, or stabilization. (A more detailed projection is found in chapter 7.) We will do so for the Orthodox, Conservative, and Reform denominations in turn and then comment on those with no denominational preference.

Researchers such as Danzger (1989), Davidman (1991), Kaufman (1991), and Waxman (1983) have pointed out that the contemporary Orthodox community has created a strong network of elementary level Jewish day schools and more advanced yeshivas for its children. However, despite an increasingly strong Jewish educational system, the Orthodox denomination has lost about one-third of its adult day school graduates to other denominations, primarily the Conservative. Nevertheless, given the above replacement birth rate and very low intermarriage rate among the Orthodox, it is likely that the Orthodox denomination has reached the bottom of its population decline. It could well begin a slow, but steady, increase in its small percentage of the American Jewish community.

The Conservative denomination has lost a substantial proportion of its young people to the Reform denomination. Defection from the Orthodox community has long been a source of membership gain for the Conservative movement, However, the current small size of the American Orthodox community, and the possibility of its growing stability, greatly reduces this historic source of new members for the Conservatives. Of course, the decline in the proportion of Conservatives may be stemmed by an increase in the proportion of its children who attend Conservative Jewish day schools. These schools seem to be particularly effective in aiding denominational retention. Nevertheless, the Conservative denomination will probably drop behind the Reform denomination in terms of denominational preferences. However, since those who prefer Conservative Judaism are more likely to be synagogue members than those who prefer Reform, there may be more Conservative than Reform Jews among future synagogue members.

If the trends up to 1990 continue into the next generation, the Reform denomination can be expected to continue its growth and to become the most common denominational preference. There is likely to be continued switching from the Conservative to the Reform denomination. Such switching, in conjunction with the considerable ability of the Reform denomination to retain its young, plus some gains from conversions associated with intermarriage (noted in the next chapter) should result in a growth in the number who prefer Reform Judaism. Such gains should more than offset the lower birth rate among Reform Jews. Gains and losses in denominational size are further discussed in chapter 6, on intermarriage, and chapter 7, on fertility and projection of future denominational size.

Finally, the grouping of those with no denominational preference is an unstable one. A substantial number of those reared with no preference later choose to be Reform Jews. However, many adults with no denominational preference, especially those involved in intermarriages, as we note in the next chapter, are not rearing their children as Jews. The proportion of the American Jewish population with no denominational preference will depend a good deal upon how many of the substantial number of Jews marrying non-Jews join its ranks. If, as we have argued, having a denominational preference is increasingly one of the important ways of participating in American society, then the future ranks of Jews with no denominational preference, especially among those married to fellow Jews, should decline, or at least remain relatively stable.

6

Denominational Preferences and Intermarriage

Permeable Boundaries Between Jews and Non-Jews

Traditionally, in the pre-Emancipation urban ghettoes and shtetls (small towns) from which Eastern European Jews, the forebears of most of contemporary American Jewry, came to the United States, marriage was seen primarily as a mechanism for satisfying the communal concern for the preservation of the Jewish people and their religion. The modern notion that marriage is essentially a means to express and satisfy the mutual romantic wishes of the couple in question was uncommon (Mayer 1985). Indeed, many marriages were arranged by the parents of the prospective bride and groom when they were relatively young (Zbrowbski and Herzog: 1952: 269–90).

Given the emphasis on marriage as a means for communal survival, intermarriage, marriage between a Jew and a non-Jew was taboo. In the conditions prevailing in Eastern Europe, intermarriages would inevitably lead to the Jewish community's loss of the new family and its children. The conversion of the non-Jewish spouse to Judaism was often forbidden by civil law. In any event, the social and economic opportunities for the Jewish community were so restricted, there would be little incentive for a religiously mixed couple to remain within the Jewish community. Thus, it is understandable that the Jewish spouse in an intermarriage was considered lost, even "dead," by his or her family. Indeed, as Tevye did for his intermarried daughter in *Fiddler on the Roof*, the prayer for the dead was often said for an intermarried child, signifying that the child was "lost" or "dead" as far as involvement with the Jewish community was concerned.

Of course, matters are quite different in the pluralistic, post-Emancipation world of the United States. Opportunities for Jews are no longer severely restricted. Conversion to Judaism is not illegal. Consequently, there is growing sentiment to reconsider long-standing views concerning conversion to Judaism (Mayer 1985: 218). Conversion is now officially welcomed, albeit to different degrees in practice, by the branches of Judaism in America. Programs to encourage the conversion of a Gentile spouse to Judaism are growing, especially within Reform Judaism. Moreover, where religious preference is so clearly an *individual* preference and a private matter, it is easy to conceive of married partners going their separate ways religiously, each partner respecting the religious choice of the other, at least until they have children, if not after. That is, "Intermarriage followed quite naturally from the emancipation of the individual . . . and signified the triumph of romantic ideology over tradition" (Mayer 1985: 86).

The frequency of marriage between a Jew and a non-Jew should vary with the degree of acceptance of the terms of Emancipation: the greater the acceptance, the greater the rate of intermarriage; the less the acceptance, the lower the rate. Thus, it would be predicted that the rate of intermarriage would vary with the degree to which a denomination is Americanized and accepts the terms of Emancipation, that is, it would be least among Orthodox Jews, higher among Conservative and highest among Reform Jews.

Predictions for Jews with no denominational preference are a bit more difficult to make in that it is unclear if their lack of a preference reflects their views on the values associated with Emancipation or if it reflects a lack of commitment to being Jewish. It is possible that many of those with no denominational preference remain committed to being Jewish ethnically, albeit not religiously. Still, if the choice of a denomination does not matter, it would seem unlikely that religion would be a factor in the choice of a spouse; hence, the rate of intermarriage among Jews with no denominational preference, all others things being equal, might even approach what it would be randomly. Since Jews are between but 2% and 3% of the entire United States population, the random intermarriage rate would be quite high. These predictions will be tested by the data presented in this chapter.[1]

Intermarriage and Denominational Preference

There are 506 intermarried couples among the respondents to the 1990 survey, slightly less than the 628 marriages examined in the last chapter in which both spouses were born into Jewish families. Of these, 83 marriages (16%) are conversionary marriages, that is, marriages in which a spouse reared as a Jew is married to one who has converted to Judaism. The majority of intermarriages, 59%, are between a Christian and a Jew. Intermarriages in which the non-Jewish spouse prefers a religion other than Christianity or Judaism or has no religious preference at all constitute 25% (126) of the intermarried couples.[2]

As shown in table 6.1, it is apparent that denominational preference makes a considerable difference with regard to intermarriage. Section A of table 6.1 shows the rate of intermarriage by current denominational preference; section B, by the denomination of one's childhood. The data in both sections A and B indicate that the less traditional one's current or childhood denomination, respectively, the more likely it is that its married adherent has married someone who was not originally Jewish.

In terms of current denominational preference (table 6.1, section A), the proportion of currently mixed marriages (marriages in which one spouse is now Jewish and the other currently is not), is a mere 4% among the Orthodox, 11% among the Conservative, 25% among Reform Jews, and 56% among respondents with no denominational preference. (Marriages in which one spouse converts, formally or informally, to Judaism, often called conversionary marriages, are not considered mixed marriages.) A similar trend is found in section B of table 6.1 when the denomination in which one was reared is considered: 9% of those reared as Orthodox are currently in mixed or religiously heterogeneous marriages, 20% of those reared as Conservative Jews, 34% of those reared as Reform Jews, and 35% of those reared with no denominational preference.

Respondents who were raised in homes with a preference for the Orthodox or Conservative denominations but who later marry a non-Jew are very likely to shift to a less traditional denominational grouping: Conservative or Reform if reared Orthodox; Reform, if reared Conservative. Where the non-Jewish spouse does not convert to Judaism, the most likely outcome is for the respondent to have no preference among the various Jewish denominations.

Among married Jewish respondents whose spouses are not Jewish (including those whose spouses prefer religions other than Judaism or Christianity and those with no religious preference), some 27% have no preference among the Jewish denominations. Among all the married Jewish respondents in the 1990 survey, only 14% say they have no denominational preference. Only 6% of the converts to Judaism are married to a Jewish spouse with no denominational preference. Some 63% of the converts are married to adherents of Reform Judaism. The findings indicate that Reform Judaism is the usual denominational preference, then, in marriages between a Jew and a non-Jew in which the latter converts.

The rate of intermarriage has increased dramatically since 1971. Lazerwitz (1981) reports the intermarriage percentages for married Jewish men from the first (1971) survey. (In 1971, there were too few interviews with intermarried Jewish women for proper statistical analysis, a point worth noting in itself.) The 1990 intermarriage percentages are compared with those for 1971 in table 6.2. Overall, the percentage in 1990 is more than four times what it was in 1971. There has also been a considerable increase in the percentage

TABLE 6.1

Intermarriage Types by Current and Childhood Denominational Preference, NJPS, 1990

A. Current Denomination	Both Spouses Born into Jewish Families	One Spouse Convert-In	One Spouse Jewish, One Spouse Christian	One Spouse Jewish, One Spouse "Other" or "None"	Base
Orthodox	93%	3%	4%	—	100%
Conservative	82%	7%	7%	4%	100%
Reform	60%	15%	19%	6%	100%
None	41%	3%	38%	18%	100%
B. Childhood Denomination					
Orthodox	85%	6%	6%	3%	100%
Conservative	73%	7%	14%	6%	100%
Reform	59%	7%	26%	8%	100%
None	60%	5%	25%	10%	100%

TABLE 6.2
Contrasting Male Intermarriages for the 1971 and 1990 NJPS Surveys

	Percent Men Intermarried				
	Overall	Orthodox	Conservatives	Reform	No Pref.
1990 Survay[a]	32%	10%	18%	43%	55%
1971 Survey	7%	3%	4%	9%	17%

[a] Includes those whose spouse is Christian, has no religious preference, or is other than Christian.

of currently intermarried Jewish men for each category. The rate of current intermarriage has more than tripled among Orthodox men and among those with no denominational preference; and more than quadrupled among both the Conservative and Reform men.

The rate of intermarriages among the Conservative men in the 1990 study is nearly twice as large as among Orthodox men. In 1971, their rates were about equal. The male Reform intermarriage rate is now over four times that of Orthodox men and well over twice that of the Conservative men.

In sum, as predicted above, the rate of intermarriage is indeed least among Orthodox Jews, somewhat greater among Conservatives and greater still among Reform Jews and those with no denominational preference. We expect these differences to be even greater between those who are synagogue members and those who are not. Synagogue membership entails a willingness to use important family resources such as time and money in its behalf and is, thus, an indicator of the seriousness of one's denominational preference and a commitment to a Jewish identity for oneself and one's family. Table 6.3 supports this prediction. Only 2% of the married Orthodox synagogue members are in currently mixed marriages, slightly more, merely 4%, of Conservative synagogue members, but more, 10%, among members of Reform synagogues. Among those who are not synagogue members, the rates of mixed marriages are much higher: nearly a quarter (24%) among Conservative Jews, over a third (37%) among Reform Jews, and over three-fifths (61%) among those with neither a synagogue membership nor a denominational preference.

Understandably, for most couples in which one partner was born into a Jewish family and the other was not, but who are now synagogue members, the originally non-Jewish spouse is now a Jew-by-choice. As seen in table 6.3, among Conservative synagogue members, some two-thirds of marriages between someone born into a Jewish family and someone who was not are now conversionary marriages, marriages in which the originally non-Jewish spouse is now Jewish. Among Reform synagogue members, 71% of marriages

TABLE 6.3

Intermarriage Types by Current Denomination and Synagogue Membership, NJPS, 1990

Denomination—Synagogue Member	Both Spouses Born into Jewish Families	One Spouse Convert-In	One Spouse Jewish, One Spouse Christian	One Spouse Jewish, One Spouse "Other" or "None"	Base
Orthodox					
Member	98%	—	2%	—	100%
Conservative					
Member	88%	8%	3%	1%	100%
Not Member	72%	4%	15%	9%	100%
Reform					
Member	66%	24%	7%	3%	100%
Not Member	55%	8%	29%	8%	100%
None—Not Member	38%	1%	41%	20%	100%

between one who was born into a Jewish family and one who was not involve
a conversion (24% of their total synagogue membership). Finally, 45% of all
conversions are found among Reform synagogue members, 22% among Conservative synagogue members, and 18% among Reform Jews who are not synagogue members. Clearly, denominational preference and synagogue
membership are related both to the rate of intermarriage and to the frequency
with which the originally non-Jewish spouse is a Jew-by-choice, now identified as Jewish.

Intermarriages Before and After 1970

Our contention is that as Jews have become more acclimated to American
society and the values of the Emancipation embodied in it, intermarriage rates
should increase; that is, rates should be highest among Reform Jews, next
highest among Conservative Jews, and lowest among Orthodox Jews, as the
above analyses show them to be. We would also expect intermarriage rates to
increase over time as more and more Jews accommodate to American society.
To determine if such is indeed the case, we contrast intermarriage rates for
three sets of marriages, those entered into: (1) before 1960; (2) between 1960
and 1969; and (3) between 1970 and 1990. For analytic purposes, only first
marriages are considered.

The trend, as shown in table 6.4, is clearly as we predict. Before 1960,
intermarriage was uncommon for both Jewish men and women. The 1960s
witnessed an increase in intermarriage rates, again for both men and women.
Since then, the rates have grown considerably, so that after 1970 only a bare
majority (54%) of both Jewish men and women married somebody born of
Jewish parents or raised as a Jew. Even excluding those (conversionary) marriages in which the originally non-Jewish spouse is now identified as a Jew,
the rate of mixed marriages since 1970 is considerably higher than the total
(mixed and conversionary) intermarriage rate was earlier.

Interestingly, as was previously noted by Mayer (1985: 230), the rate at
which the non-Jewish spouse converts is higher when the husband is Jewish
and the wife is not than it is when it is the wife who is Jewish and the husband
is not. Among the two groups with the sizeable numbers of converts, 67% of
the converts to Conservative Judaism and 71% of the converts to Reform
Judaism, are women. Perhaps these differences reflect traditional Jewish law
by which whether a child is considered Jewish or not is determined by the
mother's Jewish status, not the father's. Thus, a Jewish husband who wants
his children to be considered Jewish within traditional law would need to have
his wife convert before having children. However, a Jewish wife would not
have to make the same request; her children would be considered Jewish

TABLE 6.4
All First Marriages by Gender, Date and Type of Marriage, NJPS, 1990

First Marriages	Before 1960 Born into Jewish Families		1960–1969 Born into Jewish Families		1970–1990 Born into Jewish Families	
	Men	Women	Men	Women	Men	Women
Both Spouses Born into Jewish Families	89%	95%	84%	87%	54%	54%
Convert-in	3%	1%	5%	1%	12%	5%
Jewish-Christian	5%	3%	6%	9%	25%	31%
Jewish-None or Other	3%	1%	5%	3%	9%	10%
Base	100%	100%	100%	100%	100%	100%
n	221	314	125	129	356	315

anyway. However, in recent years, the Reform movement has rejected the tradition of matrilineal descent. Hence, the inducement for conversion among the non-Jewish wives of Reform men, may abate in the future. The number of relevant cases in our data is too small to detect if such abatement has begun.

Finally, the ratio of intermarrying Jewish men to that of women was 1.5 men to 1.0 women before 1960, 1.6 to 1.0 during the sixties, and down to 1.1 men to 1.0 women during the 1970 to 1990 period. The two ratios, based on 1990 survey data, for before 1970, are consistent with what is reported, using earlier data, on Jewish intermarriages before 1970 (Lazerwitz 1981: 33). In short, Jewish men and women are now just about equally likely to marry non-Jews.

Variables Associated with Intermarriage

Intermarriage among Jews is, then, related to both denominational preference and synagogue membership, but no longer strongly associated with gender. However, since the rate of intermarriage has changed dramatically since 1970, it is possible that the relationships we have found no longer obtain among younger Jews. Intermarriage when it is an uncommon, even deviant, occurrence may be different from what it is when it becomes more commonplace (Mayer 1985: 101–2). Thus, in this section, in order to control for differences in the historical context, we focus on marriages entered between 1970 and

TABLE 6.5
Denomination Preferences for Jewish Marriages
from 1970 to 1990, NJPS, 1990

	Marriage Types			
Denomination	Both Spouses Born into Jewish Families	Convert-In	Heterogeneous	Overall
Orthodox	12%	3%	1%	5%
Conservative	43%	27%	21%	29%
Reform	36%	63%	44%	43%
None	9%	7%	34%	23%
Base	100%	100%	100%	100%

1990, the time when intermarriage became relatively common. We begin with a review of the relationship, since 1970, between intermarriage and denominational preference. We then seek to determine if any of the other variables discussed in previous chapters are related to intermarriage.

Denominational preference of currently married respondents is clearly related, as shown in table 6.5, to whether or not one intermarried in the twenty years from 1970 to 1990. Table 6.5 uses three categories of marriage by the religion of the spouses: (1) both spouses born into Jewish families (homogeneous marriages); (2) one spouse born Jewish, the other a convert to Judaism (conversionary marriages); and 3) one spouse Jewish, the other, not (mixed or heterogeneous marriages). The respondents in the first category, prefer the two more traditional denominations, Orthodox and Conservative, more often than do respondents of either of the other two categories of marriage. Almost two-thirds of the respondents in conversionary marriages prefer the Reform denomination. Among those in mixed marriages, almost half prefer the Reform denomination and a third have no preference among the Jewish denominations.

In table 6.6, the data on recent intermarriages are reanalyzed so to provide some insight into the denominational preferences of couples married since 1970. Table 6.6 shows that for the Orthodox denomination 83% of its younger couples include spouses who were each born into a Jewish family. That percentage of two "born-Jewish" spouses is considerably higher than among the other denominations. Only somewhat more than half of families formed since 1970 who prefer the Conservative denomination include spouses who were each born into a Jewish family. Indeed, 37% of these younger Conservative families are in mixed or religiously heterogeneous marriages. Only a minority (30%) of younger Reform

TABLE 6.6
Family Types for Jewish Marriages of 1970 to 1990
by Denominational Preference, NJPS, 1990

Denomination	Both Partners Born into Jewish Families	One Partner Convert-In	One Partner Jewish, One Partner Christian	One Partner Jewish, One Partner None or Other	Base
Orthodox	83%	6%	6%	5%	100%
Conservative	54%	9%	24%	13%	100%
Reform	30%	14%	43%	13%	100%
None	15%	3%	55%	27%	100%

families include two "Jewish-born" spouses. Even when families in which one partner has converted to Judaism are included, only 44% are families in which both spouses profess Reform Judaism. Among those couples having no denominational preference, 82% are mixed or religiously heterogeneous marriages.[3]

In sum, the association between denominational preference and intermarriage holds true when we examine only marriages entered into between 1970 and 1990. The rate of intermarriage is lowest among the Orthodox, somewhat higher among the Conservative, higher still among the Reform, and highest among those with no denominational preference.

We turn now to examine whether any of the other variables discussed in previous chapters are related to intermarriage. Again the relevant analyses are confined to marriages entered into between 1970 and 1990 to control for the influence of the historical context. We begin (table 6.7) with an analysis of the percentage distribution of four important aspects of Jewish involvement and synagogue attendance, among intermarried and non-intermarried respondents of different denominational preferences. We then use multivariate, regression analyses to probe further the relationship between intermarriage and other variables.

As just indicated, information on the relationship between involvement and intermarriage and each of four important modes of involvement in American Jewish life is shown in table 6.7 for recently married couples. The four modes of involvement analyzed are: (1) synagogue membership, (2) activity in Jewish community voluntary associations, (3) involvement in Jewish primary groups, and (4) synagogue attendance. Due to the limited number of cases in our data, marriages involving a convert to Judaism cannot be differentiated by denomination.

Limitation

TABLE 6.7

Modes of Jewish Involvement of Jews Married between 1970 to 1990 by Type of Marriage, NJPS, 1990

Jewish Involvements	Both Spouses Born into Jewish Families			All Convert-In Marriages	Heterogeneous Marriages		
	Orth.	Cons.	Ref.		Cons.	Ref.	None
Synagogue Member							
Yes	83%	64%	50%	78%	22%	19%	3%
No	17%	36%	50%	22%	78%	81%	97%
Jewish Organization Activity Index							
High	76%	54%	44%	43%	12%	15%	7%
Moderate	17%	36%	28%	34%	30%	31%	25%
Low	7%	10%	28%	23%	58%	54%	68%
Jewish Primary Group Involvement Index							
High	93%	64%	39%	27%	4%	3%	2%
Moderate	7%	26%	34%	36%	15%	16%	8%
Low	—	10%	27%	37%	81%	81%	90%
Synagogue Attendance							
12 or more per yr.	80%	42%	19%	50%	8%	11%	2%
3–11	13%	30%	33%	27%	27%	16%	6%
1–2	7%	23%	37%	15%	45%	54%	54%
0 times	—	5%	11%	8%	20%	19%	38%
n (couples)	30	107	86	62	74	158	125

Among the homogeneous marriages entered into from 1970 to 1990, 83% of the Orthodox families, 64% of the Conservative families, and 50% of the Reform families claim to have synagogue memberships. Among couples in which one spouse is a Jew-by-choice, 78% claim to be synagogue members. Among the heterogeneous marriages, 22% of the Conservatives, 19% of the Reform, and but 3% of those with no denominational preference claim synagogue memberships.

The expected pattern of greatest involvement among the Orthodox and least among the Reform is also found with respect to activity in Jewish voluntary associations. Among the homogeneously married, 76% of the Orthodox report a high level of activity, as do 54% of the Conservatives and 44% of the Reform. The level of such activity (43%) among conversionary marriages is similar to that among homogeneous Reform couples. The activity levels among heterogeneous couples is considerably less (12%, 15%, and 7% respectively for Conservatives, Reform Jews, and those with no denominational preference).

The expected pattern is also found with respect to involvement in Jewish primary groups. Among the homogeneous marriages, 93% of the Orthodox, 64% of the Conservatives, and 39% of the Reform couples report a high level of involvement, as do 27% of conversionary couples. Among the heterogeneous marriages, once again the level of involvement is considerably lower: only 4% of the Conservatives, 3% of the Reform, and but 2% of those with no denominational preference report a high level of involvement in Jewish primary groups.

Finally, the pattern of involvement with respect to synagogue attendance is similar to that for the other three indices: the Orthodox attend more frequently than the Conservatives, the Reform attend the least (80%, 42%, and 19% respectively are found in the highest category of attendance). Interestingly, as with synagogue membership, the percentage of respondents in conversionary marriages in the highest category (here 50%) falls between that of Orthodox and Conservative Jews who are in homogeneous marriages. Conversionary families probably view their Jewishness more in religious than in ethnic terms. Their involvement in Jewish primary groups falls below that of Conservative and Reform homogeneous marriages. Finally, synagogue attendance among the heterogeneously married, with or without a denominational preference, is relatively low. Only 8% of the Conservatives, 11% of the Reform, and but 2% of those with no preference are found in the highest category of synagogue attendance. (These findings are in agreement with those of Lerer and Mayer 1993).

Finally, it should be noted that table 6.7, which refers to recently married couples, reveals a pattern similar to that found in equivalent tables reported in chapter 3. In both cases, the level of Jewish involvement is highest among the Orthodox, next among the Conservative, lower among the Reform, and least among those with no denominational preference. Conversionary couples are, again, likely to join synagogues and to attend services. Their level of involvement is similar to that of homogeneous Reform couples with respect to activity in Jewish voluntary associations, but somewhat below with respect to involvement in Jewish primary groups. Couples involved in mixed, religiously heterogeneous, marriages usually do not join synagogues, nor are they involved with other Jewish organizations. They seldom attend synagogue and are infrequently involved with Jewish primary groups.

Looking toward the future, the impact of intermarriage on organized American Jewish life may be somewhat muted since such life is still dominated numerically to a considerable extent by more traditionally oriented Orthodox and Conservative Jews who are less likely to intermarry. However, Reform Jews, a growing component of American Jewry and an increasingly important component of organized Jewish life, will more and more consist not only of those with Jewish backgrounds but of a significant number of converts or Jews-by-choice. The involvement of the latter in Reform synagogues is apt to equal or even exceed that of Reform Jews with a Jewish background, but their involvement in Jewish life outside the synagogue may be less. Whatever happens, Reform Jews are at the forefront of an interchange of population between American Jewry and the overall American population.

In any event, analysis of the percentage distribution of key aspects of involvement in Jewish life indicates they are influenced both by denominational preference and by intermarriage. However, such analysis does not control for the possible influence of other variables. Regression analysis, such as that discussed in chapter 4, is needed to attain the necessary controls. To further help control for extraneous factors, only two types of the four types of marriages are contrasted: those in which both spouses were born Jews and those in which one spouse is now Christian and the other was born Jewish. (Marriages in which one spouse has converted to another's religion or in which one spouse is neither Christian nor Jewish are too few for complex statistical analysis.)

With these limitations, a regression equation has been computed which reveals the statistical association between the variables and a binomial (two category) intermarriage variable which distinguishes between marriages involving two Jews (religiously homogeneous marriages) and those involving a Jew and a Christian (religiously heterogeneous or Jewish-Christian marriages). The statistical technique used is Multiple Classification Analysis (MCA). MCA searches out the association of a specific variable with the type of intermarriage while controlling for the influence of all other variables. One MCA analysis examines the influence of what we call "prior" variables (table 6.8) upon whether the Jewish respondent is involved in a religiously homogeneous or a religiously heterogeneous marriage. A second analysis (table 6.9) shows the influence of so-called "current" variables on their types of marriage.

TABLE 6.8

Regression Characteristics of "Prior" Variables
for Respondents Married from 1970 to 1990 with
Homogeneous or Jewish-Christian Marriages, NJPS, 1990

Prior Variables	MCA Beta Coefficients for Marriage Categories
Gender	.11
Age	.14
U.S. Generation	.17
Education	.05
Childhood Jewish Denomination	.18
Jewish Education	.19
Number of Marriages	.19
Geographic Mobility	.10
R^2	.15

TABLE 6.9

Regression Characteristics of "Current" Variables
for Respondents Married from 1970 to 1990 with
Homogeneous or Jewish-Christian Marriages, NJPS, 1990

Current Variables	MCA Beta Coefficients for Marriage Categories
Current Jewish Denomination	.12
Synagogue Member	.17
Synagogue Attendance	.04
Home Religious Practices	.24
Family Life Cycle	.02
Israel Orientation Index	.13
Jewish Community Organization Index	.18
General Community Organization Index	−.12
Occupation of Family Head	.07
Family Income	.06
Jewish Community Scale	.10
R^2	.37

The "prior" variables in the analysis of intermarriage are mainly those that precede adulthood, and presumably the present marriage, while those dealing with the respondent's current characteristics are called "current" variables. The prior variables include: the respondent's gender, age, education,

Jewish denomination in childhood, Jewish education, and number of marriages. The prior variables also include the number of generations the respondent's family has been in the United States and an index of the respondent's geographic mobility (table 6.8). The "current" variables, whose temporal relation to marriage is less clear, are: denominational preference, synagogue membership, frequency of attendance at religious services, religious practices in the home, activity in voluntary Jewish communal associations, an index of orientation toward Israel, stage in the family life cycle, occupation of the family head, family income in 1989 (the year prior to the survey); activity in general (non-Jewish) voluntary communal associations, and a scale ranking the size of the Jewish community in which the respondent resides (table 6.9).[4] Neither set of variables includes information covering events between high school and marriage. Such information, particularly that on dating practices, would likely provide better insight into the social processes that result in religiously homogeneous or heterogeneous marriages.

Table 6.8 shows that no prior variables are strongly associated, but some moderately associated, with whether a marriage is homogeneous or not. In order of increasing strength, they are: age, number of generations a respondent's family has been in the United States, childhood Jewish denomination, Jewish education, and the number of marriages the respondent has had.[5] Education, gender and mobility are only weakly associated with the type of marriage. For each of these so-called "prior" variables, the direction of influence is as expected. The younger the Jewish respondent, or the greater the number of generations the respondent's family has been in the United States, the greater the likelihood of a religiously heterogeneous marriage. (Women Jewish respondents are a bit more likely to be in a homogeneous marriage than a heterogeneous one.) The more traditional the childhood Jewish denomination or the more Jewish education the respondent had in childhood, the greater the likelihood the respondent is in a homogeneous marriage. Note that the association of childhood denominations is one of the four larger associations among the "prior" variables. Those who have been married more than once are more likely to now be in a heterogeneous marriage. As Goldstein and Goldstein (1996: 189–96) also find, so, too, are those who are more geographically mobile.

The equation involving the so-called "prior" variables explains only 15% of the variance between the two types of marriage (see R^2 in table 6.8). Clearly, there is a need to look at other variables for a more complete account of the characteristics associated with whether a Jewish respondent marries a Jew or a Christian.

As indicated in table 6.9, the "current" variables account for more than twice as much of the variance (with an R^2 of 37%) between the types of marriages now under consideration. The variable most highly associated with the type of marriage a respondent is in is the measure of religious practices in the home. The next highest associations are for activity in voluntary Jewish communal associations and synagogue membership. As would be expected, more religious practices at home, more activity in Jewish voluntary associations, and membership in a synagogue, increase the likelihood that the respondent is in a homogeneous rather than a heterogeneous marriage. While we cannot determine the temporal relationship between "current" variables and intermarriage, it is likely, as Mayer (1995: 419) reports, "Jews with a weakly grounded sense of Jewish identity are especially likely to intermarry."

As would be expected, the more traditional a respondent's current denominational preference and the more positively one is oriented toward Israel, the greater the likelihood of being in a religiously homogeneous marriage. (The likelihood of being in a homogeneous marriage also increases as the size of the Jewish community in which one resides increases.) On the other hand, greater activity in voluntary communal associations in the general (non-Jewish) community, is related to a greater likelihood of being in a heterogeneous marriage. Synagogue attendance, stage in the family life cycle, occupation of the head of the family, family income, and Jewish community size are only weakly associated with marriage type. Interestingly, the association with childhood denomination, shown in table 6.8, is greater than that of current denominational preference (table 6.9).

Raising Jewish Children

As is to be expected in the highly individualistic religious climate of the United States, intermarriage has a variety of outcomes with respect to whether the children of such marriages are raised as Jews (Mayer 1985: 245–77). A crucial factor for the religious socialization of children of an intermarried couple is whether the originally non-Jewish parent later identifies as a Jew (Mayer 1985: 253). In the 1990 NJPS, 97% of conversionary couples with children in their homes are raising their children as Jews. Among the mixed marriages (those marriages in which the non-Jewish spouse remains as such), just 38% are raising their children as Jews where the non-Jew is Christian and 37% where the spouse is of another religion or none at all.

The gender of the Jewish spouse also makes a difference as to whether children in an intermarriage are raised as Jews. When it is the wife who has a Jewish background, a majority (52%) report raising Jewish children; when it is the husband who has a Jewish background, only a minority (25%) are raising their children as Jews.

The perpetuation of the Jewish population, then, is not threatened by intermarriage *per se*. Fewer than 1% of respondents (25 out of 1,905) report converting from Judaism to some form of Christianity. Nevertheless, the decision of those who are intermarried, even though they themselves remain Jewish, not to raise their children as Jews does pose a threat to the perpetuation of the Jewish population in the United States. The absorption of those with a Jewish heritage into the non-Jewish world occurs not so much with the intermarriage of parents as with their decisions about how to raise their children.

Jewish Community Size and Intermarriage

Finally, we turn to another issue that may influence the ability of Jews in the United States to perpetuate their heritage, namely, the relationship between community size and intermarriage that we mentioned earlier. Fischer (1984) has stated that a critical population mass must be reached if a subgroup of the American population, such as its Jews, is to function as a viable subcommunity. For example, Cohen (1995) finds that community size is a critical factor in the success of recruitment for short-term Israel experience programs aimed at adolescents. It is also possible that community size has an influence on intermarriage rates and thus on the Jewish future.[6] We investigate that possibility here. For reasons given below, our discussion in this section is limited to Reform Jews. Since Reform Jews are often found at the boundaries between Jews and non-Jews, that restriction is not overly limiting.

In this section, we explore the extent to which respondents who prefer the Reform denomination and who live in Jewish communities of varying sizes have differing degrees of Jewish primary group involvement. Our exploration will entail the use of multiple regression analysis similar to that employed in chapter 4. The analysis for this section will control for demographic and socioeconomic factors as well as for Jewish community size. The dependent variables will be the respondent's score on an intermarriage scale and the number of close friends who are Jewish.[7] A measure of friendship with Jews is included for contrast as it is another aspect of the permeability of the boundaries between Jews and non-Jews in an open society.

Recall that, as discussed in chapter 3 (table 3.8), the concentration of the various denominations differ noticeably in Jewish communities of different sizes. For example, as noted in chapter 3, 71% of the Orthodox respondents live in the larger Jewish communities found in the metropolitan areas of New York City, Los Angeles, Miami, Chicago, Philadelphia, Boston, and Washington D.C. Sixty-six percent of Conservative respondents live in these areas, as do 57% of the Reform and 60% of those with no denominational preference. The number of Orthodox and Conservative respondents and of those with no preference in the smaller Jewish communities is too few to permit statistical analysis involving community size and other variables. For Reform Jews only (and then just barely so) are the numbers in communities of all sizes sufficient for statistical analysis.

Forty-nine percent of Reform synagogue members and 62% of Reform Jews who are not synagogue members are concentrated in the larger metropolitan areas noted above. Table 6.10 shows the results of a multiple regression analysis (MCA) for Reform Jews in which synagogue members are differentiated from nonmembers. The results indicate that for Reform Jews, the larger the Jewish population, the lower the intermarriage mean score and the larger

TABLE 6.10
Number of Close Friends and Intermarriage Score by Jewish Community
Size for Reform Jews: MCA Multiple Regression, NJPS, 1990

	Reform Jews			
	Syn. Members (MCA Adj. Means)		Not Syn. Members (MCA Adj. Means)	
Jewish Community Size	No. Close Friends Jewish	Score on Intermar. Scale	No. Close Friends Jewish	Score on Intermar. Scale
1 million plus (NYC metro area)	3.6	1.2	3.3	1.9
Around 500,000 (Los Angeles and Miami metro areas)	3.6	1.5	3.3	2.1
200,000–300,000 (Chicago, Philadelphia, Boston, Wash. D.C. metro areas)	3.6	1.5	3.1	2.1
40,000–150,000 (11 Jewish communities)	3.5	1.0	3.1	2.4
15,000–39,999 (18 Jewish communities)	3.2	1.7	2.7	3.5
3,000–14,999	3.3	1.7	2.9	2.3
Under 3,000	3.1	1.9	2.5	3.7

the average number of close Jewish friends. In Jewish communities with a population of fewer than 40,000, there is an increase in the intermarriage mean scores and a decrease for Reform Jews in the number of close friends who are Jewish. In short, the boundaries between the primary associations of marriage and friendship are stronger, among Reform Jews, in larger than in smaller communities. For Reform Jews the critical mass posited by Fischer (1984) appears to be reached in the larger communities of 200,000 or more Jews.

In the larger communities, Reform Jews, according to our findings, maintain considerable involvement in Jewish primary groups. Indeed, in communities of 200,000 or more Jews, 75% of Reform synagogue members are in homogeneous marriages (each spouse is Jewish), while only 57% are in homogeneous marriages in communities of fewer than 200,000 Jews. Among Reform Jews who are not synagogue members, the corresponding figures are 66% in the larger communities and 50% in smaller communities. Similarly, among members of Reform synagogues who live in the larger Jewish communities 54% report that all or almost all of their closest friends are Jewish, while in the smaller communities (fewer than 200,000 Jews), only 40% do so. Among Reform Jews who are not synagogue members, the corresponding figures are 38% and 18%.

Summary and Conclusions

We have found, consistent with our expectations, that denominational preference is related to the rate of intermarriage. The more traditional the denomination, the lower the rate of intermarriage. Synagogue membership is also an important factor. Members are less likely to be intermarried than nonmembers. Finally, we note that the intermarriage rate has been increasing since 1960 for all types of Jews, whatever their denominational preference or lack of one and whether or not they are synagogue members.

Intermarriage is far more common among Jewish adults who prefer Reform Judaism or who do not have a denominational preference than it is among those who prefer Orthodox or Conservative Judaism. In 1990, among those adults who were then Reform Jews, 40% had married non-Jews; among those who were then with no denominational preference, 59% were married to non-Jews. Conversely, among those reared as Orthodox Jews, the spouses of 85% of those currently married were also born Jewish. Among those currently married and reared as Conservative Jews, 73% of the spouses were born Jews. Such is the case among only 60% of those reared as Reform Jews or with no denominational preference.

The association between synagogue membership and the likelihood of marrying a non-Jew is also clear. Among married synagogue members who are currently Orthodox, 98% are married to spouses who were born Jewish. Among married Conservative synagogue members, the spouses of 88% were born Jewish, but only 72% of the spouses of Conservative Jews who are not synagogue members were born Jewish. Among adherents of Reform Judaism, 66% of the spouses of synagogue members and 55% of those who are not members were born into Jewish families. Unfortunately, the NJPS data do not allow us to determine the temporal or causal relationship between synagogue membership and intermarriage.

In any case, converts to Judaism are most often found in the ranks of Reform Judaism. Indeed, 24% of Reform synagogue members are such converts. Respondents raised as Orthodox or Conservative Jews who subsequently marry non-Jews are likely to shift their denominational preference to a less traditional denomination, usually Reform Judaism. The Jewish partner in a mixed or religiously heterogeneous marriage in which neither spouse converts often has no preference among the Jewish denominations.

Since the 1971 survey, there has been a nearly fourfold increase in the percentage of Jews married to non-Jews. Consequently, only 36% of the children of the marriages entered into from 1970 to 1990 are being reared in families in which both parents were born into Jewish families. While about half of the Jewish women who are married to non-Jewish men state they are raising their children as Jews, only about a quarter of Jewish men married to non-Jewish women claim to be raising their children as Jews. Very few Jews married to non-Jews convert to another religion.

One possible result of these various trends is that there may be a slow increase in the percentage of the Jewish population preferring the more traditional denominations. Such a result may occur if homogeneous Jewish marriages, which are more common in the traditional denominations, are more successful in raising children who become involved with the Jewish religion and the organized Jewish community.

In any case, more and more Americans are entering into religiously heterogeneous marriages. The underlying reasons (see Kalmijn 1991) for rising rates of intermarriages include secularization, individualism, and an increase in the interaction of young, single adults within their schools and workplaces with little regard for their respective religious affiliations. The result is an increasing population exchange among Protestants, Catholics, Jews, and those with no religious preference. As might be expected in an open society in which religious preference is increasingly a matter of personal choice rather than social inheritance, an achieved rather than an ascribed status, boundaries between groups are increasingly permeable and intermarriage, a "sensitive device" for detecting social boundaries (Alba 1991: 4) is on the rise.

PART III

7

A Look Toward the Future

Jewish Fertility, Births,
and Denominational Preference

We have examined the importance of decisions concerning denominational preference and synagogue membership in the lives of Jews in the contemporary United States. We have also looked at changes in Jewish life over the last twenty years and in some instances attempted to use our findings to suggest a picture of the future. In this chapter, we begin with a focus on fertility. We then compare current data with past research with the aim of projecting to the future. First, we will relate fertility to denominational preference and synagogue membership. Then we will offer a projection of what the distribution of denominational preferences is likely to be among American Jewry in the year 2010, twenty years from the time of the most recent survey.

Jewish Religiosity and Fertility

Over the years there has been much debate concerning the relationship between religiosity and fertility. There is now a considerable body of research focusing on membership in specific religious groups and on religiosity that supports the conclusion that both are significantly related to differential fertility. Mosher, Williams, and Johnson (1992) report that non-Hispanic, white Protestant women, 15 to 39 years of age, who reported weekly attendance at church services had a total fertility rate of 2.14 in contrast to a total fertility rate of 1.75 for those in the same age group who attended church less frequently. They found that non-Hispanic, white Catholic women, 15 to 39 years of age, who reported weekly attendance at communion had a total fertility rate of 1.69 in contrast to a total fertility rate of 1.62 for those of the same age group who attended communion less frequently. They also found that white women, 15 to 39 years of age, who claimed no religious preference had a total fertility rate of just 1.12.

Heaton (1986) studied Mormon religiosity and fertility. He found that Mormon couples who attended services weekly had about 1.2 more children than couples with a Mormon background who did not attend Mormon services. Heaton concluded that there are

> three aspects of religious experience which might influence fertility decisions. Acceptance of a pronatalist theology by marrying in a Mormon Temple, maintenance of a Mormon reference group through weekly church attendance, and childhood socialization in a larger family and/or with two active Mormon parents. (1986: 256)

Mosher and Hendershot (1984), in their study of national samples of married women, concluded:

> [R]eligious differentials are not artifacts of socioeconomic characteristics. . . . [T]he characteristics hypothesis does not explain the fertility of religious groups in the United States because sizable differences remain after adjustments for socioeconomic characteristics; nor is an explanation based solely on the norms of particular religious groups sufficient.

Lazerwitz (1980) studied the relationship between religiosity and fertility for married Jewish women aged 20 to 46 in the National Jewish Population Survey (NJPS) of 1971. He found that Jewish women in this age range who preferred the Orthodox or Conservative Jewish denominations and were frequent synagogue attenders expected, at that time, to have an average of 2.8 children; while those who preferred the Reform denomination expected to have an average of 2.3 children. Using the 1990 survey, we have the opportunity to compare the expected number of children for Jewish women aged 20 to 46 in 1971 with the actual number of children for a group of comparable women, aged 39 to 45 at the time of the later survey, that is, at the end of their child-bearing years.

Table 7.1 indicates the amount of variance explained in the number of children expected in 1971 by ever-married women, aged 20 to 46 years according to Lazerwitz (1980: 60–61). The table also indicates the amount of variance in the number of children actually had, nineteen years later in 1990, by a comparable group of ever-married women, now aged 39 to 65, that can be explained by the indicated predictor variables. (The automatic interaction detection [AID] technique has been used for the fertility analysis in both the earlier Lazerwitz study and ours.)[1]

Less than 10% of the variance is explained in both the number of children expected in 1971 (8%) and in the number of actual children had by 1990 (6%).

TABLE 7.1
Amount of Variance Explained for Expected and Actual Number of Children
for Jewish Women Aged 20 to 46 in 1971 and Aged 39 to 65 in 1990

Dominant Predictors	NJPS 1971 Wives 20–46 years % Var. Exp. for Expected No. Children	NJPS 1990 Ever Married Women Respondents 39–65 years % Var. Exp. for Actual No. Children
Synagogue Attendance	5%	1%
Denominational Pref.	2%	—
Synagogue Member	—	3%
Occupation of Head	1%	—
U.S. Generation	—	2%
Total Percent Explained	8%	6%

The same approach used to analyze the responses of the wives (of male respondents) who are 39 to 65 years old in 1990 explains a mere 1% of the variance in actual fertility. However, it is noteworthy that denominational preference and synagogue membership, the variables of central interest in this monograph, are among the dominant predictors in these survey years, as is synagogue attendance,.

The dominant factors associated with expected fertility in 1971 are different from those in 1990. In 1971, these factors were: frequency of synagogue attendance, denominational preference and the occupation of the head of the household. Frequent synagogue attenders who preferred the Orthodox or Conservative denominations, some 26% of the respondents, expected an average of 2.8 children. Frequent synagogue attenders who preferred the Reform denomination, 13% of the respondents in question, expected 2.3 children. Infrequent attenders with a family head scoring low on an occupational index, 18% of those in question, expected 2.3 children. Finally, infrequent synagogue attenders with a family head having a moderate to high index level on occupation score, some 43% of the group, expected 2.1 children.

Figure 7.1 presents the findings of table 7.1 in further detail. It shows the automatic interaction detection (AID) graph for the ever-married women respondents to the 1990 survey, aged 39 to 65. There are three dominant variables, synagogue membership, synagogue attendance, and number of generations in the United States. These three divide the women respondents into four almost equal groups:

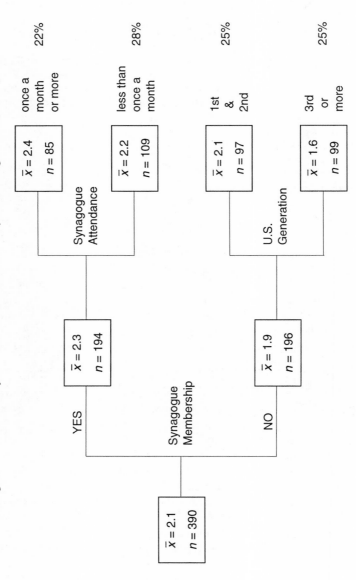

FIGURE 7.1

AID Diagram on Final Fertility for Ever Married Women Respondents Age 39–65, NJPS, 1990

Note: Amount of variance explained = 6%.

1. *Synagogue members who attend religious services once a month or more*: they have an average of 2.4 children. This group constitutes 22% of all these women.

2. *Synagogue members who attend services less frequently*: they average 2.2 children and constitute 28% of all respondents.

3. *First- or second-generation women respondents in this age range who are not synagogue members*: they comprise one of the groups with lower fertility rates and are 25% of all respondents. The women of this group have an average of 2.1 children.

4. *Non-synagogue members who are third-generation Americans*: they have an average of just 1.6 children and are 25% of all respondents.

The results, shown in table 7.1 and figure 7.1, concerning Jewish fertility are consistent with the studies cited at the beginning of this chapter. Frequent attendance at religious services is associated with having more children. Jewish women respondents (and the spouses of respondents) who are 39 to 65 years old, who are synagogue members and attend synagogue services once a month or more are the women who report higher fertility than those in the other membership and attendance level categories.

It is clear, as has been suggested earlier by Goldscheider (1989) and Della Pergola (1983), that religious involvement is associated with a complex of family-oriented factors that in turn are associated with the expectation and the actual fact of having more children. However, as Mott and Abma (1992: 92) point out, researchers have yet to determine what the causal connections are between religiosity and fertility. It is possible that having higher fertility results in greater use of churches and synagogues. It is also possible that attendance at religious services is a manifestation of a view of religion and of the family that creates a desire for more children.

A Fertility Projection: A Look at the Future

The information just presented on Jewish fertility will now be incorporated along with the findings in previous chapters on denominational preference, synagogue membership, synagogue attendance, and intermarriage in order to examine how they might influence denominational preferences in the next generation, that is, in 2010, twenty years beyond the 1990 survey. The detailed calculations for this projection model are presented in appendix D (table D.1).

We hypothesize a group of 100,000 single adult Jewish men and women living in 1990 who are distributed among the eight basic denominational preference and synagogue membership groupings (introduced in chapter 1)

TABLE 7.2
Projection of Births by Marriage Types to 2010, Based on NJPS, 1990

Denomination & Membership	Birth to J.–J. Couples	Births to Convert-In Couples	Raised J. Childr. to J.–Not J. Couples
Orthodox—Member	5,850	0	0
Orthodox—Not Member	1,300	892	182
Conservative—Member	15,130	8,403	1,156
Conservative—Not Member	8,262	582	5,016
Subtotal	30,542	9,877	6,354
%	65%	21%	14%
Reform—Member	10,246	13,477	1,778
Reform—Not Member	9,750	3,880	10,070
No Preference—Member	1,300	582	304
No Preference—Not Member	3,360	272	7,980
Subtotal	24,656	18,211	20,132
%	39%	29%	32%

as Jewish adults aged 20 to 44 are in the 1990 survey.[2] These eight groups are, in turn, subdivided by marriage types, homogeneous, conversionary, and mixed, to form a total of twenty-four (8 × 3) groups. Each of these twenty-four subgroups is again divided into two synagogue attendance categories, frequent attenders (who attend synagogue services once a month or more), and infrequent attenders (who attend less than once a month). All couples in which the respondent is a frequent attender are assumed, based on figures derived from figure 7.1, to have an average of 2.4 children and all other couples, 2.0. Finally, based on the findings in chapter 6, it is assumed that 38% of the heterogeneously married couples will raise their children as Jews.

Table 7.2 summarizes the projected births in the eight basic groupings for each of the three types of marriages, homogeneous marriages, conversionary marriages and mixed marriages. It is estimated that 65% of the children of families preferring the more traditional Orthodox or Conservative denominations, whether synagogue members or not, will be children of homogeneous marriages, 21%, of conversionary marriages, and 14% children of mixed marriages. Among the children of families preferring the less traditional Reform Judaism and among those with no denominational preferences, again regardless of synagogue membership, 39% will be the children of homogeneous marriages, 29% of conversionary marriages, and 32% the children of heterogeneous marriages. Overall, the greater number of births in homogeneous Jewish marriages among those preferring the more traditional denominations is offset by the gains from births to conversionary marriages among the less traditional groupings and in the number of children raised as Jews in heterogeneous marriages.

In sum, table 7.2 suggests the future distribution of the American Jewish population among its various denominations will depend upon: how much more the quite religious couples increase their fertility over that of the less religious couples; how the proportion of converts to the Conservative and Reform member groups changes; and how many children are raised Jewish in heterogeneous marriages.

Obviously, our effort to project to some time in the future when the hypothetical adults treated here are twenty years older is risky. Not only may each of the assumptions we make here be challenged, but we do not have data on the issue of denominational shifts after adulthood is reached. That is, to improve on our projections, some additional assumptions would have to made as to how successful each of the combinations of denominational preference and synagogue membership groupings will be in retaining their adult adherents. Only then can one take into account the possible flow from Orthodoxy to the Conservative denomination and from the Conservative to Reform Judaism. Moreover, there is a need to project to how many intermarriages will remain mixed marriages and how many will become conversionary marriages.

Summary and Conclusions

This chapter shows that a combination of synagogue membership and frequent synagogue attendance is associated with a somewhat higher fertility rate among the households surveyed.

There is some evidence to indicate that greater religious involvement is one of the factors associated with increased fertility. When the fertility data of the 1990 survey are further analyzed it is found that:

1. Synagogue membership, synagogue attendance, and number of generations in the United States are the most significant variables.

2. The combination of synagogue membership and frequent (monthly or more) attendance at religious services is associated with the highest average number of children.

Using the findings on fertility together with the information in earlier chapters, this chapter offers a projection of the Jewish population for the year 2010 based on 1990 denominational preferences, synagogue membership, frequency of synagogue attendance, and intermarriage rates among younger Jewish adults, ages 20 to 44. Adults of these ages are raising the children who will be the next generation of American Jewry.

Our projection indicates that by 2010 the Orthodox and Conservative denominations will draw 65% of their births from the children of homogeneous Jewish couples, 21% from conversionary marriages, and 14% from mixed marriages. Those identifying as Reform Jews and those with no denominational preference will, by 2010, draw just 39% of their births from children of homogeneous Jewish couples, 29% from conversionary marriages, and 32% from children of religiously heterogeneous couples.

The main conclusion to be drawn from our projection model is that the proportion preferring each of the various denominations is most affected by: (1) the greater fertility of religious couples over that of the less religious couples; (2) the number of converts gained by the Reform denomination; and (3) the number of children raised as Jews by mixed marriage couples who often have no Jewish denominational preference.

The composition of the American Jewish population of the next generation will, to a sizable degree, be a result of a substantial population exchange with the rest of the American population within a society in which interfaith boundaries are clearly permeable. This population exchange is most prominent among those who identify as Reform Jews or who have no denominational preference. Most of the non-Jewish population that joins the Jewish population will likely do so as Reform Jews. Most of those whose childhood includes a Jewish background but who will not identify as Jews when they are adults will be the children of Jews with no denominational preference.

The two larger denominational groupings, the Conservative and especially the Reform, will face the problem of coping with the consequences of permeable boundaries among America's religious groups as they struggle to socialize into their group a considerable number of children from families with one parent having been raised within the American Christian community and with family ties to that community. It is to be expected that many children with such backgrounds will have limited ties to the Jewish community.

The projection suggests that by the year 2010, 60% of the children of Conservative Jews and 40% of the children of Reform Jews will be from families in which both parents were born into Jewish families. It is also suggested that by 2010 the major change within the Jewish population, except for the Orthodox, will derive from the permeable boundaries of religious groups in the United States as adults who were not raised as Jews convert to Judaism.

8

Summation, Conclusions,
and Recommendations

As life for all Americans is different today from what it was a century ago, so too American Jewish religious and communal life is different at the end of the twentieth century from what it was at the beginning. One of the more significant changes for American Jews is that Jewish denominations are now an integral part of the denominational society of the United States. The denominations have come into being and have undergone great changes as Jewish immigrants and their descendants have acclimated themselves to American society since the middle of the nineteenth century.

Summary of Major Findings

The findings of our study generally support the contention, made in chapter 1, that in the individualistic, open, religiously pluralistic society that is the United States, decisions concerning denominational preference and synagogue membership are important for Jews in that society. Of course, in such a society, nobody is required to have a denominational preference or to join a religious organization. However, if one does either, we believe it is because doing so somehow symbolizes or expresses his or her views on important existential questions. For Jews, we contend, the choices concerning denominational preference and synagogue membership are expressions of what one believes it means to be a Jew in the United States. Many of the demographic and socioeconomic characteristics that differentiated among the various denominational preferences and synagogue membership groupings in 1971 no longer do so in 1990 (see chapters 3 and 4). In other words, those who differ in terms of denominational preference and synagogue membership, have become more alike in terms of their general sociological characteristics.

Since the United States is an open society where individuals are free to define their religious affiliations as they choose, boundaries within and between major faith groups are fluid and permeable. Thus, as we have found, it is by no means uncommon for an individual to be raised in one Jewish denomination and switch to another as an adult (see chapter 5) or even to marry somebody who is not Jewish (see chapter 6).

Nevertheless, despite and perhaps because of switching and intermarriage, the analyses discussed in this book indicate that the decision to affirm a denominational preference and/or to join a synagogue are associated with other important aspects of one's Jewish life. The adherents of the various denominations differ in terms of their Jewish involvements and activities. Denominational preference is indicative of involvement in the informal aspects of Jewish life, that is, those centered in the home or in other foci of primary group involvement. Synagogue membership, on the other hand, involves people in a web of institutional influences. Hence, denominational preference is associated with observance of religious holidays in the home and with having mostly Jewish friends; synagogue membership is associated with attendance at formal religious services and activity in Jewish voluntary associations.

While denominational preference and synagogue membership were found to be important in 1971, there have been changes from the first survey to the next. A "time" model applied to a combination of the two surveys reveals some dramatic trends (chapter 4). Synagogue attendance, home religious practices and a positive orientation to Israel all show increases from 1971 to 1990. However, involvement in Jewish primary groups and activity in both Jewish and general community organizations show decreases. The increase in synagogue attendance is found among synagogue members of all three denominational groupings as well as among Conservative Jews who are not synagogue members. Jewish involvement, compared to twenty years ago, is now more a matter of religious involvement and orientation to Israel and less a matter of whom one socializes with or works with in voluntary associations. As Jews become more accepted, their religion becomes more privatized and manifests itself at specific times, times generally associated with Shabbat or other Jewish holidays.

In 1990, as in 1971, adults who prefer the Reform denomination, whether or not they join a synagogue, are younger than those who prefer the Conservative denomination. While the Orthodox group still includes the highest percentage of foreign-born adherents and the lowest percentage with American-born parents, it now does have a sizeable number of young, American-born, adult adherents.

The Reform groupings have the highest percentage with American-born parents. Members of Reform synagogues have the highest socioeconomic status in 1990, as they did in 1971, and are now followed by Conservative synagogue members. Orthodox synagogue members have increased their educational achievements since 1971, but still have the lowest percentage with incomes of $80,000 or over.

It is clear that having a denominational preference and belonging to a synagogue has become rather prevalent among Jews in the United States. More than 85% of all respondents in 1990 specify a denominational preference; 47% claim to be synagogue members currently; an additional 19% claim past synagogue membership. All told, nearly two-thirds (66%) of all respondents are now or have been synagogue members. Those respondents who are former, but not current, synagogue members are older and have fewer children at home than those respondents who have never been synagogue members. Synagogue membership appears to be related to one's place in the cycle of family life and child rearing—less common both before and after a family is actively involved in child rearing than when it is so involved.

The rank order of Jewish religious and communal involvement found in 1971, namely, Orthodox, Conservative, Reform, and those with no preference, still holds as a general rule in 1990. Members of Orthodox synagogues are still the most involved religiously and communally. Members of Conservative synagogues are a close second. A significant exception to this rank order of scores on the various involvement indices is that Reform synagogue members now either exceed or just about equal Conservative Jews who are not synagogue members. Reform Jews who are not synagogue members and Jews with no denominational preference are the least involved religiously and communally. Members of Conservative or Reform synagogues and respondents with no denominational preference are the most active in general, non-Jewish, voluntary associations. In short, denominational preference is related to one's activity in the general, non-Jewish community.

Denominational preference is also related to another aspect of how one relates to secular society, namely, how politically liberal one is. Individuals with no denominational preference are the most likely to consider themselves politically liberal; Reform Jews who are not synagogue members are next, and they are followed by members of Reform and Conservative synagogues. Conservative Jews who are not members of synagogues and the Orthodox are least likely to consider themselves liberal politically.

An examination of the permeability of the boundaries of Jewish denominations as reflected in changes in denominational preference (see chapter 5) shows that the Reform denomination has had the most success in retaining the allegiance of those reared in it and that the Orthodox have been the least successful. The retention rates of the Conservative grouping and that of the people with no denominational preference groups fall between those of the Reform and Orthodox groupings. The Orthodox have mainly lost adults to the ranks of the Conservative denomination, while the Conservatives have lost them to Reform. Interestingly, some of those reared without a Jewish denominational preference identify with the Reform denomination as adults; somewhat fewer of them with the Conservative denomination.

These findings indicate that denominational preference does not take place in a completely free market. In particular, the tendency to change one's denominational preference may encounter some restraints; not all changes are equally likely. It is easier to cross a barrier that is not too far removed from one's earlier preference than it is to make a big leap to a denomination that is very different. The existence of restraints stemming from one's Jewish background is evident in the consistent pattern that appears when those who retain the denominational preference in which they were reared are contrasted with those who have switched denominations (see chapter 5). The amount of Jewish education, synagogue membership, and activity in Jewish voluntary associations all decrease when one compares those who stay in a denomination with those who switched into the denomination. That is, those who remain Orthodox have more Jewish education, synagogue memberships, and more activity in Jewish voluntary associations, than those who shift from Orthodox to Conservative. The latter, in turn, have more Jewish education, synagogue memberships, and organizational activity than those who remain Conservative. Those who switch from Conservative to Reform score lower on these measures, although they do score higher than those who remain Reform. Those who drop their Reform preference and enter the no preference grouping are the least educated Jewishly, have the fewest synagogue memberships and are least active in Jewish voluntary associations.

These findings raise the possibility that Jewish socialization has both a cognitive and an emotional impact on Jewish identity. Jewish socialization and, more specifically, Jewish education teach one what being Jewish means. A large number of people come to believe that their religious way of life is the "correct" or "proper" manifestation of religion. However, even when one is cognitively ready to leave one's denomination, it may be emotionally hard to make to take a giant stride. Thus, one switches to a nearby, more similar, denomination rather than to a denomination that is vastly different.

The popular media have claimed there is a return to Orthodoxy among American Jews. Our data do not support such a claim. There is, of course, a *baal t'shuva* movement (Danzger 1989; Davidman 1991), a movement of some previously nonobservant Jews into the Orthodox fold. However, their numbers are rather small. Overall, then, our data show that few adults switch to the Orthodox denomination, and the grouping is dominated numerically by those who were reared as Orthodox Jews. The Conservative and Reform groupings do include a noticeable number of switchers, although both groups are still dominated numerically by those who grew up and stayed within their ranks. Those who switch into these denominations are somewhat more religiously observant than those who grew up and stayed in them. The presence of these switchers raises the average level of religious observance of the denomination they enter. Those who move into the Orthodox denomination have potentially less impact on that denomination because they are seeking to adopt a level of religious behavior that they consider higher. They look to Orthodox Jews as role models to emulate. Such is not the case with regard to those who move to less traditional movements.

As might be expected, denominational preference and synagogue membership are related to the permeability of the boundaries between Jews and non-Jews as reflected in whether one marries a non-Jew or not (chapter 6). The less traditional the denomination one prefers, the more likely it is that one's spouse is not Jewish.

Overall, 98% of the spouses of Orthodox respondents are currently Jews, whether born as such or converts, 96% of the spouses of Conservative synagogue members are Jews, as are 90% of the spouses of married Reform synagogue members. Those married respondents who are not synagogue members are less likely to have a Jewish spouse. Among Conservative respondents, only 76% of currently married respondents who are not synagogue members are married to Jews, including Jews-by-choice (converts); 63% of currently married non–synagogue members among Reform are married to Jews; and just 39% of the currently married who have neither a denominational preference nor a synagogue membership are married to Jews.

These data again indicate that one's denominational preference reflects one's lifestyle. The religious identity of spouses is not randomly distributed. Those who prefer a less traditional denomination are more prone to marry a non-Jew and less prone to have their spouse convert.

Among the couples married between 1970 and 1990, 89% of those identified as Orthodox include two partners born into Jewish families (or who now consider themselves Jewish even though not reared as such); for those couples now identified with the Conservative denomination, 63% include spouses born into Jewish families or who are converts into Judaism. For those identified as Reform Jews, only 44% are couples who are both currently Jewish; and for those couples with no denominational preferences, only 18%.

Preference for a more liberal movement also increases with intermarriage. Many of the respondents who were raised in Orthodox or Conservative denominational homes, but who married non-Jews, shift to a less traditional denominational grouping. The Jewish individual with a non-Jewish spouse generally does not convert out of Judaism, but is apt to switch from having a denominational preference to having none. Moreover, slightly less than 40% of the children of religiously mixed marriages are being reared as Jews.

A positive sign for Jewish continuity is that a respondent whose spouse is a Jew-by-choice, or who is one him/herself, is generally a synagogue member. Moreover, they are much more Jewishly involved than those who are in religiously mixed marriages. Conversion more often appears to indicate a significant change of identity rather a change for convenience's sake.

In an effort to determine if there is a "critical mass" for the maintenance of a viable Jewish subcommunity, Jewish community size was introduced as a variable in the study of adherents of Reform Judaism, the only grouping for which numbers are sufficient for the necessary statistical analysis (see chapter 6). Regression analysis indicates that community size is an important correlate of the number of close friends who are Jewish and of the intermarriage rate. It would appear that Reform Jews can create a viable subcommunity when there is a base of 200,000 Jews in a metropolitan area. In such large communities, Reform Jews are more likely to interact with other Reform Jews and thus their scores on questions concerning Jewish primary group involvement increases.

We have attempted to project the denominational distribution to the year 2010 (see chapter 7). Our analysis indicates that synagogue membership will increase from 44% to 52%, with little, if any, of this increase being among the Orthodox (since so many are already members). The proportion of those identifying with the Reform denomination but not joining synagogues are projected to decrease slightly (−3%) as is the proportion who have neither a denominational preference nor a synagogue membership (−3%). Our projections indicate there will be no overall shift toward the more traditional sector of the American Jewish community. With respect to the overall denominational composition of the future Jewish population, the higher fertility rate of the more traditional couples could be offset by conversions into the Reform denomination and by the fact that 38% of the children of mixed, Jewish/non-Jewish, marriages will be raised as Jews.

The intermarriage rates since 1970 are changing a basic characteristic of Jewish families. It is estimated that just 36% of the next generation of Jewish children will have parents both of whom were themselves born Jewish. That is, no more than 36% will have four Jewish grandparents. The percentage is projected to be somewhat higher, 58%, in families with Orthodox and Conservative denominational preferences, and lower, 25%, in families where the preference is for the Reform denomination and in families without a denominational preference.

The Challenge of Americanization

Our study indicates that adult Jews clearly express their relationship to Judaism and to the organized Jewish community through decisions concerning denominational preference and synagogue membership. Taking such "Jewish stances" goes a long way toward expressing what the individual takes being Jewish to mean in the United States. American Jews feel the need today, as they did in 1971, to balance their in-group loyalty to Jewish ways and traditions, on the one hand, and their adjustment to American society, on the other. The Orthodox are still the least assimilationist. The Conservatives are still in an intermediate position between the Orthodox, on one side, and the Reform and those with no denominational preference, on the other. Changes, however, have taken place and the adherents of these denominations, and their synagogue members, no longer resemble the largely immigrant Jewish population of 1900. Virtually all Jews in the United States were highly Americanized by 1990. Like American Christians, the Jewish adults of 1990 differ amongst themselves in their degree of religiosity and in their involvement in the religious, charitable, and educational institutions that comprise the organized segments of their community. The decisions of American Jewish adults about their Jewishness flow out of their experiences within American society and culture.

Our analysis suggests that there may be both a small move toward increased religiosity among American Jews and a decrease in Jewish primary group involvement and activity in Jewish voluntary associations. As we have contended in chapter 1, being Jewish in America is increasingly a matter of religious preference and less a question of with whom one associates with outside of the realm of religion. It would appear that as Jews have become an integral part of American life, those who wish to remain Jewish will increasingly define Jewishness in terms of Judaism, that is, in terms of religion rather than in terms of other components of traditional Jewish life such as informal contacts with other Jews and participation in Jewish voluntary associations devoted to charitable or other causes. Furthermore, as Jews become an integral part of American society, they can also be expected to adopt the substantial level of religious life among other Americans and become more religiously involved themselves.

The process of Americanization, with all its benefits, presents a challenge to those concerned with the long-term survival of Jewish life in America. A significant portion of children with just one Jewish parent may disappear into an American secular melting pot. Moreover, Jewish fertility has been low since the end of the post–World War II baby boom. Overall, the population exchange with the non-Jewish world has resulted in Jewish losses, although these losses have been offset to some degree by converts to Judaism, especially to Reform Judaism. While the next twenty years might see an increase of conversions to Reform Judaism (and perhaps to the other denominations as well), it is expected that overall the size of the American Jewish population will remain the same, becoming a somewhat smaller percentage of a growing American population.

Recommendations for the Denominations

As researchers, our analysis of Jewish denominationalism in the United States has been dispassionate. We have sought to examine what is happening and to project what might happen in the coming years. As social scientists, we have taken a step back to look at Jewish life in the United States as it is, without any discussion of what it should be. However, in this section we discuss the implications of our findings for the various denominational preference groups and offer recommendations we would make to these groups were they to ask for our advice. We now venture our opinions, as sociologists and social psychologists, of what each denomination might do if they wish to continue to exist as a denomination and thereby further the continuity of the Jewish people in the United States. We will also have some words to say about those with no denominational preference.

Of course, we venture these opinions with some hesitance, mindful that, as Goldstein and Goldstein (1996: 325) recognize, "An omnibus survey," such as NJPS, "can provide only limited insights into the causal direction [between the variables studied] and [the] strength of Jewish identification." There is a need, therefore, for in-depth, qualitative data that "will help disentangle cause-effect relations" and "provide more information on motivational factors and on the values of Jewish ties to individuals and families" (Goldstein and Goldstein 1996: 325).

Furthermore, we recognize that, at least to some extent, the denominations are in competition with one another for the same "market." Furthermore, denominationalism is but one vehicle for religious identification. There are other ways, such as through the Federation movement, of furthering Jewish continuity outside the denominational framework. Still, as our work shows, denominationalism is a major vehicle for defining one's Jewish identity and practices. It is our position that any means of continuing Jewish identity and carrying a Jewish tradition into the future is satisfactory even if those means produce different Jewish groupings that argue about which of them represents "true" Judaism and the "right" way of being Jewish. While we recognize the potential for such argument to render Jews "a people divided" (Wertheimer 1993), we believe that the fact that Jews interpret their traditions in significantly different ways is not only to be expected, but is, in many respects, healthy. It indicates the liveliness of the tradition, its importance for its adherents, and its transformative capacity under a variety of conditions (Liebman and Cohen 1990: 174).

Jewish education is a basic variable that can be greatly influenced by the several denominations, generally through their synagogues. Jewish education is provided by many synagogues and by the Jewish day school systems. Many of these schools are clearly identified with one of the denominations or even established under their auspices. However, in some locations, particularly those with relatively few Jewish children, schools may attempt to be non-denominational.

There is evidence, reviewed by Dashefsky (1992), that Jewish education does have a meaningful influence on the decisions regarding the affiliation and identity of individual American Jews. Findings presented in chapter 5 indicate that Jewish day school education is effective in increasing the denominational loyalties of Orthodox and Conservative children when they become adults. The statistical models reviewed in chapter 4 (see tables 4.1 and 4.3) indicate that Jewish education promotes adult adherence to a denomination and to the more traditional denominations. The data also show that the more Jewish education one has in his/her youth, the more likely one is to join a synagogue as an adult. Cohen (1995), in an analysis of a comparable national survey of Jews in the United States, also concludes that all forms of Jewish education in childhood contribute to higher levels of Jewish involvement among Jewish adults. The more intense the education, the greater the result. Thus, the impact of Sunday schools on adult Jewish involvement is slight, possibly negligible, that of part-time schools is slightly positive, and that of day schools, both Orthodox and non-Orthodox, substantially greater. Other analyses of the 1990 NJPS, more focused on Jewish education, have come to similar conclusions (Fishman and Goldstein 1993; Goldstein and Fishman 1993; Lipset 1994b).

While the quantity of Jewish education is important, we would contend that the education that Jewish children receive must prepare them for life in an open pluralistic society. As Lipset (1994b: 57) writes, what is taught may be "more important than the technical factors which can be improved by more money." Traditional Jewish education in Orthodox *yeshivot* treated children as if there were no world outside the confines of the school. Many such institutions divide the educational day into morning and afternoon studies, with one part devoted to religious studies and the other, to secular subjects, but not to secular ways. Religious studies are devoted to studies of classical texts (Bible, Talmud, and books on religious ritual). There are rarely discussions of what it means to be a Jew in a secular society. There is little preparation for the dilemmas one may encounter when one participates in civil life. The main message transmitted is often to be wary of the potential influence of non-Jews, and to make sure that one behaves in accordance with traditional Jewish law (*halakha*). In terms that social psychologists use to discuss attitude formation and inoculation against competing attitudes, many Orthodox youth receive only a "one-sided" message telling them what they should do, rather than a "two-sided" message warning them about competing ideas.

However, the modern world is complex, multifaceted, and open. It is hard to prevent children and young adults from being exposed to other viewpoints.

As Meyrowitz (1985) has noted, social roles have changed in a society where the mass media bring one face to face with situations that were once hidden, or, at most, encountered only gradually as one grew older. Jewish youth encounter the non-Jewish world not only in person, but through the mass media. The relevance of religion in such a world cannot be taken for granted. An educational system that focuses only on religious texts without consideration of context, or that attempts to do nothing more than prepare a child for the Bar or Bat mitzvah rite of passage, may not adequately prepare a new generation to meet the challenge of modernity.

We suggest that the Jewish educational system not only prepare youngsters for the performance of religious ritual, but that it teach them to positively celebrate being Jewish. Education by fear of the wrath of God may be sufficient for some people to become practicing Jews, but it may not do for many others who grow up in a world in which religion is portrayed as irrational and rife with superstition and, in any case, an option one need not choose. We are by no means downplaying the importance of training in the rituals and tenets of Judaism, as interpreted by the denominations. We are saying that religious education has to prepare the children for the realities they will face in an open and largely secular society, even if their parents or teachers would prefer they not encounter those realities or think they can hide it from them. The Jewish education system, we suggest, must not only inform its students of what Jews do and believe as Jews, but should identify and explain the benefits of doing so in order to help their students to choose to be Jewish when the open society they live in does not require them to do so.

Clearly, expanded and more effective programs of Jewish education will advance the prospects for a vibrant Jewish life in America. Such programs could well be extended beyond the synagogue-based Sunday School or late afternoon, after public school, class. These may include, as Cohen (1995) suggests, an expansion of camping programs during the summer and more Jewish youth clubs such as Young Judea or denominationally based programs throughout the year. In recent decades there has been a considerable increase in Jewish Studies programs at American colleges and universities (Ritterband and Wechsler 1995). These programs, coupled with an expanded Hillel program, could reach many Jewish young adults at a critical time in their lives. College youth are removed from the direct influence of their families and their home Jewish community environment. They also find themselves in an academic setting that serves as a natural challenge to parochialism and to religious belief. An attractive, properly funded campus Jewish program in an environment that otherwise encourages a universalistic orientation might be a significant opportunity for the organized Jewish community to reach and influence a large number of young Jews who might otherwise drop out of organized Jewish life.

The development of high-quality programs requires considerable funding. There is also the need to entice highly qualified individuals to enter Jewish communal service. The cost and effort are justified because such programs would help achieve three basic aims of those interested in advancing Jewish life in America and the influence of its major denominations. These are: (1) to retain the allegiance and involvement of those who are raised within their ranks; (2) to intensify the degree of religious involvement, and to create it where it is absent now; and (3) to involve their adherents with the nonreligious aspects of the Jewish community such as involvement in Jewish primary groups and Jewish voluntary associations. The detailed analyses presented in this book indicate that the struggle for these basic aims needs to vary by denomination.

The Orthodox

The major problem for the Orthodox denominations is how to stem its historically heavy losses to other denominations, especially to the Conservative movement. Considerable childhood and adolescent religious education, in particular attendance at day schools, should aid in retaining Orthodox adherents. In addition, it would be helpful to try to integrate the geographically mobile Orthodox adherents into the local Orthodox community at their new locations.

Even more important is the establishment of an Orthodox infrastructure in a greater number of smaller cities throughout the United States. Although less mobile than other denominations (Goldstein and Goldstein 1996: 176–84), Orthodox Jews are more socially and geographically mobile than they were in the past. An increasing number are achieving higher education and are prepared to enter occupations that require them to move away from the larger metropolitan areas. Some Orthodox persons who move to smaller locations may have no choice but to affiliate with a Conservative synagogue because of the absence of one that is Orthodox.

Life for an Orthodox Jew can be expensive. The cost of buying kosher food is greater, especially in smaller cities, than that of non-kosher food. Some food products may need to be specially ordered. A non-Jewish lifestyle may be tempting and may win out if an Orthodox solution is not found. For example, one community in Ohio recently talked about subsidizing a kosher pizza shop in order to attract its Orthodox youth and prevent them from going to a nonkosher shop. More generally, national Orthodox organizations may have to help those in smaller communities meet the demands of living an Orthodox life. They may have to subsidize the cost of hiring a dynamic rabbi and establishing a quality day school education. Once the basis for a vibrant Orthodox community is established, it can become self-sufficient as it attracts additional Orthodox Jews who would be willing to move there given the religious services that are available.

There are other issues that are increasingly problematic for the Orthodox denomination. The formal or legal status of women in Jewish life, which restricts their participation in certain important functions, such as reading from the Torah at services, is one of them. Feminism has had an impact on some Orthodox women, as it has had an impact on American life in general (Greenberg 1981, 1996). As Americanization has a greater impact on Orthodox Jews, it will require creative rabbinical interpretations of religious law to reduce potential alienation. A norm of religious extremism (Liebman 1983) prevents religious legislation that can creatively keep pace with modern technology and cultural norms. The outcome of failure to accommodate to social change could be a high drop-out rate of members. Of course, greater accommodation to modernity and American ways among Orthodox Jewish Americans must be approached cautiously so as not to contradict the religious basis of Orthodox Judaism and thus threaten its vitality.

The family of Orthodox congregations does face a dilemma with regard to greater accommodation. Methods of fitting traditional religious rulings into modern life may make it easier to be an Orthodox Jew, but the rulings risk the wrath of traditional Orthodox rabbis. Contemporary Orthodox Judaism has a tendency to be extreme, and it is almost normative that it should be so (Liebman 1983).

There are also theological questions that affect Orthodox Judaism more than the other denominations (Aviezer 1990). Their almost literal acceptance of the Bible makes biblical criticism problematic. Studies in Israel indicate that a substantial number of Orthodox youth do not believe all the tenets of Orthodox Judaism, but nevertheless maintain an Orthodox lifestyle (Bar Lev, 1995). We suspect that the same may be found among Orthodox Jews in the United States. However, it is far easier here than in Israel to change denominations, for example, to join a Conservative denomination, and maintain an Orthodox lifestyle without accepting Orthodox theology. That is, while the data from the NJPS surveys do not speak to the issue, we think it likely that theological questions explain some of the movement from Orthodox to more religiously liberal denominations. The status of women, biblical criticism, and religious rulings that accommodate modern life are all matters that may push religiously involved Orthodox-reared adults into another denomination, especially the Conservative, that has dealt with these problems in a manner more to their liking.

The Conservatives

The Conservative movement has long been regarded as a "halfway house" (Sklare 1972: 229) between Orthodox and Reform versions of Judaism which possessed no distinctive ideology of its own, but rather embodied a grand coalition that accepted a series of compromises on the issues that divide Orthodoxy and Reform. Moreover, its roots are very much that of what Sklare (1972: 35) calls an "ethnic church," that is, a religious organization, "differentiated by special *descent* as well as by their doctrines or practices [emphasis in original]." The lack of a distinctive ideology may render the movement prone to schism when a given compromise no longer is seen as tolerable to some members. Thus, the compromises which the official organs of the Conservative movement devised over the issue of the ordination of women were met with the defection of some Conservatives Jews and the establishment of the Union for Traditional Judaism (Wertheimer 1993: 154–56). The institutionalization of its liberal Reconstructionist wing, which originated in the thought of Mordecai Kaplan, long a member of the Conservative movement's Jewish Theological Seminary, is another example of schism in the Conservative movement (Wertheimer 1993: 160–69). However, as we noted above, diversity, even division, among Jews may be taken as signs of a lively tradition and healthy confrontation with important issues. Thus, while such schisms may trouble the official organs of the Conservative movement, they may not presage any decline in the number of its adherents. Indeed, it may be yet another accommodation to the openness and variety of religious preference in the United States.

The ethnic roots of the Conservative movement may, however, be more a source of concern. The focus on a special or common descent rather than on common religious practices and beliefs is, in our view, challenged by the prevailing understanding of what it means to be a Jew in the United States. That understanding increasingly sees the meaning of being Jewish as focused on religion and not on ethnicity. If such is the case, then for Conservative Judaism to thrive it must identify and attract those American Jews who reject the prevailing meaning of being a Jew in the United States (see the discussion below of Strategy II) and/or find a clear and more or less distinctive religious perspective to offer adherents.

In either case, it would be important, as noted above, for the movement to improve its childhood and adolescent Jewish educational programs. The difficulty facing the Conservative movement is that of deciding what the curriculum of such education should be, what religious norms, rituals, and ideology should be stressed. Whatever the curriculum, however, we suggest that as Conservative Jews in the United States enter the twenty-first century, a focus on descent as the basis for defining who is a Jew will become increasingly difficult to maintain. Common ancestry will not suffice; a clearer understanding of common cultural and religious traditions will also be needed. Compromise and accommodation will still be called for, but the reasons for them may need to be articulated more fully. The center may still hold, the halfway house may still be attractive and habitable, but the reasons it should hold and the basis of its attraction may need to be made clearer.

The Reform

The ranks of the Reform denomination have grown as Reform Judaism attracts Jews reared in the more traditional Conservative denomination as well as converts and intermarried couples. The Reform denomination has also been the most successful in retaining the allegiance of its children. However, only a minority of those identified with the denomination are synagogue members. Moreover, the adherents of this denomination are the least religiously active and the least involved with other Jews in nonreligious activities.

We suggest the Reform movement consider two foci of increased activity: (1) outreach aimed at getting more of its adherents to join its synagogues or temples; and (2) overcome the lack of Jewish contacts and interaction among its adherents in the smaller Jewish communities.

Our data do not provide insight into why those who express a preference for Reform Judaism frequently do not join Reform temples. It may be, however, that its long-standing emphasis on prophetic Judaism, on the notion that social justice, and the liberal political policies it leads to in the "real," or secular, world, are more important concerns for Reform Jews than the maintenance of Jewish ritual and religious customs. Reform Jews, it has been said, have often rejected keeping kosher, following Jewish dietary laws, on the grounds that what goes into one's mouth is far less important than what comes out of it, that what one eats is not important, but what one says to others is. Reform Judaism's acceptance of individualism may also explain a lower rate of synagogue affiliation; the need to join an organization and the value of doing so is not always clear to a rugged individualist. However, if being a Jew increasingly means to define oneself in religious terms, and not by one's secular activity, then Reform Judaism would be well served to focus more on distinctively religious beliefs and practices than on messages that can only be implemented in the secular world.

The Reform denomination has built subcommunities within the large Jewish populations of major metropolitan areas. However, a substantial proportion of its adherents live in medium to small size Jewish communities. These smaller Jewish communities are often set within a non-Jewish population of a very sizeable metropolitan area. The adherents of the Reform denomination living in these smaller Jewish communities are often isolated from the major Reform subcommunities. Such social isolation needs to be addressed by a variety of programs which seek to overcome the inability of local Reform populations to reach a critical mass of adherents. The movement would be well served by overcoming the lack of Jewish contacts and interaction among its adherents in the smaller Jewish communities.

No Denominational Preference

Respondents with no denominational preference are only marginally involved Jewishly. They constitute an unstable grouping. The majority of those raised without a preference eventually choose a denomination. Among those staying without a preference, just 39% of those who have married have a spouse who was born Jewish and virtually none of their originally non-Jewish spouses have become Jews-by-choice. Among the 52% who have a denominational preference as adults, and who have married, 39%, have spouses who were born into Jewish families and 47% have spouses who have become Jews-by-choice. Overall, it appears that about half of those reared with no denominational preference are now involved in religiously mixed marriages. The other half either have married somebody reared as a Jew or who is now a Jew-by-choice.

It may well prove quite difficult for the Jewish community, and its denominational structure, to reach out to religiously mixed married couples who have, for the most part, decided to live outside the framework of either organized Judaism or Christianity. Given the enormous tasks the three major denominational movements have, the organized Jewish community faces the issue of whether it is better to work with those who have a denominational preference, no matter how weakly felt, than to seek to attract those who have no preference and, perhaps, no interest in being involved with Jewish life and its institutions.

For those who have a denominational preference but no synagogue membership, the door to increased Jewish involvement is still open before them. For the unaffiliated, the door away from Judaism appears to be already half closed behind them. Given the financial constraints of the denominations and the consequent need to focus resources and activities on those who are more firmly anchored in the Jewish community, it may be impractical to spend much money and effort on the nonaffiliated. There is also the question of how converts among non-Jews married to Jews would affect the delicate balance between Jews and non-Jews in the religiously pluralistic American society. Few Jews would be pleased if efforts were exerted to convert intermarried Jews to a non-Jewish religion. Nevertheless, evangelism is an old tradition in the United States. Jews may yet devise a way to proselytize among non-Jews married to Jews without stirring up a hornet's nest of unwanted Christian evangelism aimed at American Jews. Our cautious recommendation, then, is that a way be found to keep a return option open for the unaffiliated. As social scientists, we would recommend an in-depth study, using both qualitative and quantitative data gathering, comparing those who reaffiliate with Judaism with those who did not in order to understand the factors that influence their decision.

Closing Comments

The programs outlined above could help the various denominational groupings to enable their adherents to survive and thrive as Jews in the United

States. That is, they could enable current and future generations of Jews to achieve the goal set by their immigrant forbears of becoming successful, both as Americans and as Jews. The overarching problem that the generation of immigrants faced, and that contemporary American Jews face is simple: Is it actually possible to be simultaneously a successful American and a successful Jew? Historically the possibility of such a dual identity depended on the conditions that American society set for the success of its immigrant populations, Jew and Gentile alike. For Jews, the terms under which they could succeed in American society are what Marshall Sklare, the founder of the modern sociology of American Jewry, calls the American-Jewish "social contract." We have alluded to this implicit contract in chapter 1 when we wrote of the conditions and consequences of Emancipation for American Jewry. We now elaborate somewhat upon that "contract."

The "social contract" calls for American Jews to be "prepared to render unto America that which belong(s) to America" and to abstain from asking for special rights and privileges or that the public order accommodate itself to the sectarian demands of Jews as Jews (Sklare 1972: 20).

> Jewishness [is] to be a private matter—its display to be limited to the home, the synagogue, the Jewish school and similar islands of privacy. Jews [will] not routinely appear in public as Jews. When such appearances [are] made they [are to be seen as] forced upon the group, as in the case of rallies protesting anti-Semitic outrages. (Sklare 1972: 215)

To put it more succinctly, and to paraphrase the nineteenth century essayist and poet Yehuda L. Gordon, a Jew was to be "a citizen in the street, and a Jew at home."

To understand how the "social contract" that Emancipation offers Jews in the United States affects Jewish survival, we have to remind ourselves, as we did in chapter 1, of what Emancipation offers Jews and of what it asks of them. What was being offered to Jews was, and is, freedom from the restriction placed on Jews by essentially medieval conditions that restricted their political and economic rights and opportunities (Birnbaum and Katznelson 1995). It is also freedom from the burden of being a people set apart as objects of scorn, prejudice, discrimination, and hatred. For European Jewry, Emancipation came first in Western Europe, in France at the end of the eighteenth century, and in Germany, nearer the middle of the nineteenth century. For the bulk of European Jewry, which lived in the Pale of Settlement in Eastern Europe, it came only upon immigration to America, that is, at the end of the nineteenth and the beginning of the twentieth century.

Whenever and wherever it came, the offer was the same, you are to be a citizen in the street, be it a French, German, or American citizen, and a Jew at home, or in some other private domain. The offer, the "social contract," that came with Emancipation was, and is, quite appealing. It offers equal opportunity employment, equal access to the arenas of political power, and the potential end of prejudice and scorn directed at Jews as Jews. Virtually all American Jews have accepted it and have done well by it. As we have noted, the socioeconomic standing of Jews as a group is comparatively high. Yet, as with all contracts, rights entail obligations and there is a price to be paid for the advantages gained from it. The price was no more and no less than a transformation in the meaning of what it meant to be a Jew—a transformation that challenges virtually all of the supports and institutions that had worked to sustain Jewish life in the more than 1,500 years of the Diaspora in Europe. Indeed, such was the intention of Emancipation. The purpose of the "contract" that went with it was to enable Jews to accommodate to and assimilate into modern society and that, it was thought, required a transformation of what it meant to be a Jew.

The "contract" was accepted quite widely and quite readily by many Jews. After all, it meant success for a Jew as an individual, success in the economic and, if one sought it, in the political arenas of life. Still, there was a trade-off: success for Jews as individuals at the cost of a great challenge to the continued existence of the Jews as a people. The result is "the conundrum of individual Jewish success amidst the dissolution of the Jewish community" (Lipset and Raab 1995: 7). Indeed, such was one of the slogans of the French Emancipation of the Jews: to the Jew as an individual everything, to the Jew as a Jew, nothing. Given the circumstances that precipitated the Emancipation of Jews under French rule, such a slogan is not surprising. For such Emancipation was not offered solely on the grounds of the logic of the French Revolution, of liberty, equality, and fraternity. Indeed, it was not offered during the French Revolution per se, but by Napoleon afterwards.

Napoleon's offer of Emancipation to Jews under his rule was largely the result of his seeking a way to still the complaints of those in his newly conquered domains about their financial problems with Jews, namely, from the obligation of forfeiting their lands as payment to Jews to whom they owed more than they could pay (Maslin 1957: 21). Napoleon sought to prevent the mortgaging of lands to Jews whom he regarded as constituting a unique nation within the French nation. The existence of such a unique people was regarded by Napoleon as an "evil" to be prevented (Maslin 1957: 21). To his credit, Napoleon sought to solve his "Jewish Problem" by changing Jews, not murdering them. To bring about that transformation, he offered them Emancipation, the freedom and protection provided by French law.

To accomplish his end, the end of Jewish uniqueness as a people and their assimilation into the French people, Napoleon called an Assembly of (Jewish) Notables into session and presented them with a series of twelve questions (Schwarzfuchs 1979: 56ff.). The questions embodied a five-step program which would bring about the complete assimilation of Jews into French society. The steps were: (1) submission of Jews to the authority of French civil law, rather than the laws of the Talmud and Jewish tradition; (2) discouraging Jews from devoting themselves exclusively to usury and brokerage; (3) encouraging Jews to enter the crafts and other useful occupations; (4) enforced conscription into the French Army; and (5) an intermarriage rate among Jews of at least one-third (Maslin 1957: 21–25). Napoleon's program was geared ultimately to leave to Jews *qua* Jews only their dogma, their religion, and eliminate any notion, among Jews and Gentile alike, that Jews were or ought to be a unique, distinct people.

In America, such a program never had government sanction. Nevertheless, it is a consequence of the great social forces that define modern American society. Every one of Napoleon's five-point program is an established fact in the contemporary United States. Jews live under the civil law of the United States, not under distinct or separate Jewish law; Jews have economic opportunity; they serve in the armed forces; and intermarriage now occurs at a rate in excess of what Napoleon specified. Whether his program need have the result Napoleon hoped for, will be discussed later in this chapter. For now, we will remind ourselves of how the meaning of what it is to be a Jew has been transformed by Emancipation, by participation in a free, pluralistic, and voluntaristic society in the United States.

To understand the transformation, we need to be reminded of what Jewishness was in pre-Emancipation Europe. To help us recall, we quote from a nineteenth-century Orthodox rabbi, a German Jew, Samson Raphael Hirsch, who faced directly the implications of Emancipation (as quoted in Blau 1966: 79):

> Judaism is not a religion, the synagogue is not a church, and the Rabbi is not a priest. Judaism is not a mere adjunct to life: it comprises all of life. To be a Jew is not a mere part, it is the sum total of our task in life. To be a Jew in synagogue, and the kitchen, in the field and the warehouse, in the office and the pulpit, as father and mother, as servant and master, as man and citizen, with one's feelings and one's thoughts, in word and in deed, in enjoyment and privation, with needle and the graving-tool, with pen and the chisel—that is what it means to be a Jew. An entire life supported by the Divine idea and lived and brought to fulfillment according to Divine will.

In short, at the pre-immigration dawn of Emancipation, Judaism or Jewishness could not be restricted to the home, not even to the synagogue. It was an all encompassing way of life. Jewishness was not confined to its religion; there were a Jewish language, a Jewish culture, Jewish food, and more important, although not stressed by Rabbi Hirsch, a Jewish people, a people that had long been semi-autonomous and that had developed its own legal codes.

The entry into an open society raised the two very basic questions we noted in chapter 1: (1) Should a Jewish identity be a religious identity or an ethnic identity? and (2) Whether religious or not, should it be based on modern or traditional Jewish models? The distinctions that Emancipation thrust upon Jews were between the Jewish religion and the Jewish nation or people, between the sacred and the secular, and between the interests of the individual and the concerns of the community. It restricted Jewishness to the realm of the sacred, a realm that the emancipated, modern, open, and secular Western societies of Europe and America often did not respect.

The realm of religion to which Jewishness was to be confined was to shoulder alone the justification of Jewish survival and to provide the means for that survival (Greenberg 1967: 7). At the same time, religion was being threatened by secularism and other aspects of modern society. Modern secularism challenged God's active role in the world and the very notion of a sanctified life, both central to Jewish religious thought. Modern universalism, the notion that all humans are created free and equal and that all are endowed with basic human rights, often denied the legitimacy or need for particular groups. Universalism led to the view that particular groups of any type are atavistic and, historically, as the source of unwarranted divisiveness and friction within and between societies. In addition, science reveals a universe so broad and complex that the significance of any specific culture or group is diminished by the mere standard of size and perspective. Modern social science and history undermined or, by reductionism, denied the legitimacy of the religious history and affirmations of the Jews. All these aspects of a modern society then work to strike at the notion that to be a Jew can and should mean to be part of a separate and distinct people.

Those who would elect a Jewish identity, who would seek to ensure that Jews survive and thrive as Jews in a modern, free society, face great challenges. Jews in the United States have tried many strategies to meet these challenges. We will discuss the two that we think have the greatest potential. Rather than provide descriptive titles that might carry unwanted connotations, we simply call them Strategy I and Strategy II. We believe either of these strategies will appeal to the broad base of moderately affiliated and peripherally involved Jews who have an interest in "the continuity of Jewish identity both in their families and among the Jewish people generally" (Cohen 1995: 409) but who are unlikely to accept *halakha* (traditional Jewish religious practices) or to actively consider *aliyah* (emigration to Israel).

The essence of the first strategy for Jewish survival is to accept the terms of participation in an open, pluralistic, and voluntaristic society as given. It is the strategy of redefining Jewishness as nothing more than a religion and, as is the tendency in America, restricting its expression to the home and to appropriate religious settings such as the temple or synagogue and to associated organizations directed to religious education.

Since Jews in the United States live in a modern, secular society, Strategy I calls for Jewishness, now more appropriately called Judaism, to be kept unobtrusive. They can do so by applying five criteria, explicitly or implicitly, to the choice of the rituals, the practices of Judaism, that are to be retained. These criteria were first identified by Sklare and Greenblum (1979: 114) in a study of a suburban Jewish community in the 1950s.

According to these criteria, the rituals to be retained should:

1. Be capable of effective redefinition in modern terms, for example, as celebrating freedom in general, or freedom of religion in particular (Passover as a freedom festival rather than as the story of the freeing of the Jewish nation)

2. Not demand social isolation and the following of a unique lifestyle (hence no requirement to observe *kashrut*, Jewish dietary laws)

3. Be in accord with the religious culture of the larger community while providing a "Jewish" alternative when such is felt to be needed (Hanukkah at Christmas time)

4. Be centered on the child (Shavuot as the time for the confirmation of religious school graduates not as a religious holiday per se)

5. Be performed annually or infrequently (so the annual observance of Yom Kippur is acceptable, but the weekly Friday night lighting of Shabbat candles much less so)

And so,

they attend services only on the High Holidays and for family life-cycle celebrations. They celebrate Rosh Hashanah, Yom Kippur, Hanukkah, and Passover in some fashion while generally ignoring most of the other holidays on the Jewish calendar. . . . [They] tend to feel God is inactive and non-interventionist. They eschew the traditionalist religious conceptions of obligatory law and punctilious ritual observance. Instead they feel attracted to a body of available religious activities from which they feel free to select in accord with their sense of personal relevance and meaningfulness. (Cohen 1995: 408–9)

Such an expression of Jewishness or Judaism, is attractive to many Jews. It makes being Jewish easy within the context of American life. A Jew practicing this form of Jewishness certainly does not have to feel, as sometimes seems to have been the case in the past, that Jewishness is a burden to endure if you have to, but certainly not something one would have chosen had other options been available. This adapted, accommodating form of Judaism gives lie to the traditional Yiddish saying, *"Siz schwer tzu zein a Yid"* (It's hard to be a Jew). Following a Jewishly unobtrusive lifestyle, it is relatively easy to be a Jew. Indeed, under Strategy I, it may be so easy to be a Jew, it can be regarded, as Gans (1979) suggests, as a leisure time activity.

Despite its lure, Strategy I has one potentially serious flaw: it may be too easy. Anything that can be had that easily, that cheaply, may not be worth much. As Finke and Stark (1992: 271) have suggested, unless a denomination establishes "some tension with its environment" it will be unable to provide the rewards needed to sustain it. Denominations that do not demand much of their adherents may well lose out in the competition for allegiance in a free, pluralistic, competitive marketplace of religious ideas and practices, especially when such denominations are small minorities. For example, one who adopts Strategy I may find it is not something that is likely to withstand serious competition with the desires of a loving non-Jewish fiancée who wants her prospective children to live as Christians, which is, after all, easier yet, easier than meeting even the minimal demands on a Jew placed by Strategy I.

To put the matter differently, the flaw in Strategy I is that it does not adequately answer one key question: What should a Jew stand for as a Jew? That is, the twofold question of both the "vision and goal" that "define a purpose for an American Jewish community in Diaspora" (Kosmin 1994: 189) and of what difficulties one will "stand for" or endure on its behalf.

The answer Strategy I offers to what a Jew stands for, namely, religion, may not be sufficient in a modern secular society, especially not for Jews with a rather high level of secular education and economic success. That answer may be inadequate because religion is something that will not stand for much among many contemporary Jews. Encountering some relatively slight difficulty might find one willing to abandon it altogether. If being Jewish means the easy form of Judaism, why stand for anything on its behalf? Why stand for any degree of scorn or even the discomfort of being different, of participating practices that make one stand out? Why risk the loss of the love of another? Why endure personal discomfort in the name of religion when if there is no strong religious belief to support doing so? As Greeley (1972: 202) suggests, a strong "religious and theological revival among American Jews" may provide an answer to these questions. Such a revival would need to address Yinger's (1970: 523) criticism that "the liberal tendencies in religion that placed man and his welfare in the forefront of concern ran the risk of making man himself the object of worship," and of, thus, in effect, placing secular concerns above religious demands.

Such a revival may also, as Green (1994a: 5) suggests, entail some "recovery of the kabbalistic-Hasidic tradition" and "an open meeting with the philosophical and meditational traditions of the East" (Green 1994b: 21). Others (Elazar 1995; Glicksman 1995) have called for a renewal of the covenantal tradition based more on the *obligations* the parties to it accept and less on the contemporary stress on the *rights* of individual and the instrumental value of Jewish life for the fulfillment of personal goals. However, in the absence of such a revival, there may be a need for another strategy for Jewish survival in the United States.

One possible alternative, Strategy II, does not restrict Jewishness to the practice of religion, although it does not reject such practices as unimportant. It recognizes that "there is something simplistic and reductionistic in [an] emphasis on a dichotomy between the communal and the religious, especially for Jews" (Lipset and Raab 1995: 64). Thus, in addition to religion, Strategy II stresses the notion of Jewish ethnicity, of Jewish peoplehood. It stresses the idea that Jews have a distinct history and distinct values. For example, a Jew following Strategy II will know that the year 1492 is important not only as the year in which Columbus came to the New World, but also as the year in which Jews were expelled from Spain. More generally, as Eisenstadt (1992) has put it, Jews will be seen as the inheritors of a unique civilization. Moreover, its basic value challenges American individualism by proclaiming simply, as did the Jews of the shtetl, "life is with people" (Zbrowski and Herzog 1952). That is, "the traditional Jewish model is a communitarian one" (Kosmin 1994: 189). It holds, "people acquire their values and their identity through the community rather than through individual selection" and that the guiding purpose of life is defined by one's "responsibilities [to others] rather than [by] the . . . opportunity for self-fulfillment. [That is,] privatism is *not* the touchstone" (Friedman 1991: 87; italics in original). Moreover, Strategy II calls for Jews to base a major part of their Jewish identity on ethnicity—an identification and involvement with the people of Israel and the organized Jewish community. In that vein, Strategy II stresses that one Jew has a deep and abiding responsibility for other Jews. The basic tenets of such a strategy have been outlined further by Woocher (1986).

There are eight basic tenets to the "faith" of Strategy II:

1. The unity of the Jewish people is affirmed and its distinctiveness valued.

2. Each Jew individually and each Jewish community collectively is responsible for the security and welfare of all Jews.

3. The state of Israel is the symbol of the unity and mutual responsibility of the Jewish people and is, thus, a most crucial part of Jewish life.

4. Jewish tradition is of enduring worth and its perpetuation is most important.

5. Threats persist, both internal and external, to the survival of the Jewish people and its traditions.

6. *Tzedekah*, understood narrowly as philanthropy and more broadly as action on behalf of justice, is a primary mandate of the Jewish value system.

7. Active participation in American society is a virtue and is compatible with good Jewishness.

8. Individuals should have freedom of conscience with respect to most traditional norms of Jewish law. Differences with respect to these norms and with respect to classical theological affirmations should not be allowed to overshadow agreement on the first seven points. That is, while the unity of the Jewish people is stressed, pressure for uniformity in religious belief and practice is rejected.

Strategy II, like Strategy I, has its limits. The results of this study, which show a decline in participation in primary and secondary Jewish associations, indicate that the strategy may not be widely accepted. Strategy II challenges the "social contract" that calls for Jewishness to be confined to private life. It presents "a radical test of American . . . capacity to tolerate ethnic activism in support of a foreign state—something it has been willing to do to a lesser degree for others, such as the Irish and the Greeks" (Lipset and Raab 1995: 111–12). It also calls for a heightened sense of ethnicity among Jews in the United States when such a sense may be diminishing among other descendants of European immigrants (Alba 1990; Lieberson and Waters 1988; Waters 1990). Such a strategy may fall prey to a "nostalgic allegiance" that, as Gans (1979: 9) warns, may foster "a love for and pride in a tradition that can be felt without having to be incorporated in everyday behavior." Moreover, such a strategy may encourage an identity that is expressed by "'affiliating' with an abstract collectivity which does not exist as an interacting group" (Gans 1979: 8). That is, the State of Israel may be more a symbol of Jewish peoplehood than a reality with which people interact on a regular basis. Of course, for the sizeable minority of Jews with friends and family in Israel, the collectivity is not abstract, as it need not be for those who follow events in Israel very closely.

In any case, whatever the strategy adopted, whether one focuses on religion and Judaism, or one focuses as well on Jews as a people or civilization, the survival of Jews as Jews in the United States is by no means guaranteed. As Lipset (1994a: 178) notes, now, some thirteen or so generations later, a trace of the descendants of Jewish colonial families will reveal "early Jewish settler families . . . who remained Jewish for a long time, but are now Christian." The same may be said of future generations, descendants of the massive later Jewish immigration of a hundred twenty or so years ago. Jews may yet be, as Abba Eban, the noted Israeli scholar and statesman, feared, "A people who cannot take 'yes,' for an answer." Thus, it remains to be seen if Jews in the United States can continue to adapt to the positive conditions and opportunities that life in the modern, pluralistic, emancipated, individualistic, and free society in the United States of America has provided them and in which they now express their adaptations through decisions about their denominational preferences and synagogue memberships.

Appendix A

Methodology of CJF 1990 National Jewish Population Survey

Joseph Waksberg

Large-scale sample surveys are frequently carried out in a number of discrete steps and the National Jewish Population Survey (NJPS) followed such a pattern. The steps consisted of: determination of the subjects to be included in the survey; development of specific question wording; testing questions and procedures; decisions on survey procedures; preparation for data collection, including recruitment and training of staff; sample selection; data collection; weighting and other aspects of data processing; internal analysis of potential sources of errors; tabulations; analyses and preparation of reports. This methodological report concentrates on the technical aspects relating to sampling, survey procedures and data collection, weighting, and issues relating to accuracy of the data. There is a brief description of the questionnaire development. Data analysis and preparation of publications, both of the monographs and of less detailed reports, are not part of the survey methodology and are not discussed here.

General Survey Procedures

The Council of Jewish Federations (CJF) established and supports a National Technical Advisory Committee on Jewish Population Studies (NTAC). At the time the NJPS was planned, the NTAC consisted of researchers who worked for the CJF or local Jewish federations and outside demographers and statisticians interested in Jewish issues. The NTAC endorsed an initial recommendation of the October 1987 World Conference on Jewish Demography in Jerusalem to conduct a U.S. National Jewish

Population Survey (NJPS) in the spring and summer of 1990. The CJF concurred in this recommendation and agreed to support such a survey.

The choice of 1990 was a deliberate one since it placed the survey at about the same time as the 1990 U.S. Census, thereby insuring maximum comparability between the Jewish survey data and census statistics. Further, the time period chosen for the conduct of the detailed interviews, late spring and early summer, both corresponded to the timing of the Census and is a time when most college students can be reached in their families' residences or other dwelling places that are more permanent than dormitories or other college housing. The interviewing period is also the time that most sunbelt residents are in their more permanent homes.

The NTAC had independently come up with 1990 as the logical period for the survey as part of more general considerations of appropriate survey methodology. In a series of meetings in the decade leading up to 1990, the NTAC had discussed the many aspects of planning and implementing a Jewish Population Study and had submitted the following recommendations to the CJF:

- *A large scale survey of the Jewish population should be conducted in 1990.*

- *Data collection should be by telephone.* Over the past twenty to thirty years, survey researchers had demonstrated that the quality of responses to inquiries over the telephone were, for almost all subjects, about the same as for face-to-face interviews. Response rates to telephone surveys are generally lower than in face-to-face interviews, but the cost of telephone surveys is so much lower than the NTAC felt that the substantial cost advantage of a telephone survey more than compensated for the adverse effect on quality of a lower response rate.

- *A sample of 2,000 to 2,500 Jewish households should be selected by random digit dialing (RDD), without any use of Federation or other lists of Jewish households.* RDD gives all households with telephones in the United States (both Jewish and non-Jewish) a known chance of selection into the sample so that lists are not necessary. Furthermore, it was the NTAC's judgment that the effort involved in trying to construct a national list, and the likely small percentage of U.S. Jews that would be on the list, would make the construction of the list counterproductive. It should be noted that households without telephones were not intended to be covered in the survey. In 1990, about 7% of U.S. households did not have telephones. However, the percentage is undoubtedly much lower for Jewish households, and the NTAC did not believe their omission would have any detectable effect on the quality of the survey results. The survey also was to omit the nonhousehold population, principally persons in nursing homes, long-term hospital units, religious institutions, military barracks, and prisons. College students in dormitories (as well as those in private residences) were to be covered in the survey, usually as members of their parents' households.

- *Data should be collected only for the civilian population living in households*, omitting the institutional and other nonhousehold population. The survey thus would exclude those in prisons, hospitals, nursing homes, hotels, religious institutions, and in military barracks. Estimates of the relatively small number of Jews in such places were added to the survey results for the estimate of the total number of Jews in the United States. However, their characteristics would not be reflected in the breakdowns of the totals by age, sex, etc.

- *A screening questionnaire that defines and identifies Jewish households should be administered to the sample of telephone households.* Since random digit dialing produces a sample of all U.S. telephone households, non-Jewish households would then be dropped and Jewish households retained for the survey.

- *The survey should include a wide variety of topics.* The NTAC developed a broad set of questions designed to shed light on the demographic, social, and economic characteristics of the Jewish population, and to provide information on items of specific Jewish concern, such as intermarriage, Jewish education, philanthropy, observances of Jewish rituals and practices, synagogue membership, utilization of social services, volunteerism, attitudes to certain issues of Jewish concern, and so forth. The questions were divided into two groups: (a) ones for which reasonably accurate information for all household members could be provided by any adult in the household (e.g., age, education, observance, etc.) and (b) questions for which the accuracy of proxy responses would be in doubt (e.g., attitudes). For the first set of questions, data would be obtained for all members of the sample households. For the second group, the NTAC recommended that one adult be selected at random in each sample household and that the sample for these items should be considered as consisting of only the selected persons.

A second, and independent, partition of the questions was also made. In order to reduce the considerable interview length, the questionnaire was divided into a "core" component, to be asked in all sample households, and "modules" to be asked in subsamples of households. More specifically, respondents were randomly allocated to three equal subsamples, and each subsample was assigned one of the three following areas of inquiries: (1) Jewish identity; (2) social services; and (3) philanthropy.

- *After the survey information was collected, weights should be inserted into the data file.* The weights should be constructed so that when they are used in tabulations of the survey data, they provide approximately unbiased estimates of the U.S. Jewish population in each category shown in the tabulations.

- *The individual responses to the survey questionnaire as well as the appropriate weights should be entered onto a computer tape.* Copies of the tape would be available for researchers interested in making detailed studies of particular aspects of Jewish life.

- *A high priority was put on speed of data processing, tabulations of the data, and publication of the major results*, first in a summary report highlighting the major findings in the survey, and then in a series of analytic studies focusing on particular topics.

- *The survey should be conducted outside of CJF or its member organizations.* More specifically, a contract would be let by competitive bidding to a company experienced in the conduct of such statistical studies.

The CJF approved the NTAC recommendations, provided a budget for the survey, and asked the NTAC to make the necessary arrangements. A Request for Proposals (RFP) that described the work to be done, the procedures outlined above, and the scope of work was prepared and distributed to interested statistical and market research companies. A subcommittee of the NTAC reviewed the proposals submitted by organizations that were interested in carrying out the survey, and selected the ones that were judged best. These organizations were invited to make personal presentations of their plans and their experience in such activities before the subcommittee. A contract was then awarded to a team consisting of ICR Survey Research Group and Marketing Systems Group (also known as Genesys Sampling Systems). The Marketing Systems Group was responsible for the sample selection and all weighting and estimation phases of the project. ICR was responsible for all other aspects of the survey, from questionnaire pre-testing through data collection, coding, and data tape preparation.

The choice of ICR and Marketing Systems Group was based on a number of factors: understanding of the requirements of the study, the reputation of the team in doing high quality work, experience with large-scale telephone sample surveys, an existing staff of experienced telephone interviewers and a system of training and supervising them, a capable statistician to oversee the sampling and related activities, and cost. A main and overriding advantage of the team was the fact that they carried out, for other sponsors, a weekly RDD national household sample survey of 2,000 households. They agreed to add the screening questions that identified Jewish households to the questionnaire then in use. It was estimated that the approximately 100,000 households screened over the course of a year would supply the 2,500 responding Jewish households desired in the final sample. (The screening actually covered more than a year, and consisted of over 125,000 households which yielded over 5,000 households that indicated the presence of a Jewish member.) By attaching the screener questions to an existing national sample survey, the NJPS was able to avoid the expense of selecting and interviewing the very large sample needed to locate 2,500 Jewish households. Instead, the survey incurred only a fairly modest marginal cost of the added time to administer the screening questions. If the NJPS had to pay the entire cost of selecting and screening more than 100,000 households, the additional cost probably would have been well over $1,000,000.

An additional advantage of using the ICR's ongoing weekly survey was that it provided flexibility in achieving the desired sample size. The amount of screening necessary to achieve a sample of 2,500 Jewish households could only be approximately estimated in advance. With the weekly samples screened by ICR, a cumulative tally of Jewish households could be kept, and the weekly samples terminated before the end of the year if fewer than 100,000 households provided the required sample size, or it could be continued for longer than a year if that was necessary.

Sample Selection

The telephone numbers selected for the NJPS were based on random digit dialing (RDD), and are a probability sample of all possible telephone numbers in the United States. The sampling procedure utilized a single-stage sample of telephone numbers within known residential working banks (the first two digits of the four-digit suffix, e.g. 212-555-xxxx). Telephone exchanges were strictly ordered by census geographic variables (i.e., Division, Metro/Non-Metro, Central City/Suburban, etc.) creating a sample frame with fine implicit geographic stratification. This procedure provides samples that are unbiased and in which all telephones have the same chance of selection. Since the random digit aspect allows for the inclusion of unlisted and unpublished numbers, it protects the samples from "listing bias"—the unrepresentativeness of telephone samples that can occur if the distinctive households whose telephone numbers are unlisted and unpublished are excluded from the sample. The RDD sample is referred to as the "screening sample." It consisted of 125,813 households that were asked whether any household member was Jewish. (See Section 4 for specific questions.) All qualified Jewish households were followed up with requests for the detailed interviews.

The household sample selection was accompanied by an automated scheme for scheduling callbacks for telephone numbers at which there was no response to the initial call. A three-callback rule was followed—the timing of the callbacks was scheduled by the computer to cover various times of the day, but within a narrow time frame. This narrow time frame was required by the short field period for each weekly survey. There were actually two weekly sample surveys, with 1,000 households in each survey. One weekly survey ran from Wednesday evening through Sunday evening; the second from Friday evening through Tuesday evening. The initial call and callback schedule ensured a minimum of two weekend attempts (if necessary) on each sample number.

The tight time schedule for the screening interviews undoubtedly reduced the response rate, as compared to a survey with more time for callbacks. (For example, persons on vacation during the survey week were never given an opportunity to respond.) However, the NTAC believed that the advantages of using an ongoing survey for screening outweighed the disadvantages.

Presurvey Operations

Two major sets of activities preceded the data collection. They consisted of the development and testing of the survey questions, and the interviewer training and briefing.

Development and Testing of Survey Instruments

Three stages of data collection were planned: screening, recontact and in-depth interviewing. The questionnaires for all three phases were initially developed by the NTAC. These documents were then edited, reformatted and programmed for CATI interviewing by ICR staff. The development phase included several questionnaire drafts and a series of "live" pretests.

CATI stands for Computer Assisted Telephone Interviewing. It is a system in which the questionnaire has been entered into a computer, each interviewer is provided with a computer screen and keyboard, and the questions to be asked appear on the screen instead of having to be read from a paper questionnaire. The responses are entered directly into the computer. In addition to speeding up the data processing, CATI has the capability of carrying out editing for consistency and completeness of data and flexibility of operations. Almost all large-scale telephone surveys are now done via CATI.

All interviewing in both the Screening, Recontact/Validation, and the Main Study Phases were conducted by professional interviewers via computer-assisted telephone interviewing (CATI). From an interviewing standpoint, the CATI system removes the potential for interviewer error relative to skip patterns and possible response options. Moreover, the CATI system provides inherent response editing capabilities relative to both range edits and conditional requirements based upon prior responses. Computerized questionnaire control allows interviewers to better establish rapport with respondents and concentrate on responses rather than attempting to contend with the extreme complexity of the Recontact and Main Study questionnaires.

Finally, CATI capabilities allowed for access to up-to-the-minute interviewing production measures including production rates, refusal and refusal conversion rates, and results of dialing attempts.

In each pretest, personnel from NTAC and ICR monitored interviews as they were being conducted. Any unforeseen deficiencies in question content, sequencing, and nomenclature were corrected during this stage. In most cases, indicated changes were incorporated immediately, providing pretest capabilities during the same pretest session.

The final CATI questionnaires were reviewed and tested extensively by both NTAC and ICR personnel prior to "live" interviewing. In addition, the pretest data served as a "live" test of output, data format, edit checks, and so on.

Interviewer Training and Briefing

All interviewers selected to work on the 1990 NJPS were personally briefed, trained and supervised during all hours of interviewing. In addition to participating in the standard ICR ten-hour interviewer training session, all interviewers who worked on the survey participated in a detailed briefing session developed specifically for this study.

This special briefing included an item-by-item discussion of each question and module contained in the interview; a discussion of special respondent "handling" for specific interview situations, including providing the CJF's telephone number to respondents who questioned the authenticity of the survey and suggesting that the CJF be called; and a review of areas and issues relating to Jewish heritage including customs, holidays, and proper pronunciation of Hebrew words and phrases that interviewers would be likely to encounter during the course of the study. In addition to the briefing, written interviewer aids were provided and made available during all hours of interviewing.

Organization of Data Collection Activities

For approximately one year preceding the survey, beginning in April 1989, ICR conducted Stage I of the National Jewish Population Survey (NJPS). This entailed incorporating a series of four screening questions into its twice weekly general market telephone surveys. The screening questions determined Jewish qualification and thus were the basis for the recruitment of households. The four screening questions in Stage I were asked in the following order:

1. What is your religion? If not Jewish, then . . .

2. Do you or anyone else in the household consider themselves Jewish? If no, then . . .

3. Were you or anyone else in the household raised Jewish? If no, then . . .

4. Do you or does anyone else in the household have a Jewish parent?

This screening stage of the survey obtained information on the religious preference of 125,813 randomly selected adult Americans and the Jewish qualification of their respective households. It was determined initially that 5,146 households contained at least one person who qualified as "Jewish" or Jewishly affiliated as determined by the screening questions. Stage II, the inventory stage, consisted of attempts to recontact Jewish households to requalify potential respondents and solicit participation in the 1990 NJPS. The households classified as Jewish in the last three months of screening were omitted from Stage II because the Stage III interviewing was to follow so closely. Stage II included 4,208 households. During Stage II, a number of households that were initially classified as Jewish dropped out of the survey sample due to changes in household composition or to disqualification based upon further review.

Stage III, the final interviewing stage of the survey, yielded a total of 2,441 completed interviews with qualified respondents. The statistics reported here are drawn from these households. Through a process of scientific weighting procedures utilizing all 125,813 Stage I interviews, the sample of Jewish households represents about 3.2 million American households nationally.

The survey interviews collected information about every member of the household. Thus, the study was able to ascertain important personal information about 6,514 persons in the surveyed households. Appropriate weighting procedures indicate that the number of persons in the surveyed households represents about 8.1 million individual Americans, a number of whom are not themselves Jewish, reflecting the mixed composition of the households in the Jewish sample.

Data Collection: First Two Phases— Screening and Recontact and Validation

Phase I: Screening

The entire screening phase was conducted as part of the ICR Survey Research Group's twice weekly telephone omnibus survey. The use of a telephone omnibus vehicle as opposed to a custom survey has obvious cost advantages; on the other side, there may be trade-offs relative to response rates; length of field period; placement of the screening questions on Jewish identity within the ever changing instrument, and so forth. However, these were felt to be small.

As mentioned earlier, 125,813 screeners were completed for this project. Although no formal disposition of call results is available, it is known that the proportion refusing to participate in any given weekly survey averages about 45%. In order to assess the potential bias resulting from this response rate, two separate analyses were conducted. They are described in Section 9.

Phase II: Recontact and Validation

The second phase of the study was conducted with respondents from Jewish households identified during the initial Screening Phase. This phase was designed to validate the initial screening process; initiate contacts with qualified households to explain the purpose of the study and gain cooperation; and provide a means of keeping in touch with the qualified respondents given the extended time period between the initial screening and final interview.

The primary informational objectives of the Recontact/Validation Phase were as follows:

1. Validate that the respondent/household was, in fact, Jewish

2. Explain the purpose of the call and encourage respondents to participate in the in-depth study during the summer of 1990

3. Collect detailed household data relating to age, sex, and relationship of each household member, and type of residence and location

4. Request and secure a third party reference to assist in the future recontact for the in-depth study

Recontact Phase interviewing was conducted over a 52-week period, from April 7, 1989, through April 2, 1990. The process was continuous, with most recontacts occurring within two weeks of the initial qualification in the Screening Phase.

Upon successful recontact, the household member who participated in the Screening Phase was asked to re-verify the Jewish character of himself/herself and other household member relative to:

- Being Jewish

- Considering himself/herself Jewish

- Being raised Jewish

- Having Jewish parent

Respondents were asked to participate in an in-depth Main Study Phase interview to be conducted at a later date. This recruitment included an explanation of the study, the size of the study, an explanation of how and why they were selected to participate, and the naming of CJF as the study sponsor.

Substantial efforts were made to "convert" respondents who refused to participate. Respondents who refused to participate at the introduction or during the interview itself, were recontacted by specially trained interviewers. These interviewers used specially developed and proven techniques to convert refusals into participants. In some cases, alternative respondents within a given household were recruited to participate. In addition to specially trained interviewers, letters of explanation were mailed to refusals in an effort to establish credibility for the study and, in turn, to increase likely participation.

A household inventory of requalified Jewish households was created; this roster of household members included age and sex, along with each member's relationship to the primary contact person. Specifically, four questions were asked about each household member:

1. Name

2. Age and sex

3. Relationship to the respondent

4. Religious qualification

Additional information relating to household characteristics was also requested; specifically, the type of household unit (e.g., multiple family, single unit, apartment, etc.) and whether this particular unit was the primary residence or a seasonal or similar recreational dwelling.

Finally, information about third-party references (i.e., a relative or close friend) was requested for use in the event that respondents could not be reached at their original location. This third-party information was utilized to "track" the original respondents during the final phase of interviewing.

Not every Jewish household identified in the Screening Phase was included in the Recontact Phase. Specifically, households identified during the final three months of screening were excluded because of the rather short time until onset of the full national survey; it was thought that the risk associated with alienating respondents by attempting multiple contacts over a very short period of time outweighed the few households likely to be lost due to relocation.

In total, 4,208 Jewish households identified in the Screening Phase were included in the Recontact Phase. The results of attempted recontact are shown below. It should be noted that there was no strict callback rule, but rather "nonrespondent households" were continually recycled, with many receiving twenty attempts or more.

About 80% of the screened and qualified households were successfully contacted and re-interviewed; of these, 15.5% did not requalify, and 6.3% disavowed knowledge of the previous interview. Just over 9% refused the Recontact interview.

None of the original respondent households were excluded from the 1990 survey based on results of the Recontact Phase; the purpose here was to facilitate tracking of respondents and increase ultimate cooperation, not to requalify, validate, and reject sample households. Although the Recontact data were retained,

TABLE A.1
Results of the Recontact Validation Phase

	Number	Percent
Total	4,208	100.0%
Requalified and Willing to Participate	2,124	50.5
Requalified and Not Willing	316	7.5
Not Requalified	652	15.5
No Such Respondent	266	6.3
Refused at Start	315	7.5
Refused During Interview	75	1.8
Language Barrier	27	0.6
Nonworking	135	3.2
Nonhouseholds	20	0.5
No Contact	278	6.6

all sample households (including those that failed to qualify in Phase II) regardless of the outcome were again attempted during the final phase of interviewing.

Phase III: Main Study—Data Collection

In the spring and summer of 1990, the third and final phase of data collection was undertaken. The survey instrument itself was initially developed by the NTAC, jointly pretested with ICR, and prepared for CATI interviewing by the ICR.

In the Main Study Phase, households that were identified as being Jewish in the screening phase were recontacted between May 8, 1990, and August 12, 1990, in an effort to complete the in-depth, detailed information requested on the Jewish character of the household, its members, and related issues. Due to the considerable interview length (approximately thirty minutes), the questionnaire was divided into two parts: the "core" questionnaire and three shorter questionnaire "modules."

The core questionnaire was asked of all respondents. In addition to this core, respondents were randomly assigned to one of three groups and asked a series of more detailed questions relating to one of the following areas of inquiry (referred to as modules):

1. Jewish identity

2. Social services

3. Philanthropy

The Screening Phase had identified a total of 5,146 Jewish households over more than fifteen months of interviewing, and surveying a total of over 125,000 households. As table A.2 shows, 49% of these resulted in completed Phase III interviews; just over 15% refused to participate; and in only 13% of the cases was it impossible to contact any household members.

The most difficult and puzzling result however, were the roughly 18% of respondents and/or households that failed to requalify; all of these respondents were recontacted a second time during Phase III, and all failed to validate their replies in the Screening Phase. Sections 7 and 9 contain a discussion of this group of respondents and describe how they were used in estimating the size of the Jewish population.

It was also a standard practice to attempt conversion of all refusals, so that all of this group represents "double refusals." All telephone numbers reported as nonworking were verified and attempts to secure new numbers were made, although this was not very successful. There was no limit on number of followup attempts, which explains the relatively low proportion of No Answer and Busy sample dispositions (< 4%).

Weighting Procedures

Overview of Weighting Procedures

After the survey information was collected and processed, each respondent was assigned a weight. When the weights are used in tabulations of the

TABLE A.2
Results of the Main Study Phase

	Number	Percent
Total	5,146	100.0%
Nonworking	366	7.1
Nonhousehold	63	1.2
No Answer/Busy	191	3.7
Respondent No Longer There	23	0.4
Answering Machines	101	2.0
Refused at Start	670	13.0
Refused During Interview	126	2.4
Language Barrier	21	0.4
Ineligible	146	2.8
Not Requalified	908	17.6
Deleted/Not Used Interviews	25	0.5
Completed Interview	2,506	48.7

survey data, the results automatically provide estimates of the U.S. Jewish population in each category shown in the tabulations.

The weighting method first insured that key demographic characteristics of the adult population of the total weighted sample of the 125,813 screened responding households matched the most current estimates of these demographic characteristics produced by the Census Bureau. The weighting procedure automatically adjusted for noncooperating households, as well as for those who were not at home when the interviewer telephoned and for households who did not have telephones or had multiple lines.

A second step in the weighting was carried out on the questionnaires completed in the recontact and validation phase and the main study phase of the study. This step made the weighted totals of completed questionnaires in each phase of the survey conform to the geographic and demographic profile of Jewish households at the earlier phases.

In addition, a separate weighting routine was established for each of the modules that was based on a subsample of the full set of Jewish households, so that the weighted total of each module corresponded to the full sample.

Detailed Description of Weighting

There were four stages in the preparation of the screening sample weights. First, households with more than one residential telephone number were assigned weights designed to compensate for their higher probabilities of selection—one-half for households with two telephone numbers, and one-third for households with three or more numbers. Secondly, cooperating households were poststratified, using 18 geographic strata—9 Census Divisions, and 2 categories for in or out of metropolitan areas. In the third stage, a weight was derived by poststratifying the weighted counts of the population in the sample households, using geographic-demographic strata, to the best current estimates of those strata. The strata comprised Census Region (4), age by sex (12), education of respondent (3), and race, that is, white or other (2). The fourth stage was geographic poststratification at a state, metropolitan statistical area (MSA), or county level, depending on the size of the area. Individual counties with 75,000 or more households became individual strata. The remaining counties were grouped by individual MSAs or, when necessary, linked to a larger county (over 75,000 households) within the same MSA. Counties outside MSAs were grouped at the state level.

Following the weighting processes described above, the completed screener interviews were classified by their initial level of Jewish qualification and the results of the subsequent data collection efforts. During the various interviewing phases, a significant number of Jewish households that were initially considered qualified, subsequently became classified as non-Jewish. The largest proportion of these households were originally qualified because

TABLE A.3
Qualified Jewish Households in Screener
by Reporting Status in Validation Interview

Reporting Status of Later Interviews	Basis of Qualification in Screener				
	Total	Religion	Consider	Raised	Parents
Total	3,753,000	1,737,000	1,347,000	195,000	474,000
	100.0%	46.3%	35.9%	5.2%	12.6%
Known Jewish	1,896,000	1,167,000	460,000	80,000	189,000
Households	100.0%	61.6%	24.2%	4.2%	9.9%
Refused	506,000	242,000	176,000	29,000	59,000
Phase III	100.0%	47.8%	34.8%	5.7%	11.7%
Other	563,000	200,000	246,000	29,000	88,000
Nonresponse	100.0%	35.4%	43.8%	5.1%	15.7%
Not Qualified	789,000	128,000	466,000	57,000	138,000
	100.0%	16.2%	59.1%	7.2%	17.5%

the respondents or others in the households "considered" themselves to be Jewish. Table A.3 details weighted respondents by the basis for qualification and response category in the Phase II follow-up interview.

The critical issue was how to treat the "not qualified" in estimating the total number of Jewish households. The extreme alternatives were to ignore the requalification information altogether, essentially treating the "not qualified" as refusals; or taking the additional information at "face value" and reducing the estimates of Jewish households by 789,000, to just under 3 million.

Of course, there was a wide range of options in between. To aid in the evaluation of this situation, a DJN (Distinctive Jewish Name) analysis was conducted on the respondents qualified through the screening process. The first step in this process was obtaining a reverse match for these telephone numbers; for each telephone number corresponding to a household that was listed in the white pages of any U.S. telephone directory, the name and address of the subscriber was obtained. The surnames were then matched against a data file of distinctive Jewish surnames provided by the NTAC. The results are shown in Table A.4.

As is evident from table A.4, the Not Qualified segment exhibits strikingly different proportions of DJNs from the other groups. Based on this and related information, the determination was made that all respondents originally qualified on the basis of religion were most likely refusals, and should

TABLE A.4
Percentage of Sample with Distinctive Jewish Surnames
(Base = Qualifiers with a Located Surname)

Reporting Status of Later Interviews	Basis of Qualification in Screener				
	Total	Religion	Consider	Raised	Parents
Known Jewish Household	16.7	23.3	5.6	10.5	4.8
Refused Phase III	13.8	20.0	8.0	9.5	7.8
Other Nonresponse	10.9	21.2	4.9	6.7	3.8
Not Qualified	2.6	8.6	1.5	0.0	1.6

TABLE A.5
Final Estimates of Jewish Households
Reflecting Adjustments to "Not Qualified" Call Results

Reporting Status of Later Interviews	Basis of Qualification in Screener				
	Total	Religion	Consider	Raised	Parents
Total	3,208,000	1,737,000	963,000	148,000	360,000
	100.0%	54.1%	30.0%	4.6%	11.2%
Known Jewish Household	1,896,000	1,167,000	460,000	80,000	189,000
	100.0%	61.6%	24.2%	4.2%	9.9%
Refused Phase III	506,000	242,000	176,000	29,000	59,000
	100.0%	47.9%	34.8%	5.8%	11.6%
Other Nonresponse	563,000	200,000	246,000	29,000	88,000
	100.0%	35.4%	43.8%	5.1%	15.7%
Not Qualified	244,000	128,000	82,000	10,000	24,000
	100.0%	52.4%	33.6%	4.1%	9.9%

remain as qualified Jewish households; conversely, among the other groups, the unweighted ratios of DJNs indicated a likely true qualification rate of 17.5%.

On the basis of these assessments, the estimated Jewish households were adjusted to those shown in table A.5. The impact of these adjustments were to reduce the estimates of Jewish households from 3.753 million to 3.208 million, a reduction of about 14.5%.

The adjustments to the weighted estimates of Jewish households required a two-phase adjustment to the weighted data set:

1. The indicated proportions of Not Qualified Respondents needed to be weighted downward to the indicated totals, while non-Jewish households required a compensatory weight to maintain Total Household in the entire screening sample.

2. The completed Phase III interviews were then weighted to the estimates of Total Jewish Households, for analyses based on Jewish households only.

The first step, was accomplished by stratifying based on Census division, and within division, by (1) non-Jewish qualifiers; (2) households qualified in the screener as Jewish based on other than religion, who became "not qualified" in Phase III; and (3) all other Jewish households. The second group represent those respondents whose estimate of Jewish affiliation was to be adjusted in this process. The revised weights were substituted in the individual data records, completing reconciliation of the full screener data set.

The procedure described above was carried out for the full sample and is therefore applicable to the core questionnaire that was administered to all sample households. However, each sample data record also includes a module weight in addition to the household and population weights for the core questions. The weighting procedure for the modules duplicated that of the previous section; a poststratification scheme incorporating census region and level of Jewish qualification. A simple expansion factor, to weight each module's sample total in each cell was computed, multiplied by the household weight, and incorporated into the sample record.

Separate population weights were also developed for the statistics obtained from the randomly selected adult in each household. Essentially, these weights incorporated the household weights multiplied by the number of adults in the sample households.

Application of Weights

Given the character and complexity of the survey instrument itself, a determination as to which of the weights described above to utilize for a particular statistic is not always apparent. The following explanation and examples should help in eliminating uncertainties.

Household weights should be used for developing estimates in the following types of situations:

1. Where the analysis, table, or distribution being produced is clearly based on household demographics. Examples include:
   - The number of households by level of Jewish qualification
   - Distributions of households by number of children, number of adults, number of Jewish adults, age of oldest member, or household income distributions
   - Household distributions based on qualification of one or more members; such as "Are you or any member of your household currently a member of a synagogue or temple?"

2. Where the analysis or distribution utilizes variables constructed from the roster of household members. Examples include:
   - Age or educational attainment of all household members or, subsets of all members
   - Country of origin, or employment status, of all household members, or adult household members

The Population Weights are applicable only in those situations where the respondent answers to a specific question about himself or herself are to be utilized to represent all adult members in Jewish households. For example:

- Opinions about various public issues

- Distributions of Jewish religious denomination, or Jewish ethnicity

- Personal attendance at Jewish religious services

In certain rare situations users may need to devise their own weighting schemes to establish a fully weighted sample base. This is most likely to occur when the adult members of a sample household exceed the number for which data was requested. For example, detailed information as to marital status was requested for only four members eighteen years of age and older. If a particular sample household had five members, there are a number of options depending upon one's objectives and the characteristics of the household:

- A balance line of "not-reported" could be incorporated into the tables being produced.

- The simplest weighting method would be to weight each of the four responses by 1.25 in addition to application of the household weight. Depending, however, upon the characteristics of the member for which no data is available, alternative approaches might prove more desirable.

- If the missing number's data represented one of three adult children, a better approach might be to weight the data for the two children for which data is present by 1.5, while keeping the parent's weight at 1.0.

- Alternatively, one could compensate for the missing member information on an overall basis. For example, one could categorize all qualified members by age, sex, region, etc. using the household weights; categorize those for which data was reported in a similar matrix using the household weight; and finally computing a weight for each cell that would increase the base of those responding to the weighted total in the first matrix.

In most cases, the bias created by simply ignoring the small discrepancies will be minimal. However, the user needs to make these decisions on a case-by-case basis, possibly trying alternative methods and comparing the results.

Finally, the module weights should obviously be used for tabulations of items in any of the modules regardless of whether simple totals of module items are tabulated or there are cross-classifications with other nonmodule items.

Accuracy of Data

Nonsampling Errors

All population surveys are subject to the possibility of errors arising from sampling, nonresponse, and respondents providing the wrong information and the NJPS is no exception. The response rate to identify potential Jewish households, was approximately 50%. This is lower than most surveys that make efforts to insure high quality strive to achieve. (The low response rate was partially caused by the contractor's need for each set of sample cases assigned for interview to be completed in a few days. This made intensive followup in the screener impractical.) The concern over the effect of nonresponse on the statistics is not so much on the size of the nonresponse since this is adjusted for in the weighting, but on the likelihood that nonrespondents are somewhat different from respondents. Although variations in response rates by geography, age, sex, race, and educational attainment were adjusted for in the weighting, there was still the possibility that Jews and non-Jews responded at different rates.

To test whether this occurred at an important level, the telephone numbers of approximately 10,000 completed interviews and for about 10,000 nonrespondents were matched against telephone listings to obtain the household names, and the percentage of each group having distinctive Jewish names was calculated. The percentage for the completed cases was 1.38% and for the nonrespondents was 1.29%. The difference between the two is well within the bounds of sampling error. Although distinctive Jewish names account for a minority of all Jews, this test does provide support for the view that nonresponse did not have an important impact on the reliability of the count of the Jewish population.

In regard to errors in reporting whether a person is Jewish, previous studies indicate that the errors are in the direction of understating the count of the Jewish population, although the size of the understatement does not seem to be very large. A particular concern in the NJPS was the fairly large number of cases where respondents in households reporting the presence of one or more Jews in the screening operation, reversed themselves in the detailed interview. Of all households reported as having Jews in the screener, 18% were reported as nonqualified in the detailed interview. There was a possibility that this was a hidden form of refusal, rather than errors in the original classification of the households or changes in household membership.

A test similar to the one on refusals was carried out for the nonqualified households. The telephone numbers for the 5,146 households who were reported as Jewish in the screening interview were matched against telephone listings, and those with distinctive Jewish names (DJN) were identified. The detailed results of the match are reported in Section 7. They can be summarized as follow: in households that reported themselves as Jewish in the detailed interviews, 16.8% had DJNs. The rates were slightly smaller for refusals (13.9%) and for those who could not be contacted (10.9%). However, the percentage was only 2.9% for households that were reported as not Jewish in the detailed interview. It is, of course, possible that DJN households are less reticent than others in acknowledging to a telephone interviewer the fact that all or some of the household members are Jewish, but the evidence is that under reporting did occur, but not to a very serious extent. An adjustment in the weights of about 8% was made to account for the unreported Jews in the estimates of the total number of Jews. Since questionnaire information was not obtained for them, the statistics on characteristics of Jews may be subject to small biases if the Jewish nonqualifiers are very different from those who responded.

As mentioned earlier, other studies have reported that there is some understatement of reporting of Jewish heritage in interviews surveys. No adjustments were made for such possible understatement since firm data on its size does not exist. As a result, the estimate of the size of the Jewish population is probably somewhat on the low side.

It is not possible to quantify the effects of the relatively high nonresponse rates, the possibility that some respondents might have deliberately misreported their religious affiliations, errors arising from misunderstanding of the questions, or other problems in the data. As indicated above, the test done with the presence of Distinctive Jewish Names did not detect any important problems. Furthermore, comparisons of the estimates of total Jewish population with the results of local area surveys carried out in or near 1990, did not show any important discrepancies. The screener questionnaire that inquired about Jewish affiliations also identified other major U.S. religious groupings, and estimates of their membership corresponded reasonably well with independent estimates of the membership.

Consequently, all of the tests we were able to carry out failed to turn up any major problems in the data. However, it seems reasonable to assume that persons who did not respond are somewhat different from respondents, and the other potential sources of error must also have had some impact. When comparisons are made, either over time, or among subgroups of Jewish persons (e.g., between those with a relatively high level of Jewish education and others, persons with synagogue affiliation and unaffiliated, etc.), it would be prudent to avoid analyses or explanations of small differences, even if they are statistically significant. However, the evidence is that large and important differences do reflect real phenomena, and can be relied on.

Sampling Variability

Sample surveys are subject to sampling error arising from the fact that the results may differ from what would have been obtained if the whole population had been interviewed. The size of the sampling error of an estimate depends on the number of interviews and the sample design. For estimates of the number of Jewish households, the sample size is 125,813 screened households. The screened sample was virtually a simple random sample. As a result, it is very likely (the chances are about 95%) that the number of Jewish households is within a range plus or minus 3% around the estimate shown in this report. For estimates of the Jewish population, the range is slightly higher since sampling variability will affect both the estimate of the number of Jewish households and of the average number of Jews in those households. The 95% range is plus or minus 3.5%. These ranges are the limits within which the results of repeated sampling in the same time period could be expected to vary 95% of the time, assuming the same sampling procedure, the same interviewers, and the same questionnaire.

Unfortunately, due to the complex nature of the sample design and weighting method used in estimating the characteristics of the Jewish population, it is not possible to give a simple formula that will provide estimates of the standard errors for all types of estimates. To begin with, there are three basic samples embedded in the survey:

1. The household sample can be considered as the equivalent of a simple random sample of 2,441 households.

2. For population statistics based on data reported for all household members, the sample size is 6,514. However, for most estimates of this type, the standard errors will be greater than what would be achieved with a simple random sample of 6,514 because of the presence of intraclass correlation, that is the tendency of household members to be more alike than would be the case of persons chosen at random. The intraclass correlation introduces a design effect that should be superimposed on the simple formula for the standard error.

3. Population statistics based on data reported for only one household member, selected at random, are also based on a sample size of 2,441. However, since the chance of selection of any person depends on the number of adults in the household the sample is not equivalent to a simple random sample of 2,441. The varying probabilities of selection also create a design effect.

The standard error of an estimate of a percentage can be approximated by:

$$\sqrt{D.p.(1-p)/Rn}$$

where p is the estimated percentage, D is the design effect, R is the proportion of Jews in the segment for which percentages are computed, and n is the sample size, that is, 2,441 or 6,514. When percentages are computed of all Jewish households or persons, R is equal to one; when the base of the percentage is a subgroup of all households or persons (e.g., households observing certain rituals, all females, persons in a particular age group) the value of R is the fraction of all households or persons in that subgroup.

The value of D is one for household statistics. For population statistics, the value will depend on the item being estimated. Although it is possible to calculate an estimate of the value of D for each item (or alternatively, a relatively unbiased estimate of the standard error), we assume most analysts will not want to make the fairly extensive effort needed for such calculations. Guidelines for approximating D follow.

- As stated earlier, D can be considered equal to one for household statistics.

- For items based on data reported for all household members, D will be in the range 1 to 2.7. It will be close to one for percentages based on a subset of the Jewish population (e.g., adult males, currently widowed persons, persons born abroad, disabled, etc.). At the other extreme, the value will be close to 2.7 on items for which household members are likely to have similar characteristics (e.g., the percentage of Jews who belong to conservative congregations). The 2.7 is the average size of Jewish households, and when D has this value, the effect on the standard error is to treat the statistic as a household item with a sample size of 2,441 rather than a population item. For other types of percentages, the value of D will be somewhere in the 1 to 2.7 range; the more alike members of a household are likely to be, the greater should be the value of D used in the calculations.

- The value of D is about 1.2 for items based on data reported for only one adult in the household. This design effect reflects the effect on sampling errors of having varying probabilities of selection, depending on the household size. For example, adults living in one-adult households will have twice the chance of selection as those in two-adult households, three times the chance as those in households containing three adults, etc.

It should also be noted that the value of n is lower for items in the modules asked for a subsample of respondents than for other items. Since the modules are based on a one-third subsample, the sample size of 2,441 and 6,514 are reduced to 814 and 2,171. When the sample sizes used in the base of percentages are obtained by simply counting the number of records used in the calculations, the count automatically provides the value of Rn, and it is unnecessary to calculate R, or to be concerned over whether or not the item is one of the modules.

Appendix B

Total Survey Errors and the Comparison of the 1971 and 1990 Surveys

As suggested in appendix A, the process used to obtain a probability sample of survey respondents, such as is the basis of this work, always includes some sampling error. However, not all the errors encountered in survey work are a result of the sampling process. An important class of errors, called nonsampling errors, arises out of such things as inadequate questions, refusals to be interviewed, incomplete respondent answers, inability to contact the proper respondents, clerical errors in processing or coding interviews, and mistakes in data processing or analysis. "Nonsampling" errors would still be there even if the entire population were interviewed, and, thus, there were no sampling errors.

Nonsampling errors can be classified into two basic divisions: (1) random errors, and (2) biases. Random errors tend to cancel each other out in the long run. They include clerical mistakes in coding or data processing and minor interviewer errors. Biases consist of errors that have a cumulative effect and do not cancel out.

The total error in a survey—the result of the various sampling errors, random errors, and biases of a survey—is found by adding together the squares of their respective measurements and then taking the square root of this sum. In other words, the effects of all sorts of survey errors can be measured by the formula:

Total error = $\{[SE \text{ (sampling)}^2 + R \text{ (interviewer)}^2 + R \text{ (measurements)}^2 + R \text{ (coding)}^2 + R \text{ (analysis)}^2 + R \text{ (others)}^2] + [\text{Bias (sampling)} + \text{Bias (interviewer)} + \text{Bias (measurements)} + \text{Bias (coding)} + \text{Bias (analysis)} + \text{Bias (others)}]^2\}^{1/2}$

where $SE \text{ (sampling)}^2$ refers to the variance resulting from the sampling process; R stands for the random error effects of the indicated survey activities; $Bias$ stands for the biasing effects of the indicated survey activities.

169

FIGURE B.1
Combining Variable Errors and Biases to Get Total Error

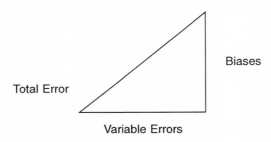

The square root of the sum of the sampling variance and the squares of the errors arising from the other sources of random error is usually referred to as the variable error.

These several error sources can be depicted by a right-triangle, as shown in figure B.1. In this diagram total error (the hypotenuse) is equal to the square root of the sum of the squares of the variable errors and the square of all the bias sources (the legs of the triangle). The illustration shows that survey errors cannot be controlled by a concern with sampling errors alone for much of the actual error in a survey can, and usually does, arise out of the other phases of the survey process. Fortunately, variable error can be reduced by increasing sample size. Unfortunately, biases cannot be reduced this way since they do not result from the sampling process.

Among the most common sources of biases in the data are those which result from failure of a prospective respondent in a sampled housing unit to be interviewed either because they refuse to be interviewed or cannot be found after a specified number of callbacks. Few, if any, survey measurements other than its geographic location can be made on such missed housing units or on the missing within–housing unit respondents.

The nonresponse rate is the major source of measurement bias in the 1990 survey. In the main, it is a consequence of the two-stage approach used to obtain survey respondents. The first stage obtained a very large sample of housing units by use of a random digit dialing sample design procedure. These housing units were then screened to determine if they included eligible Jewish residents.

Later, in another survey stage, those housing units found in the first stage to include one or more Jewish residents were recontacted. The goal was to interview one Jewish adult selected by a probability process from among all the Jewish adults in each eligible housing unit.

The overall or final response rate is the product of the response rates at each of the two stages. In the proceeding appendix section, the survey response rate has been estimated to be 50%.

Kish (1965: 535–71) gives several criteria by which to judge the import of a survey's nonresponse bias. He points out that

> a small nonresponse is unlikely to produce a large effect. . . . For estimating its effect on survey statistics, the size of the nonresponse must be linked somehow to estimates of differences between responses and nonresponses.

The 50% nonresponse rate of NJPS is, however, not small. We turn, therefore, to an attempt to judge if there are apt to be important differences between respondents and nonrespondents. Some clues may be found in the 1971 survey.

The earlier 1971 survey found that Jews not known to local Jewish communities, that is, Jews not on local Jewish federation lists, had lower response rates than Jews known to local federations. Those not known to federations had a 73% response rate; those known to federations, had an 82% response rate. Lazerwitz (1986) studied the differences between Jews not on federation lists who had or did not have what are known as Distinctive Jewish Names (DJNs), names commonly found among Jews and often associated with Jews. He concluded that those with Distinctive Jewish Names tended to be more traditionally inclined than those without such names.

Furthermore, in both national surveys, 1971 and 1990, those contacted for interviews were clearly told that the surveys were sponsored by the National Council of Jewish Federations. Presumably, those who agreed to be respondents were more interested in federations as a form of Jewish organization and in helping its work than those who refused to be interviewed.

All told, then, it seems reasonable to assume that Jewish nonrespondents are more marginal to Jewish life and their local Jewish communities, as represented by the local federation, than are Jewish respondents. For example, nonrespondents ought to be less likely to be synagogue members.

Using this judgment about synagogue membership and working with several different estimates on synagogue membership for nonrespondents, it is possible to develop estimates of total survey error. Among the 1,905 adult Jewish respondents to the 1990 survey that form the basis of this book, 47% were synagogue members. We can estimate the bias in the sample for each of three different possible levels of synagogue membership among nonrespondents: (a) that none (0%) of the nonrespondents are synagogue members; (b) that they join at half the rate of respondents, that is, 24%; or (c) at two-thirds the respondent's rate, that is, 31%.

The bias for the measure of synagogue membership is the difference between the reported synagogue membership in the survey minus the sum of the response rate (0.50) times the rate of synagogue membership (0.47) among respondents and the product of the response rate (0.50) and the rate (0.00, 0.24 or 0.31) at which nonrespondents are assumed to join synagogues.

172 JEWISH CHOICES

Thus, if adult respondent synagogue membership is 47% and we assume (a), that the nonrespondent synagogue membership is 0%, the bias is: $0.47 - [(0.50)(0.47) + (0.50)(0)] = 0.47 - (0.235 + 0) = 0.235$ or 24%.

If, however, we assume (b), that the nonrespondent synagogue membership rate is 24%; then the bias is: $0.47 - [(0.50)(0.47) + (0.50)(0.24)] = 0.47 - (0.235 + 0.12) = 12\%$.

Finally, if we assume (c), that the nonrespondent synagogue membership is 31%, then the bias is: $0.47 - [(0.50)(0.47) + (0.50)(0.31)] = 0.47 - (0.235 + 0.155) = 8\%$.

We can now calculate the total survey error for each of the three levels of assumed nonrespondent adult synagogue membership. The sampling error for 47% is 1.3% using the formula given in the preceding appendix, namely, $\sqrt{(1.2)(0.47)(0.53)/1,905}$. With a sampling error of 0.013, under assumption (a) with its bias of 0.24 (no nonrespondent synagogue membership), then Total Error $= \sqrt{0.000169 + 0.058} = 24\%$; under assumption (b), with its bias of .12, the Total Error $= \sqrt{0.000169 + 0.016} = 13\%$; under assumption (c), with a bias of 0.09, Total Error $= \sqrt{0.000169 + 0.0081} = 9\%$.

In all three calculations, the bias is greater than the small sampling error. Depending on the assumed level of synagogue membership among nonrespondents, the total survey error can vary from 9% to 24%. Those working with the statistics of the 1990 survey should take into account the likelihood of a total survey error that may be larger than the more easily computed sampling error. For example, rather than stating that synagogue membership is 47% plus or minus the sampling error of 1.2%, synagogue membership may be 47% plus or minus the 9% total error, assuming (c), a synagogue membership rate among nonrespondents two-thirds that of respondents.

When Dealing with Differences

Usually, analysts of the findings of the 1990 survey are concerned with the difference among two or more survey statistics rather than with individual statistics. Kish (1965: 536) states that "an important relative bias can occur only if the effect of nonresponse bias on one class mean is much different from that on the other," since biases tend to cancel each other out. For example, if a percentage of concern in one sample is 0.37 and in another it is 0.63, then the "real" difference between the two is:

$$(.37 \pm \text{bias}_1) - (.63 \pm \text{bias}_2) = (.37 - .63) \pm (\text{bias}_1 - \text{bias}_2)$$

To generalize, the difference between any two survey statistics, no matter what their biases, is the sum of the difference between the statistics and between their respective biases. If these biases are reasonably similar, the net bias of the difference can be considerably reduced. In addition, the sampling error of any difference is the square root of the sum of their separate variances. Working with a difference in percentages reveals both an increase in the sampling error of such a difference together with a decrease in its bias as an example from table 3.2 of chapter 3 shows.

Table 3.2 shows that 72% of Orthodox Jews are synagogue members while just 43% of Reform Jews are synagogue members in 1990. Suppose the nonresponse bias for Orthodox Jews is 15%, and, for Reform Jews is 30%. Then, their difference is not simply 29% (72% − 43%) but rather (72% ± 15%) − (43% ± 30%) = (72% − 43%) ± (−15% + 30%) = 29% ± 15%. Again, the smaller the nonresponse bias as the proportion of synagogue members among nonrespondents approaches that for respondents, the less their statistical difference need change to reflect the bias.

Using the 1971 Survey to Judge the Bias of the 1990 Survey

Given the design differences between the 1971 and 1990 surveys, considerable effort is required to compare properly their results as we have tried to do. Fortunately, both surveys obtained probability samples of the American Jewish population. (The sample design for the first survey is detailed by Lazerwitz, 1974a, 1974b. The second survey's sample was obtained by Random Digit Dialing among all United States residential telephones.)

Moreover, each survey randomly selected a sample household respondent from among the adult Jewish household residents. The first survey did so by use of the Kish (1949) selection table technique. The second survey used an equivalent approach called "The Next-Birthday Method of Respondent Selection" (Salmon and Nichols 1983), which was applied to all adult Jewish household residents.

When attention is turned from the selection of respondents to specific questions, other differences between the two surveys may also be noted. The wording of questions, especially with respect to the time frame involved, often differs in the two surveys. For example, with regard to frequency of synagogue attendance the 1971 survey asked: "How many times, if any, did (Person) attend Jewish religious services during the past twelve months?" A different wording was used in the 1990 survey which asked" "About how often do you personally attend any type of synagogue, temple, or organized Jewish religious service?" The two questions use different words to elicit the desired information about the same "fact," the frequency of attendance at Jewish religious services. A specific time frame is mentioned in 1971 but not in 1990.

To ensure that differences in the wording of questions are not themselves the source of the differences between the responses to the two surveys, rather than differences in the "facts" referred to by the questions, every question used in contrasting the two surveys must be carefully scrutinized. Occasionally, differently worded questions about the same topic have been accepted as sufficiently equivalent to justify comparing responses to them. For example, it was assumed that the specific time frame of twelve months mentioned in 1971 is akin to the unknown time frame used in the second survey in the questions on attendance at Jewish religious services.

Overall, the major difference between the two surveys stems not from their sample design or from questions wording, but from their response rates. The first survey had a 79% response rate and yielded 5,790 interviews. The second survey obtained a 50% response rate for its 2,441 interviews. Fortunately, as we shall see, this difference is not a meaningful impediment to comparing the results of the two surveys.

One way of determining if valid comparisons can be made between the results of different surveys is to use equivalent statistics from a survey with a higher response rate (Kish 1965: 528–32). In our case, we take advantage of the fact that there are nineteen years between these two surveys on the same population group. That is, we project 1971 results nineteen years into the future and contrast them with actual 1990 results. Specifically, we reconstruct the samples in each year so as to include comparable aged groups.

Two steps are needed to accomplish the desired reconstruction. After taking them, we will be in a position to compare the results of the two surveys for similar age groups. First, we eliminate all respondents sixty years old and older from the 1971 interviews. By 1990, they would be eighty years or older and unlikely to have been included in the sample since many would have passed away or have been institutionalized by 1990. (Institutionalized individuals were not interviewed). The remaining 1971 respondents would, then, be 40 to 79 years old by 1990.

Second, we eliminate all those under forty years of age from the 1990 sample. Such people would have been too young to be included in the first survey. Of course, our reconstruction would be improved if life table survivor rates were applied to the 1971 data. Also, we are assuming compatible rates of Jewish characteristics for the two survey populations.

Table B.1 shows that the percentages projected for the 1971 survey (with its 79% response rate) and the corresponding 1990 percentages are surprisingly close. In all, nine comparisons have been made. Among them, responses to the four questions on keeping separate meat and dairy dishes, membership in Jewish organizations, denominations, and synagogue membership, are quite close. Their average difference or "bias" is a mere 2%. The percentage distributions for the question on lighting candles at Hanukkah

TABLE B.1
Contrasting Various 1971 and 1990 Survey Percentages on Equivalent Age Groups
(Questions and Percentages)

	Separate Meat and Dairy Dishes		No. Jewish Org. Memberships				Jewish Denominational Preference				Light Hanukkah Candles		Kosher Home		Fast on Yom Kippur		Among Friends, Number Jewish			Syn. Membs.		Synagogue Attendance			
	Yes	No	0	1-2	3-4	5+	Orth.	Cons.	Ref.	None	Yes	No	Yes	No	Yes	No	None/Few	Some	Most/All	Yes	no	0	1-5	6-24	25+
1971 Respondents who are 40 to 79 years by 1990 (n = 3,973)	18%	82%	58%	30%	9%	3%	8%	43%	34%	15%	82%	18%	25%	75%	50%	50%	10%	26%	64%	50%	50%	28%	34%	27%	11%
1990 Respondents 40 years and over (n = 1,104)	16%	83%	60%	28%	9%	3%	6%	42%	37%	15%	71%	29%	18%	82%	59%	41%	13%	31%	56%	49%	51%	17%	34%	31%	18%

time differs by 11%; that for keeping a kosher home by 7%; fasting on Yom Kippur by 9%; having most or all Jewish friends by 8%; and attending synagogue twenty-five or more times by 7%. Interestingly, the direction of these differences is not the same in all cases. With respect to lighting candles at Hanukkah time, keeping a kosher home, and Jewish friends there is a decline from 1971 to 1990; with respect to fasting on Yom Kippur and synagogue attendance, there are increases. The average difference or "bias" for these latter questions is −10%.

Taken as a whole, these questions do not indicate a consistent or sizable bias. The replies are close enough to warrant careful analysis work with the 1990 survey. Then, too, many of the statistics studied here are more complex than mere percentages. Kish (1965: 527) points out that the impact of a survey bias, such as those arising from nonresponse, is considerably lessened for contrasts between two means or percentages than for a single percentage. Moreover, the impact of bias can be considerably reduced when using regression coefficients, as we often do.

Furthermore, the variables of central interest to this study are slowly changing ones such as denominational preference, synagogue membership and synagogue attendance. Respondents and nonrespondents likely differ little on such slowly changing variables so that the potential nonresponse bias would be considerably reduced.

To summarize, it would appear likely that for the variables of concern here, especially in light of the use of powerful statistical models, and the consistent change patterns, the nonresponse bias in the 1990 survey is not serious enough to inhibit meaningful analysis or conclusions.

The Weighting System Used in This Monograph

The 1990 NJPS employs a rather complicated weighting scheme, as indicated in the preceding methods appendix (see also Marketing Systems Group 1991, section 7). In part, the scheme is designed to meet two important needs: (1) to compensate for possible varying number of telephone lines per sample housing unit; and (2) to compensate for the varying number of Jewish adults per sample housing unit. In addition, a number of other weights are employed that are regular features of the standard, and complex, sample used by the market research firm that did the sample design and field work for the 1990 survey. For instance, weights are used since most firm samples will include approximately equal numbers of male and female respondents. That is, a weighting scheme is used to adjust for the fact that the housing units in the adult population contain more women than men. The regular sample design also has built into it a design feature called "sample balancing." It results in compensating for the number of nonresponse housing units and adults. It also adjusts for a number of other variables such as region, respondent education, age, or race. Finally, the product of all these weights and adjustment procedures have been converted to a housing unit weight and a population weight for each housing unit. For the 1990 survey these weights have been transmitted along with all the other data to those who analyze survey results.

Finally, while adjusting for nonresponse housing units is feasible for the estimate of population sizes, it is not useful for estimates of Jewish adult characteristics measured by means, variances, regression coefficients, and the like. It is axiomatic in social science survey analysis that weighting schemes do not compensate for missing data due to nonresponses to a survey.

Thus, our analyses of the data of the 1990 NJPS do not need to use the quite complex weighting scheme discussed in appendix A. The data used in the analytic work in this monograph are, instead, weighted by the number of adult Jews in each sample housing unit, which can be obtained from the survey itself. (The transmitted survey data do not include the number of telephone lines per sampled housing unit. Fortunately, the bias from neglecting this weight factor is relatively small and does not add significantly to the difficulties of analyzing the data.)

Table B.2 shows that the use of a weighting scheme based on the number of Jewish adults per sample housing units is equivalent to the weighting scheme developed for the 1990 survey.

It also reports the total adult (or population) weights for the complex weighting scheme and for the simplified approach used here together with household weights and sample sizes. Note that the complex weighting system uses the full 2,441 interviews while the simplified scheme is based upon just the 1,905 households that have at least one Jewish adult and excludes the 536 interviews with households none of whose adults are Jewish (but at least one adult had one Jewish parent).

The simplified weighting scheme differs considerably, on a household basis from the complex scheme on synagogue membership. However, when the 536 households that we do not regard as including a Jewish individual and who, thus, do not have a synagogue membership are included, the household synagogue membership percentage slips to 31%. However, with respect to denominational preference of adults, the percentages are similar regardless of the weighting scheme. Finally, with respect to synagogue attendance, if the 536 interviewees who would very likely never attend a synagogue service are added into the "not at all" attending category for the simplified weighting scheme, the two sets of percentages are again quite close. These figures indicate that the major weighting factor for Jewish adults derives from the number of Jewish adults per household and not nearly as much from the other weight factors in the complex scheme.

TABLE B.2
Contrasting the Complex and Simplified Weighting Schemes
for the 1990 NJPS Survey

	Complex Scheme	Simplified Scheme
1. Total Adult (Population) Weights	608,303	3,014
2. Total Household Weights	318,582	1,905
3. Sample Size	2,441	1,905
4. Has a Synagogue Membership		
a) Household basis	27%	40%
b) With the 536 non-Jewish households add in with zero memberships	—	31%
c) Jewish adult basis	—	47%
5. Denominational Preference: Jewish Adults		
Orthodox	6%	6%
Conservative	38%	37%
Reform	41%	39%
No preference	15%	18%
6. Synagogue Attendance: Jewish Adults*		
Not at all	31%	29%
1–2 times per year	31%	30%
A few times per year	17%	18%
Once a month	7%	9%
More than once a month	14%	14%

* The 17% coded "not ascertained" excluded in complex scheme.

How the 1971 and 1990 Surveys
are Similar and Different

Sample Designs

The 1971 survey employed a multistage, clustered, stratified, sample design to obtain a probability sample of the 1971 American Jewish population. The 1990 survey employed a Random Digit Dialing (RDD) design to obtain a probability sample of the 1990 American Jewish population. Since both samples were probability samples, their difference can best be seen in the sampling errors generated by their sample designs. Like cluster samples in general, the 1971 survey has a larger sampling error than the 1990 survey, whose design gives a sampling error relatively near to simple random sampling. As detailed in Lazerwitz (1974b), the sampling error for the 1971 survey is 3.5 times its simple random sampling equivalent. In the section on sampling variability in appendix A, Waksberg reports the sampling error for the 1990 survey to be $\sqrt{1.2} = 1.1$ times its simple random sampling equivalent for Jewish adults. However, for items for which household members have similar characteristics, such as synagogue membership, sampling error can increase to $\sqrt{2.7} = 1.6$ times its simple random sample equivalent.

Response Rates

A major difference between the two surveys are their response rates. The 1971 survey had a response rate of 79%. The 1990 survey had a response rate of 50%.

Contrasting Survey Statistics

If we contrast, say, a 50% Jewish adult statistic from the 1971 survey with a 50% Jewish adult statistic from the 1990 survey we get:

Total Survey Error for Differences between 1971 and 1990 = $\{(\text{var}_{90} + \text{var}_{71}) + [(\text{statistic}_{71}) - \text{its bias}_{71} - (\text{statistic}_{90}) - \text{its bias}_{90}]^2\}^{1/2}$

First, using the generalized sampling error tables for 1971 found in Lazerwitz (1974b), which gives 12.25 as the design effect for the first NJPS survey and a statistic of 0.50 for respondents together with 5,700 interviews, the variance for 1971 is: $(0.046/2)^2 = 0.000529$. Then, using the sampling error formula presented in the sampling variability section of appendix A of 0.50 for respondents with 2,000 interviews, and the 1990 design effect of 1.2, the variance for 1990 is: $(0.5)(0.5)(1.2)/2,000 = 0.3/2,000 = 0.000150$.

Hence, the sum of the variances for these two surveys is: $\text{var}_{71} = 0.000529$ and $\text{var}_{90} = 0.000150/0.000679$.

Then, if it is assumed that the corresponding statistic for nonrespondents is 0.24 for both survey years, together with the 79% response rate of 1971 and the 50% response rate of 1990, then the bias of 1971 is: $(0.50) - [(0.79)(0.50) + (0.21)(0.24)] = 0.50 - [(0.40) + 0.050] = 0.50 - 0.45 = 0.05$.

The bias for 1990 is then: $(0.50) - [(0.50)(0.50) + (0.50)(0.24)] = (0.50) - [(0.25) + (0.12)] = 0.50 - 0.37 = 0.13$.

The overall bias is, then, $0.13 - 0.05 = 0.08$; and total survey error becomes: $[(0.000679) + (0.08)^2]^{1/2} = (0.000679 + 0.0064)^{1/2} = (0.007079)^{1/2} = 0.084$.

Note that the total survey error for this hypothesized set of data differences consists of a variance contribution from the 1971 survey that is 3.5 times as large as the 1990 variance contribution, but a bias contribution from the 1990 survey that is 2.6 times as large as that for the 1971 survey. For practical purposes then, total survey error is dominated by the larger 1971 survey variance and the larger 1990 nonresponse bias. The RDD sampling technique of 1990 reduces survey variance, but this gain is offset by the nonresponse level of this later survey.

Quality of Field Work

The RDD telephone approach to interviewing provides better data quality during the course of interviews since interviewers are at one location, use a computer screen for interview questions, and have response categories also appearing on the computer screen together with being under the watchful eye of the interviewer supervisors. All these advantages of the 1990 survey over the more "traditional" field interviewing approach of the 1971 survey have been offset by the nonresponse rate of the 1990 survey.

Appendix C
Model Indices Cited in Chapter 4

The nine components of Jewish attitudes and behavior dealt with in this work are based upon those previously examined in Lazerwitz (1973, 1978), Lazerwitz and Harrison (1979), Harrison and Lazerwitz (1982), and York and Lazerwitz (1987). The components and their measurements are described below:

1. Childhood Jewish characteristics   Domination raised in; the degree of denomination involvement of one's parents

2. Jewish education   Amounts and types of Jewish education received through young adulthood

3. Denominational preference   Denominational preference in childhood and at present

4. Synagogue membership   Past and present synagogue membership

5. Attendance at religious services   Frequency of attendance at religious services

6. Home religious practices   Lighting candles on the Sabbath and during Hanukkah; attendance at a *seder* on Passover; the extent to which the kosher laws are observed in home; fasting on Yom Kippur

7. Involvement in Jewish primary groups   The extent to which one's friends and neighbors are Jewish; the extent to which marriage has been confined to Jews

8. Membership in Jewish voluntary associations	The number of memberships in Jewish voluntary associations; amount of activity in such voluntary associations; committee memberships and offices held in such associations; financial contributions to or raised for such organizations; amount of time spent in working for such Jewish organizations
9. Attitudes and activities regarding Israel	Attitudes toward and trips to Israel

Secular and Non-Jewish Attitudes and Activities

In addition to a concern with respondents' Jewish attitudes and activities, we have examined attitudes and behavior beyond the boundaries of Jewish institutions. In 1990 such survey items cover memberships in general (non-Jewish) community voluntary associations, self-definition as a political liberal or conservative, fertility, and intermarriage.

Forming Index Scores and the High, Moderate, and Low Categories

The questions pertaining to the nine dimensions of Jewish attitudes and activities, the secular dimensions of activity in general community voluntary associations, and political orientation were all formed into scores and subsequently categorized as high, moderate, or low.

The 1971 survey contained similar dimensions. Since a major goal of this monograph is to contrast the results of the 1990 survey with the 1971 survey, the same method of scoring and categorizing scores into high, moderate, and low levels used in analysis of the 1971 survey was used again in our analysis of the 1990 survey data. The use of similar scoring and categories enhances comparability between analyses of the two NJPS surveys.

To illustrate how the scoring and categorization has been done, we will refer to the components of the dimension of home religious practices. Eight survey questions are relevant to this dimension:

1. Did a respondent refrain from eating on the "Fast of Esther?"

2. The frequency of lighting Sabbath candles in a respondent's home

3. The frequency of attending Passover *seders*

4. Did a respondent's home observe the kosher laws?

5. Did a respondent's home have separate dishes for dairy and meat foods?

6. The frequency of Hanukkah lights' being lit in a respondent's home

7. The extent to which a respondent refrained from handling money on the Sabbath

8. The extent to which a respondent fasted on Yom Kippur

For the 1990 survey, then, the eight home religious behavior questions were scored, as they had been with the 1971 survey data, as follows:

- The responses to questions on lighting Sabbath candles, lighting Hanukkah candles, attending *seders*, keeping kosher, having separate dishes have the same codes and were scored as follows: "Always," 3 points; "Usually," 3 points; "Sometimes," "Never," "Don't know," or refusal, 0 points.

- Responses to the question on the Fast of Esther were coded and scored as follows: "Yes," 5 points; "No," "Don't know," and refusal, 0 points.

- The responses to the question on refraining from handling money on the Sabbath were scored as follows: "Yes, does not handle money," 3 points; "No, handles money," "Don't know," and refusal, 0 points.

- Responses to the question on fasting on Yom Kippur were scored: "Yes," 5 points; "No," "Have health problems," "Sometimes," "Don't know," and refusal, 0 points.

The next step was to add together the scores for the responses on the eight questions. The resulting overall score formed the dependent variable version of this dimension for regression analysis. Next, the scores for the 1,905 respondents were arrayed from the highest score down to the lowest. The percentile for each respondent's score was noted and then, as nearly as possible, the respondents who formed the first third (percentile 1 to 33 or so) were coded as 1, "high." The respondents falling into the middle third (right after the first cut down to the 67th percentile or so) were coded as 2, "moderate." The remaining respondents were coded as 3, "low." The high, moderate, low categorization was used when home religious behavior was treated as an independent variable. For illustrations of how this method has worked in practice, refer to Lazerwitz (1973, 1978), and York and Lazerwitz (1987).

The various demographic and socioeconomic variables were coded as follows:

- *Gender*
    1: Male
    2: Female

- *Age*
    - 1: 60 years of age and over
    - 2: 40 to 59 years
    - 3: 20 to 39 years of age
- *Generations in the United States*
    - 1: Foreign-born
    - 2: Born in the United States, but one or both parents foreign born
    - 3: Parents born in United States, but two or more grandparents foreign-born
    - 4: Three or more grandparents born in the United States
- *Marital Status*
    - 1: Currently married
    - 2: Has never been married
    - 3: Currently widowed, divorced, or separated
- *Family Life Cycle*
    - 1: One or more children 5 or younger
    - 2: One or more children 6 to 17
    - 3: No children 17 years of age or younger

The socioeconomic variables were coded as follows:

- *Education*
    - 1: Did graduate studies and/or has a graduate or professional degree
    - 2: University degree, but no graduate studies
    - 3: No university degree
- *Occupation*
    - 1: Professional or scientific occupations
    - 2: Technicians, elementary or high school teachers, administrators, managers
    - 3: All other occupations
- *Annual Income*
    - 1: $80,000 or more
    - 2: $40,000 to $79,999
    - 3: Under $40,000 per year

The following questions were used to form the remaining Jewish and communal involvement variables (home religious behavior has been given above):

Jewish Education

- What was the major type of schooling you received for your formal Jewish education?

- All together, how many years of formal Jewish education did you receive?

- Did you have a Bar or Bat Mitzvah celebration or Jewish confirmation when you were young?

- During the past year did you participate in any adult Jewish education programs?

- Do you have any paid subscriptions to Jewish periodicals, newspapers, or magazines?

Synagogue Attendance

- About how often do you personally attend any type of synagogue, temple, or organized Jewish religious services? The responses were scored as follows: "Not at all," 0 points; "Once or twice a year," "Only on special occasions," or "Only on high holidays," 1 point; "A few times a year," 3 points; "About once a month," 5 points; "Several times a month," "About once a week," or "Several times a week," 9 points.

Jewish Primary Groups

- Among the people you consider your closest friends, would you say that none, few, some, most, or all are Jewish?

- Which of the following best describes the Jewish character of your neighborhood: very Jewish, somewhat, little, not at all Jewish in character?

- How important is it to you that your neighborhood have a Jewish character: very important, somewhat, not very, or not at all important?

- If your child were considering marrying a non-Jewish person, would you strongly support, support, accept, be neutral, oppose, or strongly oppose the marriage?

- Did you or anyone in your household attend a Purim carnival or celebration this year?

- During the Christmas season does your household have a Christmas tree all the time, usually, sometimes, or never?

Activity in Jewish Community Voluntary Associations

- To how many Jewish organizations other than a synagogue or temple do you belong?

- In 1989, did you and/or other members of your household together contribute or give gifts to Jewish philanthropies, charities, causes, or organizations?

- In 1989, did you and/or other members of your household together contribute or give gifts to the Jewish Federation or UJA?

- How many hours in an average month do you spend in these Jewish volunteer activities?

- How much in 1989 did you and/or other members of your household together contribute or give to Jewish charities?

Israel Orientation

- Did you or anyone in your household celebrate Israel Independence Day in any way this year?

- Have you any close friends or immediate family living in Israel?

- How many times have you been to Israel?

- What is the longest time you spent in Israel?

- Has anyone in your household age six to twenty-five ever been to Israel?

- If you were to move to another country, what country would that be?

Activity in Non-Jewish Community Voluntary Associations

- To how many organizations that were not specifically Jewish did you pay dues in 1989?

- In 1989, did you and/or other members of your household together contribute or give gifts to philanthropies, charities, organizations, or causes that are not specifically Jewish?

- If so, how much was that?

- How many hours in an average month do you spend in these non-Jewish volunteer activities?

The Political Scale Question

- On a political scale, do you consider yourself generally very liberal, liberal, middle-of-the-road, conservative, very conservative?

Appendix D

Computation of the Projections in Chapter 7, Table 7.2

We hypothesis a group of 100,000 single adult Jewish men and women in 1990 who are distributed among the various basic denominational preference and synagogue membership groupings as are Jewish adults aged 20 to 44 in the 1990 survey. That distribution is shown in table D.1. Column 1 presents the percentages, while column 2, the number, in each of the eight adult groupings.

Columns 3, 4, and 5, respectively, give the percentages of each of three types of marriages:

1. Both spouses born into Jewish families (column 3)

2. One spouse born into a Jewish family, the other a convert to Judaism (column 4)

3. One spouse born into a Jewish family, the other not Jewish (column 5)

These figures are derived from the marriage and intermarriage rates for Jewish adults between the ages of 20 and 44. The next three columns, 6, 7, and 8, convert the percentages into the corresponding number of couples. The number of couples need not add up to the original number of adults since it takes two Jews to form one Jewish-Jewish couple, but just one Jew is involved in an intermarried couple. For example, the 18,000 single Jewish adults who prefer the Reform denomination and who actually join a Reform synagogue (the fifth grouping listed) translate into 4,770 all-Jewish couples, 6,120 Jewish-convert couples, and 2,340 mixed married couples. Adding these numbers together, while counting the 4,770 all-Jewish couples twice, yields the original number, 18,000, of Jewish adults in the appropriate line of column 2.

Since the combination of synagogue membership and synagogue attendance are the factors most closely related to fertility according to our regression equations, it is incorporated into our calculations. Synagogue attendance

TABLE D.1

Projection of Births by Denominational-Synagogue Membership Groupings

Grouping			Marriage Types			Number of Couples			% "Freq." Attenders		
	(1)	(2)	(3)	(4)	(5)	(6)	(7)	(8)	(9)	(10)	(11)
1990 Dist.	Adult Cohort %	Adult N	J:J %	J:C %	J:nJ %	J:J	J:C	J:nJ	J:J	J:C	J:nJ
Orthodox											
Member	5%	5,000	100%	0%	0%	2,500	0	0	85%	—	—
Not Member	2%	2,000	65%	23%	12%	650	460	240	0%	0%	0%
Conservative											
Member	19%	19,000	72%	20%	8%	6,840	3,800	1,520	53%	59%	0%
Not Member	15%	15,000	54%	2%	44%	4,050	300	6,600	10%	0%	0%
Reform											
Member	18%	18,000	53%	34%	13%	4,770	6,120	2,340	37%	57%	0%
Not Member	25%	25,000	39%	8%	53%	4,875	2,000	13,250	0%	0%	0%
No Preference											
Member	2%	2,000	65%	15%	20%	650	300	400	0%	0%	0%
Not Member	14%	14,000	24%	1%	75%	1,680	140	10,500	0%	0%	0%

Key: J:J: Each spouse born into a Jewish family.
     J:C: Marriage involving a convert to Judaism.
     J:nJ: Marriage of a Jew to a person who is not Jewish.

is divided into two categories, "frequent," once a month or more, and "infrequent," less than once a month. Columns 9, 10, and 11 show the percentage of frequent synagogue attenders for each of the types of couples, Jewish-Jewish, Jewish-convert, and mixed, for each of the eight basic groupings of denominational preference and synagogue membership.

At this point a major statistical limitation is encountered. The numbers of Jewish adults aged 20 to 44 have been distributed among twenty-four categories: eight basic groupings (four denominational groupings times the two categories of synagogue members and nonmembers) times the three types of marriage. The resultant sample size in any one of the twenty-four subgroups may be too small to permit the computation of reasonably stable estimates of synagogue attendance levels. Hence, the next best thing was done: the attendance figures for all Jewish adults, regardless of age, have been used. When this is done, the numbers are large enough for reasonable estimates of synagogue attendance for each of the twenty-four subgroups. Using the entire pop-

TABLE D.1 *(continued)*

Grouping	Number of Couples by Attendance					Number of Couples Raising Jewish Children		Number of Children Raised Jewish		Next Generation	
	(12)	(13)	(14)	(15)	(16)	(17)	(18)	(19)	(20)	(21)	(22)
1990 Dist.	J:J	J:J	J:C	J:C	J:nJ	Freq. Attend.	Other Attend.	at 2.4 Births	at 2.0 Births	Total	%
	Freq.	Other	Freq.	Other							
Orthodox											
Member	2,125	375	0	0	0	2,125	375	5,100	750	5,850	5%
Not Member	0	650	0	460	240	0	1,187	0	2,374	2,344	2%
Conservative											
Member	3,625	3,215	2,242	1,558	1,558	5,867	5,304	14,081	10,608	24,689	22%
Not Member	405	3,645	0	300	6,600	405	6,444	972	12,888	13,860	13%
Reform											
Member	1,765	3,005	3,488	2,632	2,340	5,253	6,447	12,607	12,894	25,501	23%
Not Member	0	4,875	0	2,000	13,250	0	11,850	0	23,700	23,700	22%
No Preference											
Member	0	650	0	300	400	0	1,093	0	2,186	2,186	2%
Not Member	0	1,680	0	140	10,500	0	5,806	0	11,612	11,612	11%
									Total	109,742	100%

ulation as a base, 53% of the members of Conservative synagogues, for example, who are in all-Jewish couples marriages are said to be frequent synagogue attenders, as are 59% of Jews married to converts, but none of the Conservative synagogue members married to non-Jews.

The percentages in columns 9, 10, and 11 are then used to generate the numbers in columns 12 through 16. Each of these columns represents the combination of four variables: denominational preference, synagogue membership, type of marriage and frequency of synagogue attendance. The original hypothetical cohort of 100,000 adults is now divided into 48 subgroups ($4 \times 2 \times 3 \times 2$) with, possibly, different levels of fertility.

On the basis of the findings above, all frequent synagogue attending couples will be assumed to have an average of 2.4 children and all other couples, 2.0. Since 97% of the Jewish-convert couples report that they are raising their children as Jews and 38% of mixed married couples report that they are doing so, we assume 100% of frequent attenders in conversionary marriages will raise Jewish children; that 97% of infrequent attenders in conversionary marriages will do likewise; and that 38% of mixed married couples will raise Jewish children. The numbers which result from these assumptions, the number raising their children as Jews, are found in columns 17 and 18. That is, column 17 shows the number of couples raising Jewish children who are frequent synagogue attenders for each of the eight basic groupings. Column 18 shows the corresponding number for infrequent synagogue attenders. This section uses the distinction between frequent and not frequent levels of synagogue attendance to obtain the total number of frequent and not frequent attenders by denominational-membership groupings. The number in column 17 is the sum of columns 12 and 14 since we assume all of the children of frequent synagogue attenders in homogeneous marriages will be reared as Jews. The number in column 18, for infrequent synagogue attenders, represents the sum of column 13, all of the intramarried Jewish couples, added to 97% of the conversionary marriages and 38% of the mixed couples, a sum reflecting the expected number who will raise their children as Jews.

The number of children expected to be raised as Jews can now be calculated by multiplying the number in column 17 by 2.4, the number of children expected among frequent synagogue attenders, and the number in column 18 by 2.0, the number expected for infrequent synagogue attenders. The number of children expected to be raised as Jews, for each combination of denominational preference and synagogue membership is found in columns 19 and 20, and then added to produce the numbers in column 21 and formed into percentages to produce column 22.

Notes

1. Denominations in American Religious Life

1. For a discussion of the classification of Protestant denominations, see Smith (1990, 1992). His (1992) tripartite division of Protestant denominations into fundamentalist, moderates, and liberals parallels the division among the Jewish denominations into Orthodox, Conservative, and Reform Judaism.

2. A Sociohistorical Overview of American Jewish Denominations

1. The ultra-Orthodox community of B'nai Brak in Israel serves as an interesting contrast. The religious leaders in this major Orthodox community have forbade the socializing of boys and girls in pizza and *falafel* (an Israeli fast food) shops. They have even forbade evening sit-down restaurant service for young singles. However, the norm in this Orthodox community still calls for arranged marriages at a relatively early age, so the need to have a place for singles to meet may be less pressing.

2. However, while few in number, Reconstructionists Jews do hope to become a fourth American Jewish denomination. Like Conservative Judaism from which it derives, Reconstructionist Judaism represents a wholly American response to the tension between tradition and modernity. Founded by Mordecai M. Kaplan, a faculty member of the Conservative Jewish Theological Seminary, Reconstructionism views Judaism as a civilization whose preeminent quality is its religion. That is, Kaplan argued, Jews constitute a people whose civilization and religious culture need reconstruction as a result of the undermining of tradition by modernity. This reconstruction has taken the form of de-emphasizing the supernatural in Judaism and emphasizing ritual enhancement, ethics, and aesthetic contributions. Initially, Reconstructionism represented a theological school of thought at the Jewish Theological Seminary. It has now developed its own organizational basis by forming the Federation of Reconstructionist Congregations and Havurot (1954), the Reconstructionist Rabbinical Seminary (1968), and the Reconstructionist Rabbinical Association (1974). (For an excellent review of the early development of Reconstructionist Judaism in the United States, see Liebman 1970.)

3. A General Description of the Adherents
of American Jewish Denominations

1. Other analyses of 1990 NJPS frequently use households, not individuals, as their unit of analysis and include interviews with all 2,441 respondents rather than just those we have defined as Jews. Consequently, the results of these analyses may differ somewhat from what is presented here. Such differences, however, are more apt to involve percentage differences than more complicated statistical analysis such as regression analysis prominent in this study. For example, if the 1,905 households are the basis of analysis, the percentage of (household) synagogue membership is found to be 40%. If the 2,441 individual interviews are the unit of analysis, the household rate of membership is 31%.

2. These additional 536 households are referred to as including "adults of Jewish parentage with another religion" in the initial report on the 1990 survey (Kosmin et al. 1991: 6). Since our focus in this study is on Jewish choices of those identifying themselves as Jews—that is, on their denominational preference, or lack thereof—we have excluded respondents who regard themselves as having been born Christian and as having remained so, that is, as not being Jews.

3. For a more detailed explanation of the formation of scales and indices, see chapter 4 and appendix C.

4. The issue of statistical significance for within and between the two surveys is extremely complex. It involves questions of total survey error and survey variance such as discussed in appendices A and B. It is our informed judgment that the differences noted in this chapter are too consistent to be random events.

5. Note that in table 3.4, the entries for categories with three subcategories, membership distribution, age, and marital status, add up to 100%.

6. Our major concern when forming categories of community size was to ensure there was a sufficient number of interviews in each category to permit sophisticated statistical analysis as is done in Rabinowitz, Lazerwitz, and Kim (1995).

4. The Components and Consequences
of Jewish Involvement

1. All statistics derived from the various path analysis equations are adjusted for colinearity. To simplify our discussion, the repeated use of the term "adjusted" is avoided.

2. For further information on how the scale scores and the index categories were calculated, see appendix C.

3. For the 1971 survey, betas with an absolute value of 0.07 or more (0.07 or more, or − 0.07 or less) are statistically significant ($p < 0.05$). For the 1990 survey, betas with an absolute value of 0.12 or more are significant statistically ($p < 0.05$). For

the combined survey, statisticaly significance ($p < 0.05$) is attained by betas with an absolute value of 0.05 or more. However, we regard only absolute values of 0.10 or more as sociologically meaningful.

The plus or minus (directional) signs used for a given beta reflect the values of the means of the subcategories of the two involved variables. For example, when computing the impact of a variable such as membership in Jewish organizations on the level of activity in general or non-Jewish organizations, we find that the level of activity in non-Jewish organizations increases with increasing numbers of memberships in Jewish organizations, hence a positive or plus sign. Specifically, the level of general activity is 4.1 among those in the low category of Jewish organizaional memberships, 7.2 among those in the moderate category, and 10.3 among those with a high category of Jewish memberships.

4. Details on the results of regression analysis of data from the 1971 NJPS can be found in: Lazerwitz (1973, 1978); York and Lazerwitz (1987); and Lazerwitz, Winter, and Dashefsky (1988).

5. Increased synagogue attendance may not unambiguously reflect an increase in religiosity. It may, for example, reflect greater attendance associated with preparation for a child's Bar/Bat Mitzvah and not with the religiosity of the parent. The conclusion offered here should be checked in the findings of future surveys directed at probing such matters.

5. Jewish Denominational Switching

1. A fuller explanation of the formation of model indices for both sets of predictor variables is found in chapter 4 and the appendix.

2. Following the convention developed by Lazerwitz (1978, 1980) and York and Lazerwitz (1987), beta coefficients between −0.09 and 0.09 are regarded as weak and not statistically relevant; beta coefficients from 0.10 to 0.19 or from −0.10 to −0.19 are considered of moderate strength; and those with a value greater than 0.20 or less than −0.20, are regarded as strong. If a test of statistical significance is applied, betas with an absolute value of 0.12 or more (0.12 or more; −0.12 or less) are significant ($p < 0.05$).

3. Of course, we do not know whether the denominational switching or the birth of a child came first.

4. For further information on denominational switching among American Jews, see Lazerwitz (1995a).

5. The dominance of Conservative Judaism among second-generation American Jews is discussed in Sklare's (1972) classic analysis of the denomination.

6. Denominational Preferences and Intermarriage

1. The analysis of intermarriage in this chapter is largely limited to the relationship between denominational preference and intermarriage. Other aspects of intermarriage

are examined by Lazerwitz (1995b) and will be covered extensively by another work in this series of monographs on the 1990 NJPS.

2. Among the 2,441 interviews of the 1990 survey, 25 were with former Jews who had converted to Christianity. Their marriages are not considered here given our focus on Jewish denominational preferences.

3. It takes two Jews to form one couple in which the spouses are each born Jewish, but only one Jew to form a religiously heterogeneous family. Hence, rates based on couples may differ from those based on individuals. In the former case, where two Jews form a religiously homogeneous marriage, and one enters an intermarriage, the intermarriage rate is 50%, one of two couples. However, if only individuals are considered, the rate is only 33% (one Jew of the three intermarried).

The reader is reminded that given the coding scheme used here for age and generations-in-the-U.S., those who are older and those who are first or second generation-in-the-U.S. are more likely than those who are younger or who are later generation Americans, respectively, to be in religiously homogeneous marriages.

4. The index of Jewish primary group involvement has been excluded from the analysis reported in table 6.9. When it was included, it dominated the equation and had a very large beta value. However, it is to be expected that those who have intermarried have both Jewish and non-Jewish primary group networks, the latter likely involving their non-Jewish relatives or friends of the non-Jewish spouse. Thus, intermarried Jews should have fewer involvements in Jewish primary networks compared to Jews in homogeneous marriages.

5. The categorization of beta coefficients introduced in chapter 4 applies here: values between −0.11 and 0.11 are termed "weak," those with an absolute values of between 0.12 and 0.19, are "moderate," and those with an absolute value of 0.20 or more are "strong."

6. The importance of community size has also been shown by Rabinowitz, Lazerwitz, and Kim (1995), who have analyzed the association of Jewish community size and Jewish involvement using both the 1971 and 1990 NJPS. They found that in 1971 synagogue membership and activity in both Jewish and non-Jewish voluntary organizations decreased as the size of the Jewish community increased, while Jewish community size was not associated with synagogue attendance or with home religious practices. Involvement in Jewish primary groups, however, increased as the size of the Jewish community increased. Moreover, they found that involvement in Jewish primary networks is even more sharply associated, that is, increases faster, with increasing Jewish community size in 1990 than it did in 1971. Furthermore, they found that in 1990, home religious practices, unlike in 1971, increased with Jewish community size. The relationship between other aspects of Jewish involvement and Jewish community size are essentially the same in 1990 as they were in 1971.

7. In table 6.10, a married respondent is scored "1" if both the respondent and the spouse were born into Jewish families; "2," if the respondent or the spouse is a convert to Judaism; "4," if one of the couple is a Christian; and "5," if one of the couple has no religious preference or prefers a religion other than Judaism or Christianity.

7. A Look Toward the Future

1. Our analysis of the 1990 survey is a bit different from that of Mott and Abma (1992). They included those Jewish women respondents who were 18 to 44 years old regardless of marital status. Their regression approach was ordinary least squares. We do not include women who have never married or women who are eighteen or nineteen years old. We also include information on the spouses of male respondents. The age limit of twenty is used because it is the limit used in the 1971 survey with which we want to compare our results. The statistical techniques used here have some technical advantages over that used by Mott and Abma in that they allow one to deal a bit better with colinearity, the use of ordinal and nominal scale measurements and interaction effects.

2. We also assume that the denominational preferences and synagogue memberships, fertility, and intermarriage rates for these adults will remain stable until the year 2010 and that they will marry and can bear children.

References

Abrahams, Israel. 1969. *Jewish Life in the Middle Ages*. New York: Atheneum.

Agus, Jacob. 1975. "The Reform Movement." Pp. 5–30 in *Understanding American Judaism,* Vol. 2, edited by Jacob Neusner. New York: KTAV.

Alba, Richard D. 1990. *Ethnic Identity: The Transformation of White America*. New Haven, Conn.: Yale University Press.

———. 1991. "Intermarriage and Ethnicity among European Americans." *Contemporary Jewry* 12: 3–19.

Andrews, Frank, James Morgan, and John Sonquist. 1969. *Multiple Classification Analysis*. Ann Arbor: Institute for Social Research, University of Michigan.

Andrews, Frank, and Robert Messenger. 1986. *Multivariate Nominal Scale Analysis*. Ann Arbor: Institute for Social Research, University of Michigan.

Aviezer, Nathan. 1990. *In the Beginning: Biblical Creation and Science*. Hoboken, N.J.: KTAV.

Babchuk, Nicholas, and Hugh Whitt. 1990. "R-Order and Religious Switching." *Journal for the Scientific Study of Religion* 29: 246–54.

Bar Lev, Mordechai. 1995. "Reasons for Leaving Orthodoxy." Symposium on Religion and Deviance, Bar Ilan University, March 29.

Bellah, Robert N., Richard Madsen, William M. Sullivan, Ann Swidler, and Steven M. Tipton. 1985. *Habits of the Heart: Individualism and Commitment in American Life*. Berkeley: University of California Press.

Birnbaum, Pierre, and Ira Katznelson (eds.). 1995. *Paths of Emancipation: Jews, States and Citizenship*. Princeton, N.J.: Princeton University Press.

Blalock, Hubert. 1969. *Theory Construction: From Verbal to Mathematical Formulations*. Englewood Cliffs, N.J.: Prentice Hall.

———. 1979. *Social Statistics* (2nd rev. ed.). New York: McGraw-Hill.

Blau, Joseph. 1966. *Modern Varieties of Judaism*. New York: Columbia University Press.

Bromley, David (ed.). 1988. *Falling from the Faith: Causes and Consequences of Religious Apostasy*. Beverly Hills, Calif.: Sage.

Bulka, Reuven P. (ed.). 1983. *Dimensions of Orthodox Judaism*. New York: KTAV.

Carroll, Jackson W. and Wade Clark Roof. 1993a. "Introduction." Pp. 11–27 in *Beyond Establishment: Protestant Identity in a Post-Protestant Age*, edited by Jackson W. Carroll and Wade Clark Roof. Louisville, Ky.: Westminster/John Knox Press.

———. 1993b. "Epilogue." Pp. 343–61 in *Beyond Establishment: Protestant Identity in a Post-Protestant Age*, edited by Jackson W. Carroll and Wade Clark Roof. Louisville, Ky.: Westminster/John Knox Press.

Cohen, Steven M. 1983. *American Modernity and Jewish Identity*. New York and London: Tavistock.

———. 1995. "Geographic Variations in Participation in Israel Experience Youth Programs: The CRB Foundation Geo-Coded Survey." *Journal of Jewish Communal Service* 71: 212–20.

Cohn, Werner. 1958. "The Politics of American Jews." Pp. 615–26 in *The Jews* edited by Marshall Sklare. New York: Free Press.

Cornwall, Marie. 1989. "The Determinants of Religious Behavior: A Theoretical Model and Empirical Test." *Social Forces* 68: 572–92.

Danzger, Herbert. 1989. *Returning to Tradition: The Contemporary Revival of Orthodox Judaism*. New Haven, Conn.: Yale University Press.

Dashefsky, Arnold. 1992. "What We Know about the Effects of Jewish Education on Jewish Identification." Pp. 103–14 in *What We Know About Jewish Education*, edited by Stuart G. Kelman. Los Angeles: Torah Aura Press.

Davidman, Lynn. 1991. *Tradition in a Rootless World: Women Turn to Orthodox Judaism*. Berkeley: University of California Press.

Della Pergola, Sergio. 1983. "Contemporary Jewish Fertility: An Overview." Pp. 215–38 in *Papers in Jewish Demography, 1981* edited by Uziel Shmelz, Paul Glikson, and Sergio Della Pergola. Jerusalem: Avraham Harmon Institute of Contemporary Jewry, Hebrew University.

Eisenstadt, S. N. 1992. *Jewish Civilization: The Jewish Historical Experience in Comparative Perspective*. Albany: State University of New York Press.

Elazar, Daniel. 1995 "The Future of American Jewry." *Contemporary Jewry* 16: 110–21.

Encyclopedia Judaica. 1971. Jerusalem: Keter.

Fein, Leonard J., Robert Chin, Jack Daucher, Bernard Reisman, and Herzl Spiro. 1972. *Reform Is a Verb*. New York: Union of American Hebrew Congregations.

Feingold, Henry L. 1995. "From Equality to Liberty: The Changing Political Culture of American Jews." Pp. 97–188 in *The Americanization of the Jews* edited by Robert M. Seltzer and Norman J. Cohen. New York and London: New York University Press.

Finke, Roger, and Rodney Stark. 1992. *The Churching of America, 1776–1990: Winners and Losers in Our Religious Economy*. New Brunswick, N.J.: Rutgers University Press.

Fischer, Claude. 1984. *The Urban Experience* (2nd ed.). New York: Harcourt Brace Jovanovich.

Fishman, Sylvia Barack, and Alice Goldstein. 1993. "When They Are Grown, They Will Not Depart: Jewish Education and the Jewish Behavior of American Adults." Research Report No. 8. Waltham, Mass.: Brandeis University, Cohen Center for Modern Jewish Studies.

Friedman, Howard I. 1991. "Response to Henry Feingold." Pp. 81–89 in *Jewish Identity in America* edited by David M. Gordis and Yoav Ben-Horan. Los Angeles: Wilstein Institute of Jewish Policy Studies.

Furman, Frida. 1987. *Beyond Yiddishkeit: The Struggle for Jewish Identity in a Reform Synagogue*. Albany: State University of New York Press.

Gans, Herbert J. 1979. "Symbolic Ethnicity: The Future of Ethnic Groups and Cultures in America." *Ethnic and Racial Studies* 2: 1–20.

Glazer, Nathan. 1989. *American Judaism* (2nd ed.). Chicago: University of Chicago Press.

———. 1995. "The Anomalous Liberalism of American Jews." Pp. 133–43 in *The Americanization of the Jews*, edited by Robert M. Seltzer and Norman J. Cohen. New York and London: New York University Press.

Glicksman, Allen. 1995. "The Future of the American Jewish Community: *Lo Zu Haderech*." *Contemporary Jewry* 16: 122–25.

Glock, Charles Y., and Rodney Stark. 1965. *Religion and Society in Tension*. Chicago: Rand McNally.

Goldscheider, Calvin. 1986. *Jewish Continuity and Change: Emerging Patterns in America*. Bloomington: Indiana University Press.

———. 1993. "A Century of Jewish Fertility in an American Jewish Community: Cohort Trends and Differentials." Pp. 129–44 in *Papers in Jewish Demography, 1989* edited by Uziel Schmelz and Sergio Della Pergola. Jerusalem: Avraham Harman Institute of Contemporary Jewry, Hebrew University.

Goldstein, Alice, and Sylvia Barack Fishman. 1993. "Teach Your Children When They Are Young: Contemporary Jewish Education in the United States." Research Report No. 10. Waltham, Mass.: Brandeis University, Cohen Center for Modern Jewish Studies.

Goldstein, Sidney, and Alice Goldstein. 1996. *Jews on the Move: Implications for Jewish Identity*. Albany: State University of New York Press.

Gordon, Milton. 1964. *Assimilation in American Life*. New York: Oxford University Press.

Greeley, Andrew. 1972. *The Denominational Society: A Sociological Approach to Religion in America*. Glenview, Ill.: Scott, Foresman.

————. 1991. "American Exceptionalism: The Religious Phenomenon." Pp. 94–115 in *Is American Different? A New Look at American Exceptionalism* edited by Byron E. Shafer. New York: Oxford University Press.

Greeley, Andrew, and Michael Hout. 1988. "Musical Chairs: Patterns of Denominational Change." *Sociology and Social Research* 72: 75–86.

Green, Arthur. 1994a. "New Directions in Jewish Theology in America: David W. Berlin Lecture in American Jewish Affairs." Ann Arbor: Frankel Center for Judaic Studies, University of Michigan.

————. 1994b. "Judaism for the Post-modern Era: Samuel H. Goldenson Lecture." Cincinnati: Hebrew Union College-Jewish Institute of Religion.

Greenberg, Blu. 1981. *On Women and Judaism: The View from Tradition*. Philadelphia: Jewish Publication Society of America.

————. 1996. "Ultra-Orthodox Women Confront Feminism." *Moment* 21 (June): 36–37, 63.

Greenberg, Irving. 1967. "Identity in Flux: Will American Jewish History Culminate in Renewal or Escape from Freedom into Dissolution?" *Congress Bi-Weekly* March 20: 8–16

Hadaway, Christopher. 1978. "Denominational Switching and Membership Growth: In Search of a Relationship." *Sociological Analysis* 39: 321–37.

Hadaway, Christopher, and Penny Long Marler. 1993. "All in the Family: Religious Mobility in America." *Review of Religious Research* 35: 97–116.

Hammond, Phillip E. 1992. *Religion and Personal Autonomy: The Third Disestablishment in America*. Columbia: University of South Carolina Press.

Hargrove, Barbara. 1989. *The Sociology of Religion: Classical and Contemporary Approaches* (2nd ed.). Arlington Heights, Ill.: Harlan Davidson.

Harris, Jay M. 1994. *"How Do We Know This?" Midrash and the Fragmentation of Modern Judaism*. Albany: State University of New York Press.

Harrison, Michael, and Bernard Lazerwitz. 1982. "Do Denominations Matter?" *American Journal of Sociology* 38: 356–77.

Heaton, Tim. 1986. "How Does Religion Influence Fertility? The Case of Mormons." *Journal for the Scientific Study of Religion* 25: 248–58.

Heilman, Samuel. 1992. *Defenders of the Faith: Inside Ultra-Orthodox Jewry*. New York: Schocken.

Heilman, Samuel, and Steven M. Cohen. 1989. *Cosmopolitans and Parochials: Modern Orthodox Jews in America*. Chicago: University of Chicago Press.

Helmreich, William. 1982. *The World of the Yeshiva: An Intimate Portrait of Orthodox Jewry*. New York: Free Press.

Herberg, Will. 1960. *Protestant-Catholic-Jew: An Essay in American Religious Sociology*. Garden City, N.Y.: Doubleday Anchor.

Horowitz, Bethamie. 1994. "Findings from the 1991 New York Jewish Population Study." *Contemporary Jewry* 15: 4–25.

Johnstone, Ronald J. 1988. *Religion in Society: A Sociology of Religion* (3rd ed.). Englewood Cliffs, N.J.: Prentice Hall.

Kalmijn, Matthijs. 1991. "Shifting Boundaries: Trends in Religious and Educational Homogamy." *American Sociological Review* 56: 786–800.

Kaufman, Debra. 1991. *Rachel's Daughters: Newly Orthodox Jewish Women*. New Brunswick, N.J.: Rutgers University Press.

Kelley, Dean. 1977. *Why Conservative Churches Are Growing*. New York: Harper & Row.

Kish, Leslie. 1949. "A Procedure for Objective Respondent Selection within the Household." *Journal of the American Statistical Association* 44: 380–87.

———. 1965. *Survey Sampling*. New York: Wiley.

Kosmin, Barry A. 1994. "The Need for a New Model for Jewish Continuity: A Response to Lipset's Remarks." *Contemporary Jewry* 15: 187–92.

Kosmin, Barry A., and Seymour P. Lachman. 1993. *One Nation under God: Religion in Contemporary American Society*. New York: Harmony Books.

Kosmin, Barry A., Sidney Goldstein, Joseph Waksberg, Nava Lerer, Ariella Keysar, and Jeffrey Scheckner. 1991. *Highlights of the CJF 1990 National Jewish Population Survey*. New York: Council of Jewish Federations.

Lazerwitz, Bernard. 1961. "A Comparison of Major United States Religious Groups." *Journal of the American Statistical Association* 56: 568–79.

———. 1964. "Religion and Social Structure in the United States." Pp. 426–39 in *Religion, Culture and Society* edited by Louis Schneider. New York: Wiley.

————. 1973. "A Multivariate Model of Religious Identification and Its Ethnic Correlates." *Social Forces* 52: 204–20.

————. 1974a. "The Sample Design of the National Jewish Population Survey." New York: Council of Jewish Federations.

————. 1974b. *Sampling Errors and Statistical Inference for the National Jewish Population Survey.* New York: Council of Jewish Federations.

————. 1977. "The Community Variable in Jewish Identification." *Journal for the Social Scientific Study of Religion* 16: 361–69.

————. 1978. "An Approach to the Components and Consequences of Jewish Identification." *Contemporary Jewry* 4: 3–8.

————. 1979. "Past and Future Trends in the Size of American Jewish Denominations." *Journal of Reform Judaism* 26: 77–82.

————. 1980. "Religiosity and Fertility: How Strong a Connection?" *Contemporary Jewry* 5: 56–63.

————. 1981. "Jewish-Christian Marriages and Conversions." *Jewish Social Studies* 43: 31–46.

————. 1986. "Some Comments on the Use of Distinctive Jewish Names in Surveys." *Contemporary Jewry* 7: 83–91.

————. 1995a. "Denominational Retention and Switching among American Jews." *Journal for the Scientific Study of Religion* 34: 499–506.

————. 1995b. "Jewish-Christian Marriages and Conversions: 1971 and 1990." *Sociology of Religion* 56: 433–43.

Lazerwitz, Bernard, and Michael Harrison. 1979. "American Jewish Denominations: A Social and Religious Profile." *American Sociological Review* 44: 656–66.

————. 1980. "Comparison of Denominational Identification and Membership." *Journal for the Scientific Study of Religion* 19: 361–67.

Lazerwitz, Bernard, J. Alan Winter, and Arnold Dashefsky. 1988. "Localism, Religiosity, Orthodoxy, and Liberalism: The Case of Jews in the United States." *Social Forces* 67: 229–42.

Lerer, Nava, and Egon Mayer. 1993. "In the Footsteps of Ruth: A Sociological Analysis of Converts to Judaism in America." Pp. 172–84 in *Papers in Jewish Demography, 1989* edited by Uziel Schmelz and Sergio Della Pergola. Jerusalem: Avraham Harmon Institute of Contemporary Jewry, Hebrew University.

Levine, Betty C. 1986. "Religious Commitment and Integration into a Jewish Community in the United States." *Review of Religious Research* 27: 328–43.

Lieberson, Stanley, and Mary C. Waters. 1988. *From Many Strands: Ethnic and Racial Groups in Contemporary America*. New York: Russell Sage Foundation.

Liebman, Arthur. 1978. *Jews and the Left*. New York: Wiley.

Liebman, Charles S. 1970. "Reconstructionism in American Jewish Life." *American Jewish Yearbook* 71: 2–99.

———. 1973. *The Ambivalent American Jew: Politics, Religion, and Family Life in American Jewish Life*. Philadelphia: Jewish Publication Society.

———. 1975. "A Sociological Analysis of Contemporary Orthodoxy." Pp. 131–74 in *Understanding American Judaism*, vol. 2, edited by Jacob Neusner. New York: KTAV.

———. 1983, "Extremism as a Religious Norm." *Journal for the Scientific Study of Religion* 22: 75–83.

Liebman, Charles S., and Steven M. Cohen. 1990. *Two Worlds of Judaism: The Israeli and American Experience*. New Haven, Conn.: Yale University Press.

Lipset, Seymour Martin. 1960. *Political Man*. Garden City, N.Y.: Doubleday.

———. 1994a. "Some Thoughts on the Past, Present and Future of American Jewry." *Contemporary Jewry* 15: 171–81.

———. 1994b. "The Power of Jewish Education." Wilstein Institute Research Report. Los Angeles: Wilstein Institute for Jewish Policy Studies.

Lipset, Seymour Martin, and Earl Raab. 1995. *Jews and the New American Scene*. Cambridge, Mass.: Harvard University Press.

Marketing Systems Group. 1991. *Survey of American Jews: Methodological Report* (October). Philadelphia.

Maslin, Simeon, J. 1957. *An Analysis and Translation of Selected Documents of Napoleonic Jewry*. Cincinnati: Hebrew Union College–Jewish Institute of Religion.

Mayer, Egon. 1985. *Love and Tradition: Marriage between Jews and Christians*. New York and London: Plenum Press.

———. 1995. "From an External to an Internal Agenda." Pp. 417–35 in *The Americanization of the Jews* edited by Robert M. Seltzer and Norman J. Cohen. New York: New York University Press.

Meyrowitz, Joshua. 1985. *No Sense of Place: The Impact of Electronic Media on Social Behavior*. New York: Oxford University Press.

Mosher, William, Linda Williams, and David Johnson. 1992. "Religion and Fertility in the United States: New Patterns." *Demography* 29: 199–214.

Mosher, William, and Gerry Hendershot. 1984. "Religious Affiliation and the Fertility of Married Couples." *Journal of Marriage and the Family* 46: 671–77.

Mott, Frank, and Joyce Abma. 1992. "Contemporary Jewish Fertility: Does Religion Make a Difference." *Contemporary Jewry* 13: 74–94.

Newport, Frank. 1979. "The Religious Switcher in the United States." *American Sociological Review* 44: 528–52.

Niebuhr, H. Richard. 1929. The Social Sources of Denominationalism. New York: Henry Holt.

Rabinowitz, Jonathan, Bernard Lazerwitz, and Israel Kim. 1995. "Changes in the Influence of Jewish Community Size on Primary Group, Religious, and Jewish Communal Involvement: 1971 and 1990." *Sociology of Religion* 56: 417–32.

Ritterband, Paul. 1993. "The Social Basis of American Jewish Religious Organization." Pp. 165–71 in *Papers in Jewish Demography, 1989* edited by Uziel Schmelz and Sergio Della Pergola. Jerusalem: Avraham Harmon Institute of Contemporary Jewry. Hebrew University.

Ritterband, Paul, and Harold Wechsler. 1995. *Jewish Learning in American Universities*. Bloomington: Indiana University Press.

Roof, Wade Clark. 1972. "The Local-Cosmopolitan Orientation and Traditional Religious Commitment." *Sociological Analysis* 33: 1–15.

———. 1976. "Traditional Religion in Contemporary Society: A Theory of Local-Cosmopolitan Plausibility." *American Sociological Review* 41: 195–208.

———. 1978. *Community and Commitment: Religious Plausibility in a Liberal Protestant Church*. New York: Elsevier.

———. 1993. *A Generation of Seekers: The Spiritual Journey of the Baby Boom Generation*. New York: Harper Collins.

Roof, Wade Clark, and Dean Hoge. 1980. "Church Involvement in America: Social Factors Affecting Membership and Participation." *Review of Religious Research* 21: 405–26.

Roof, Wade Clark, and William McKinney. 1987. *American Mainline Religion: Its Changing Shape and Future*. New Brunswick, N.J.: Rutgers University Press.

Rosenblum, Herbert. 1983. *Conservative Judaism: A Contemporary History*. New York: United Synagogues of America.

Salmon, Charles, and John Nichols. 1983. "The Next-Birthday Method of Respondent Selection." *Public Opinion Quarterly* 47: 270–76.

Sarna, Jonathan D. 1986. "American Jewish Community Takes Form." Pp. 3–5 in *The American Jewish Community*, edited by Jonathan D. Sarna. New York: Holmes & Meier.

Schnapper, Dominique. 1983. *Jewish Identities in France*. Chicago: University of Chicago Press.

Schwarzfuchs, Simon. 1979 *Napoleon, the Jews and the Sanhedrin*. London and Boston: Routledge and Kegan Paul.

Sherkat, Darren, and John Wilson. 1992 "Status, Denomination and Socialization Effects on Religious Switching and Apostasy." Research Paper, Department of Sociology. Nashville, Tenn.: Vanderbilt University.

Siegel, Seymour. 1977. *Conservative Judaism and Jewish Law*. New York: The Rabbinical Assembly.

Silverman, William. 1994. "Seven Movements in Pursuit of Market Share: Speculation on the Future of American Jewish Denominations." Paper presented at a meeting of the Association for the Sociology of Religion, Los Angeles.

Sklare, Marshall. 1971. *America's Jews*. New York: Random House.

————. 1972. *Conservative Judaism: An American Movement* (new augmented ed.). New York: Schocken.

Sklare, Marshall, and Joseph Greenblum. 1979. *Jewish Identity on the Suburban Frontier: A Study of Group Survival in the Open Society* (2nd ed.). Chicago: University of Chicago Press.

Smith, Tom W. 1990. "Classifying Protestant Denominations." *Review of Religious Research* 31: 225–45.

————. 1992. "Are Conservative Churches Growing?" *Review of Religious Research* 33: 305–29.

Sonquist, John, Elizabeth Baker, and James Morgan. 1971. *Searching for Structure (Alias AID III)*. Ann Arbor: Institute for Social Research, University of Michigan.

Sullins, D. Paul. 1993. "Switching Close to Home: Volatility or Coherence in Protestant Affiliation Patterns." *Social Forces* 72: 399–419.

Swatos, William H. Jr. 1981. "Beyond Denominationalism? Community and Culture in American Religion." *Journal for the Scientific Study of Religion* 20: 217–27.

Thomas, John. 1963. *Religion and the American People*. Westminster, Md.: Newman Press.

Tiryakian, Edward A. 1993. "American Religious Exceptionalism: A Reconsideration." *Annals of the American Association of Political and Social Sciences* 527: 40–54.

Wald, Kenneth D. 1987. *Religion and Politics in the United States*. New York: St. Martin's Press.

Warner, R. Stephen. 1993. "Work in Progress toward a New Paradigm for the Sociological Study of Religion in the United States." *American Journal of Sociology* 98: 1055–93.

Waters, Mary C. 1990. *Ethnic Options: Choosing Identities in America*. Berkeley: University of California Press.

Waxman, Chaim. 1983. *America's Jews in Transition*. Philadelphia: Temple University Press.

———. 1996. "Sociological Perspectives on the Rabin Murder." *Jewish Education* 62: 23–31.

Wertheimer, Jack. 1993. *A People Divided: Judaism in Contemporary America*. New York: Basic Books.

Winter, J. Alan. 1985. "An Estimate of Affordability of Living Jewishly." *Journal of Jewish Communal Service* 61: 247–56.

———. 1989. "Income, Identity and Involvement in the Jewish Community: A Test of an Estimate of the Affordability of Living Jewishly." *Journal of Jewish Communal Service* 65: 149–56.

———. 1991a "Income and Involvement in the Jewish Community: Do Identity, Marital Status, or a Child in the House Matter? *Journal of Jewish Communal Service* 68: 17–23.

———. 1991b. "Religious Commitment, Zionism and Integration in a Jewish Community: Replication and Refinement of Levine's Hypothesis." *Review of Religious Research* 33: 47–59.

———. 1992. "The Transformation of Community Integration Among American Jewry: Religion or Ethnoreligion? A National Replication." *Review of Religious Research* 33: 349–63.

Woocher, Jonathan S. 1986. *Sacred Survival: The Civil Religion of American Jews*. Bloomington: Indiana University Press.

Wuthnow, Robert. 1988. *The Restructuring of American Religion: Society and Faith Since World War II*. Princeton, N.J.: Princeton University Press.

Yinger, J. Milton. 1970. *The Scientific Study of Religion*. New York: Macmillan.

York, Alan, and Bernard Lazerwitz. 1987. "Religious Involvement as the Main Gateway to Voluntary Association Activities." *Contemporary Jewry* 8: 7–26.

Zbrowski, Mark, and Elizabeth Herzog. 1952. *Life Is with People: The Culture of the Shtetl*. New York: Schocken.

Subject Index

Name Index